Bali's Silent Crisis

Bali's Silent Crisis

Desire, Tragedy, and Transition

Jeff Lewis and Belinda Lewis

LEXINGTON BOOKS

A division of
ROWMAN & LITTLEFIELD PUBLISHERS, INC.
Lanham • Boulder • New York • Toronto • Plymouth, UK

LEXINGTON BOOKS

A division of Rowman & Littlefield Publishers, Inc.
A wholly owned subsidiary of The Rowman & Littlefield Publishing Group, Inc.
4501 Forbes Boulevard, Suite 200
Lanham, MD 20706

Estover Road
Plymouth PL6 7PY
United Kingdom

British Library Cataloguing in Publication Information Available

Library of Congress Cataloging-in-Publication Data

Lewis, Jeff, 1964–
  Bali's silent crisis : desire, tragedy, and transition / Jeff Lewis and Belinda Lewis.
     p. cm.
  Includes index.
  ISBN-13: 978-0-7391-2820-6 (cloth : alk. paper)
  ISBN-10: 0-7391-2820-5 (cloth : alk. paper)
  ISBN-13: 978-0-7391-3243-2 (electronic)
  ISBN-10: 0-7391-3243-1 (electronic)
  1. Bali Island (Indonesia)—Social conditions. 2. Bali Island (Indonesia)—
History. 3. Bali Island (Indonesia)—Economic conditions. I. Lewis, Belinda,
1960– II. Title.
  HN710.B3L49 2009
  306.09598'62—dc22   2008052228

Printed in the United States of America

∞™ The paper used in this publication meets the minimum requirements of
American National Standard for Information Sciences—Permanence of Paper for
Printed Library Materials, ANSI/NISO Z39.48–1992.

Contents

Illustrations and Tables

PLATES

TABLES

Acknowledgments

We would like to thank Dr. I Nyoman Darma Putra, whose expert guidance has been critical for the writing of this book. We would also like to acknowledge significant support provided by the School of Applied Communication, the Global Cities Institute at RMIT University, and the Faculty of Medicine, Nursing, and Health Sciences at Monash University. Special thanks to Professor Paul James, Professor John Handmer, Dr. Damian Grenfell, and Professor Helen Keleher for their ongoing support and faith in this project.

We express our gratitude to the many people who participated in the interviews and whose experiences and insights have provided the foundations for this book. Particular thanks are due to Governor I Made Mangku Pastika, Satria Naradha, Gede Nurjaya, Donna Holden from the Bali Rehabilitation Fund, Brad Otto from Burnett Indonesia, Viebeke Lengkong, Professor Muninjaya, Professor Wayan Ardika, and other academic staff from Udayana University.

Personal thanks to our dear and enduring friends, Reika and Gede Narmada, everyone at Lusa Inn, Legian, especially Wayan, Ketut and his wives Made and Ketut. Thanks especially to George and Anne Marie Paterson for their boundless enthusiasm and grace.

We would also like to thank the following people for permission to use their photographs and artwork: Alit Widusaka (Traditional Balinese *Arja*, plate 3.5), I Nyoman Wija (Traditional *Joged* performance, plate 3.7), Putu Ebo (*Bye Bye Bali* cartoon, plate 4.3), I Made Rai Warsa from *Radar Bali* (*Joged* dancers protest, plate 3.9), and Thea Linke (Cremation ceremony, cover). We would also like to thank Jordana Hill and Ainslie Jackel for their careful transcription of the interviews and Elizabeth MacDonald for her editing assistance. We express our appreciation to the Lexington Books team, particularly Patrick Dillon for his faith in our project and willingness to publish this book and Michael Sisskin for his valuable advice and support.

Sincere and special thanks to Jay and Sian for their incredible friendship, encouragement, and assistance—and for their extraordinary adventurousness during our not-always-comfortable trips across Bali and Indonesia.

Introduction

Jeff Lewis

> We have our own censorship. It's part of our culture right. In our culture, one value is that everybody knows when to control their speech. So self-censorship is at the core of our culture.
>
> —Palguna, Denpasar, 2005

I first visited Bali as a teenager in the 1970s. A few surfers from my hometown were making a surf movie set on this mythical island and had invited me along to help out. It was just a few years after the completion of the new Ngurah Rai airport and Hotel Bali Beach, which would open the island's tourism industry to the high spending markets of Europe, Australia, and the United States. In the first major tourism plan for Indonesia, it was imagined that Bali's exotic and mystical culture would attract a new brand of five-star tourist who could fly direct to the island, journey along the new highway to Sanur, and stay in the island's only luxury hotel—constructed out of Japanese wartime reparation funds.

Our journey, however, took us to Kuta Beach, a small fishing village on the island's southwest coast. Lightly populated with low-rise guesthouses and cheap restaurants, Kuta was in those days a haven for young surfers and backpackers seeking some authentic experience of the East, its tropical beaches, and exotic (sometimes narcotic) forms of spiritual transcendence. For the young visitors, sensual imaginings of primitive lifestyles and languid, bare-bodied natives seemed to subsume the actual conditions of contaminated foods, dirty water, and frequent bouts of diarrhea. The rituals, ceremonies, and nightly spectacle of incandescent sunsets elevated the squalor in which most islanders lived, creating a beautiful

1

motif of community and belief to which the Westerners felt strangely sup-plicant. Fortified by anthropologists like Miguel Covarrubias and films like *Morning of the Earth*, this generation of visitors became entranced by the vision of a tropical idyll that seemed to precede their actual knowl-edge and understanding. The low-voltage globes that pulsed over restau-rant tables in Poppies Lane, under which they shared their experiences, might have been a totem around which they assembled the marginal il-lumination of their knowing—a dull vision, a meager glimpse of the ex-traordinary complexity of a world beyond the electric light.

Most of us in those days understood very little of the shadows of crisis and violence that had beset the island's history and which continue, even into the present, within the chambers and vortex of its cultural conditions and collective psyche. Suharto's political genocide (1965/1966), for exam-ple, which resulted in as many as 100,000 Balinese deaths, was subsumed within a cascade of idyllic discourses promoting the island as a peaceful and harmonious paradise. These discourses seemed to contribute to the ob-fuscation of the horrors, not only for the visitors, but for the Balinese them-selves whose lives had been ripped into a bloody morass of political terror. Less than a decade later in the early 1970s, the Balinese who were living around the southern tourist zones had, in fact, marshaled their creative and dramatic skills in order to convince the visitors that all was well on the is-land of the gods, and that their friendly, happy demeanor was not a mask but a genuine expression of their cultural disposition. And little doubt there was some semblance of verisimilitude in the performance but we could not have guessed in those early years of mass tourism that these extraordinary people were bearing the burden of profound cultural and psychological ca-tastrophe.

On one sepia evening in Kuta, I saw a glimpse of it in the eyes of my hosts. There had been a strange air of anticipation all day; small groups of men and women had been huddling and speaking in lowered voices, their eyes darting sideways at any disturbance or the sound of a passerby. We were all aware of the unease in the village, and were expecting that it was a prologue to some immaculate ceremony—a wedding or the cremation pro-cession for a regal figure. However, by late in the afternoon the houses and huts that lined the main roadway from the airport to Denpasar were abloom with national flags and spectacular red and white lanterns. A con-voy of trucks began to block the road, releasing their cargo of armed sol-diers in khaki fatigues. Some were carrying the lanterns and flags; others were shouting to occupants of the houses, barking orders and marshaling them into the streets. The children too were bundled into the street, their wide brown eyes blinking with terror as they looked into the dimming light. I was standing with a group of other visitors on Bemo Corner. Some-one was suggesting we retreat to our losmen, while others were taking photos of this strange congregation. For most of us, though, there was just a sense of cold dread. The sun had set, and the faces in the crowd had turned to a spectral and featureless mass.

Finally, the source of the gathering revealed itself: a cavalcade of armed vehicles, followed by motorcycles bearing the national flag, and then the black limousine and President Suharto. The crowd cheered on command and the children waved their hands in the air. After the convoy passed, they all dropped their eyes and returned to their houses. I managed a single glimpse of the tyrant, still wearing the general's uniform and gazing, without emotion, at his loyal subjects. As the presidential vehicle approached Bemo Corner, I remember wondering what Suharto would think of this little gaggle of untidy, young Westerners. But his gaze appeared to move straight through us, with neither acknowledgment nor interest.

In the thirty years since that evening, this part of the island has changed markedly. Suharto's personal and state development projects have transformed the physical and cultural landscape of the Badung district, the area encompassing Kuta, Sanur, and the Bukit Peninsula. Especially since the 1980s, this part of Bali has become invaded by large hotels, resorts, golf courses, shopping plazas, and nightclubs. The once-sleepy zones around Kuta have become a frenetic entertainment cosmopolis, abundant with a seemingly ceaseless capacity for change, growth, and ever-mutating services and styles. The fishing village and hippie enclave has evolved into a seething morass of pulsing music, desire, bodily displays, and pleasure. For Westerners in particular, the Badung Bali represents a hedonistic playground and psychocultural landbridge to the "exotic East." As many observers have noted, the island has become symbolically inscribed as a "paradise," a "morning of the world" in which tradition and culture have been transformed into tourist commodities within the phalanx and ecstasy of global consumer capitalism.

And yet, as we have already intimated, the social and cultural history upon which this ecstasy has been constructed is replete with disjunctive elements—conflict, violence, trauma, and a deep and abiding condition of doubt. Thus, the woof and weave of Bali's evolving culture is textured by a darker dynamic, a horror that blends itself in barely visible threads through the pattern of the island's propagated pleasure. This horror is not fixed in a single or distinctly aberrant event that might be simply exorcized in the progress of history and modernization; it is rather an historical theme which evinces itself through times of crisis and radical social change. To this end, Bali resembles most cultures, although the extremes of its propagated pleasures seem to amplify the conditions of its bleak and percussive negative intensity. That is, Bali's elevated beauty seems to render its horrors even more terrible. What we failed to see in the 1970s, though our imaginings consistently marshaled us to the edge of this revelation, was the darkness that perpetually and necessarily adheres itself to the hyperbole of the island's intrinsic marvels and its extraordinary beauty.

At one level, therefore, the Islamic militant attacks of 2002 and 2005 can be understood as part of the continuity of this horror, this crisis. Over the past century, in particular, Bali's historical evolution has been implicated in an increasing integration and alignment with the Western political and cultural imaginary, including the Western-based pleasure industries. Inevitably, Bali has also been implicated in the contentions associated with cultural transformation, including the most recent incarnation of the global "war on terror." In a long history of Balinese-Javanese tension, the bombings were not an historical aberration, but represented a vector in this complex cultural weave. Bali's engagement with the Western imaginary incited an act of violence which has a profound connection with broader amplitudes of history, social change, and crisis.

BALI AND MODERNIZATION

It is clear that the current manifestation of crisis being experienced in Bali is associated with development and the island's alignment with a Western-based economy of pleasure (consumer capitalism) and forms of cultural practice. This movement from an agricultural economy and lifestyle to more developed, Western-styles of social organization is generally called modernization; globalization is the transformation associated with global participation in world economy and forms of cultural interaction. These transformations are not, however, a simple exercise of surrendering tradition to a Western lifestyle and way of being. Indeed, there is no absolute divide between tradition and the modern, and hence we use the notion of modernization and globalization, denoting a process of change, rather than a state of closure or arrival. Even the most durable cultures have been subject to change and readjustment, often responding to external influences or the impact of internal social or environmental crisis.[1] In Bali, such crises extended over a long history, including the period of regional feudalism and increasing interaction with traders, travelers, diplomatic envoys, cultural influences, and various forms of external military incursion.

Largely because of their significant military superiority and alien cultural practices, the Dutch colonists were among the most significant of these external influences. While the Balinese had experienced considerable pressure from regional powers, the Dutch proved a more formidable enemy in many respects, conquering the northern part of the island in 1849 and the remainder in 1908. While Bali was far from an isolated or solipsistic kingdom before colonial conquest, the Dutch brought a new intensity of change, especially after 1908, which radically impacted upon the economic, political, and cultural practices of the island. In this sense, colonization was one of those historical events (and processes) which brings revolutionary or accelerated change. Thus, while Adrian Vickers and other cultural historians insist that the process of modernization for Bali has been occurring over a very long period of time and through a general progression, it is clear that colonization and other major historical ruptures have contributed to an acceleration of change, most particularly in terms of the momentum of modernization and globalization.[2]

Indeed, while there have been seemingly inexhaustible debates about the actual meaning of "modernization," our use here is relatively straightforward. Modernization is a mixed progression of trends and elements, some of which are consonant and continuous, others of which are contradictory and disjunctive. While there can be no sense in which this progression has a destination, since "being modern" is an indefinite and perpetually advancing condition, the source of current forms of modernization is a European-American style of economy, politics, lifestyle, and culture. We also readily acknowledge that beyond this identifiable source, modernization is being experienced in very different ways by many different national groups: the modernizations of Japan, South Korea, Singapore, and Taiwan, for example, are both similar and dissimilar to the source cultures of "the West." To this end, we are deliberately avoiding a prescriptive dating of the modern epoch (modernity) and its possible occlusion (postmodernity).

And indeed, while there is a tendency to speak of modernization as a relatively integrated temporal process, it is actually replete with inconsistencies and contradictions. To this end, being modern is not the antithesis of being traditional; rather, the concept of tradition has itself been invented by modern societies and social groups in order to situate their current and future conditions. That is to say, events, customs, and elements of the past are selected by modern groups in order to "ground" themselves, their culture and identity—as well as their ideologies—in the dignity and origin of history (the writing of the past). This creation of tradition is usually part of a social group's political and cultural strategy, most often to assert their own interests over others. It is common, for example, that social groups such as a "nation" seek to create a sense of tradition around their foundation, their specific political ideology, and the glory of the people. While not limited to autocracies, this strategy is spectacularly evident in Hitler's Third Reich where the great tradition of the Aryan people was used as a justification for the slaughter of the European Jews.

In Bali these same battles over the meaning and value of the past are occurring between various social groups. At its simplest, a sense of "tradition" is often invoked by those groups who want to resist high levels of tourism development and its related environmental and cultural damage. In the period following the first bombings of 2002, for example, a number of activist community groups invoked a sense of "the old Bali" to promote their political and environmental causes. The same sense of tradition, however, is generally mobilized by tourism operators and promoters who consistently deploy motifs of Balinese music and dance to attract tourists to the paradise isle.

Such contentions around the meaning of history, in fact, characterize the more general demeanor of modernization. Sourced from the early eighteenth-century Enlightenment period, the cultural consciousness that characterizes modernization is frequently often regarded as—rational, secular, progressive, and highly individualistic. These attributes are nevertheless contradicted by other "modern" qualities, including the "irrationality" of religion, spiritualism, Romanticism, experimental arts, and various modes of social and political violence. Moreover, the formation of mass society and its diverse forms of collective ideology (socialism, nationalism, imperialism) directly challenge the profound intensity of capitalist-based individualism and the apotheosis of consumer choice. Modernization generally, and as it directly applies to Bali, is fraught with a complex and dynamic cultural instability, one which perpetually predisposes its ever-evolving newness to various conditions of crisis and change.

BALI AND TRANSFORMATION

Thus, while we are arguing that crisis, transformation, and pleasure are key elements of the modernization process, the disposition, meaning, and experience of these changes vary considerably across social groups and cultural localities. The focus of this book is the recent phase of modernization in Bali, a phase that begins with the genocide killings in 1965/1966, which occur almost simultaneously with the arrival of mass tourism to the island. These events mark an accentuated phase of crisis which is more generally connected to the experiences of colonization and decolonization in the twentieth century. The genocide killings and contemporaneous lurch into mass tourism occur as a historical flash point, drawing into unrestrained violence many of the agonisms that had accompanied the Dutch and Japanese occupation and the difficult struggles associated with Indonesian independence. Like the living infant who subsumes the violence and agony of its birth, the renaissance Bali of mass tourism has attempted to create a sense of self, which outshines the impurity of its inception. Thus, this recent phase of Bali's modernization is constituted around a crisis that remains "forbidden," as it deems to threaten the basis of economic development and the purity of vision by which the culture imagines itself.

Indeed, a great paradox of Bali's transformation has been the survival of the paradise motif within a context of its own implausibility. That is, while the notion of a mystical paradise continues to be represented in tourism brochures and the imaginings of many visitors, the cultural and environmental elements which have sustained this imagining have been seriously degraded. The Balinese themselves, along with many in the 1970s' generation of international pilgrims, have seriously interrogated the validity and value of the paradise motif, arguing in many cases that it is a mythical projection which merely distorts a fundamental and irresolvable tension for Bali between traditionalism and modernism. According to this argument, mass tourism has clearly produced significant economic benefits for the Balinese, providing employment and development opportunities as well as significant reductions in the overall poverty rate (from 16 percent to 4 percent). However, for many commentators, including many Balinese, the price of this economic improvement has been the degradation of the island's natural and cultural environment—the very qualities which attracted tourists in the first place.

This dialectic, in fact, dominates much of the current discussion on Bali, including discussions about the "tragedy" of the Bali bombings and the significance of Indonesia's political transition to a democratic, civil society. Consternation over Bali's rapid and rapacious growth becomes confused, however, as it invokes the tradition-modern dichotomy as an explanation for all that is going awry with their island paradise. Indeed, as the proponents of growth invest their faith in tourism and even higher levels of development, skeptics frequently invoke a nostalgic, almost puritanical, faith in traditional rituals and lifestyles which had sustained the Balinese economy and culture for centuries prior to the Western invasion. In either case, these contending perspectives are being forged around an ideology which is unmistakably *modern*—as we noted above, the dichotomy of modern-tradition is itself a creation of modern thinking which creates a glorious past in order to justify a particular trajectory into the future. Even traditionalists, in this sense, are "modern" as their traditions are created in contention with a particular type of modernism they reject in favor of another. This is a theme to which we will frequently return during the course of this book.

Bali's particular form of modernization, which has been largely carried by the island's absorption into the Dutch-Indonesian state and ultimately the global economy, has largely skipped the phase of industrialization, moving directly to the advanced condition of symbolic exchange. This "paradise" aesthetic, in fact, has become the island's central exchange commodity within this new form of culture-based consumer capitalism. In this sense, the crisis of Bali is fundamentally associated with its *meaning* and the different ways in which these meanings are created by different social groups. *Bali's Silent Crisis* is an attempt to unravel these complex meanings and to deconstruct them at their source. This book combines the wisdom of various disciplines and analytical approaches. We draw our sources from history, anthropology, literature, political studies, news reporting, formal interviews, and a broad range of firsthand accounts. While our most recent work has focused on community recovery after the Bali bombings,[3] we have been formally and informally studying Bali for many decades. Our interests, therefore, are both personal and professional, but this book is dedicated to our close friends, including Gede Narmada, I Nyoman Darma Putra, our many colleagues at Udayana University, and the innumerable Balinese people who have graced us with their friendship and love over many years.

This crisis, therefore, is one in which we are all implicated. Even through the dreamy idealism of the 1970s, the young travelers were contributing to the reshaping of the island, its people, and its culture. While the tourism boom didn't begin in earnest until the 1980s, the earlier visitors were all laying the foundation for that superhighway of change. The misty meanderings of the "old Bali" simply could not resist the powerful forces that were marshaling at the door of globalization. Our vision of a durable and elevated idyll simply crumbled beneath the pressure of the World Bank, Suharto's avarice, and the hunger and horror which we failed to see in the eyes of our hosts. We had no sense of the rupture we were bringing, nor of the incredible transformations that would follow and for which we were the harbinger. And while many Balinese themselves claim to be largely unaffected by history and the rupture of radical social change, there is no doubt that even this delusion is a symptom of psychological and cultural trauma. Indeed, it is evident, as the studies in this book illustrate, that events like the bombings are neither incidental nor accidental: they are manifestations of a cultural crisis by which the fates, as in a Greek tragedy, produce their inevitable horror.

Bali is a complex and splendid culture that is rich with creativity, ritual life, and spectacle. But it is also a culture that is bound to a deep and enduring pain. It is, perhaps, the aesthetic force of these contrasting intensities which ultimately represents the island's profound appeal as a tourist destination and site of scholarly intrigue. Where culture is an assembly of sometimes unified and sometimes distinctly contending meanings, Bali appears iconic—a special place that defies and indeed outshines its own propagated image. Bali is not a paradise, but a place of glorious spirits, fallen angels, and demons—a place in which desire and disaster are compounded in a powerful social, cosmological, and human drama.

NOTES

1. This point is perhaps best illustrated by the example of Australian Aboriginal culture, which is generally regarded as the most durable of all human cultures, ex-

tending over a period of between 40 and 70,000 years. While the archaeological record is very patchy it seems that the Aboriginal toolkit and basic social system and way of life remained consistent for much of that period, at least until the end of the last Ice Age and the rising of the seas. The environmental changes wrought by the rising seas and the loss of fertile territory created new pressures on the indigenous culture compelling a change in the weaponry and toolkit, which affected the economic practices of the Aborigines.

2. See Adrian Vickers's introduction in *Being Modern in Bali: Image and Change*, ed. Adrian Vickers (New Haven, Conn.: Yale University Southeast Asia Studies, 1996).

3. See Jeff Lewis and Belinda Lewis, "Transforming the Bhuta Kala: The Bali Bombings and Indonesian Civil Society," in *Interrogating the War on Terror*, ed. Deborah Staines (Newcastle-upon-Tyne, UK: Cambridge Scholars Press, 2007); Jeff Lewis, "The Bali Bombings and the Terror of National Identity," *European Journal of Cultural Studies* 9, no. 2 (2006); Belinda Lewis and Jeff Lewis, "After the Glow: Challenges and Opportunities for Community Sustainability in the Context of the Bali Bombings" (Paper presented at the First International Sources of Insecurity Conference, Melbourne, November 2004), ed. Damien Grenfell (Melbourne: RMIT Publishing, 2004), search .informit.com.au/documentsummary;dn=876201933383235;res=E-LIBRARY (accessed 15 May 2008); Jeff Lewis and Belinda Lewis, "The Crisis of Contiguity: Communities and Contention in the wake of the Bali Bombings" (Paper presented at the First International Sources of Insecurity Conference Melbourne, November 2004), ed. Damien Grenfell (Melbourne: RMIT Publishing, 2004), search.informit.com.au/documentsummary;dn=876183300411977;res=E-LIBRARY (accessed 15 May 2008); Jeff Lewis, "Globalizing Jihad: The Bali Bombings at the End of Paradise," in *Language Wars: The Role of Media and Culture in Global Terror and Political Violence* (London: Pluto Press, 2005).

1

Temple of Doom

Shadows in the New Bali

The situation in Bali was extremely bad, because the people of Bali were unhappy with the existing system of government and asked that it be changed quickly. Killings, beatings, arson, theft, banditry, kidnapping and so on were taking place everywhere so that the general situation in Bali became chaotic.

—Nyoman Pendit, 1954

I had visualized a rugged, winding trail leading over-hill and down-dale and ultimately reaching the world renowned surf break, Uluwatu. Once there I would paddle out through the cave, my hand knifing the glassy, utterly transparent water covering the colorful, almost fluorescent reef. Taking off on the wave of my choice, the line-up devoid of goons, I would receive tube after tube, each one becoming longer and deeper than the one before it. The vision began to crack when we pulled up beside a giant billboard advertising cigarettes. . . . On the side of the hill facing the break was a row of concession stands while in the water forty surfers battled to drop in on each other's three foot waves.

—Tom Boyle, *Surfer Magazine*, 1978

These people are so gentle, so loving and beautiful. It is so wrong. They should take the terrorists out and feed them to the dogs. Bali is such a beautiful and peaceful place. They are very spiritual people. Why do these animals want to ruin it for all of us. For Australians. We come here to play, to dance, to make love on the sand. We come here because we love the people.

—Annette, October 2005

11

SOLDIERS OF THE DEAD

Ibu Sewitri is visited by the dead. She sits on a flat timber bench, her fingers twisting the stems of flowers into *canang*, offerings to the gods who protect the family and their homes from the *bhuta kala* demons who lurk in shadows and threaten constantly to cast all human life into calumny and chaos. Ibu Sewitri is sixty-two years old. She has seen much evil in her life, but also much goodness. Ibu Sewitri is famous in the family and the village because she is visited by the dead. She is not a *dukum* white witch, nor does she work in spells or magic trances. But as she works, her eyes darken and, through memory or visitation, she speaks the words of the dead. The children who are in the compound sing songs that are playful but impolite. "*Nenek tuah dan teman teman mati.*" "Old grandmother and her dead companions." Their parents chide them, but watch ruefully as Ibu Sewitri drifts once more into the other world.

Forty years before, in the same courtyard, Ibu Sewitri had watched the murder of her brother and young husband. She had made love to her husband four times during the first week of their marriage; then on the seventeenth of May 1966 Bapak Made Lasawan, a senior official in the region and member of the Indonesian Nationalist Party (PNI), burst into the courtyard with twelve armed men. Sewitri's young husband had been active in the PKI communist party and was accused of treason. His throat was cut as Ibu Sewitri pleaded for his life. With her husband's blood still pooling onto the bricks in the center of the compound, Pak Lasawan then commanded a strip search of all the young women in the family. Communist women were said to have the letters PKI tattooed on their labia and Bapak Lasawan was going to cut the throat of any communist whore. It was known that Lasawan had at one time sought marriage with Ibu Sewitri, but his suit was refused as he already had two wives and his caste origins were unclear. During the attack, Lasawan and two other men dragged Ibu Sewitri behind a wall and raped her. They beat her unconscious and then dragged her back to the courtyard where she lay with the corpses of her husband and younger brother who, it seems, had tried to protect her.

It may be that Ibu Sewitri is one of the more fortunate survivors of the Balinese genocide. While there are many disputes about the actual figure, it is feasible that around 100,000 people were killed in the purges. In a systematic, state-sponsored campaign of physical and sexual terror, Sewitri had at least survived. Her entire marriage family had been slaughtered and while many women had been left destitute by the killings, she had at least been absorbed back into her own family. In her district of Badung, in fact, whole villages had been destroyed and thousands were rounded-up and massacred. Anyone who had benefited from the central government's new land reforms or had expressed sympathy for socialist ideals was killed. Children were beaten to death. Women were humiliated, raped, and murdered. In some cases, as in the attacks on Ibu Sewitri and her brother, the violence was almost gratuitous, payback for some meager offence that was part of the normal vicissitudes and petty disputes of village life. In either case, district leaders like Bapak Lasawan, whose land had been threatened by the reforms, had turned blood-lord, working with General Suharto's paracommandos to wreak vengeance and establish the authority of the New Order regime across Bali and all of the Indonesian archipelago.[1]

On the surface, at least, the story seems clear enough. President Sukarno, the leader of the Indonesian nationalist movement which ousted the Dutch colonialists through an independence war (1945–1949), had failed to unite the nation and improve living conditions. While it is generally believed that Sukarno was growing increasingly sympathetic to socialist ideas and the Indonesian Communist Party (*Partai Komunis Indonesia*), in particular, his efforts to reform the country's agricultural sector stimulated significant discontent among the powerful landholders and elite. During the 1960s accelerating inflation and the faltering of the land reforms were also contributing to a deepening division within Sukarno's own government and sections of the military elite. Sukarno, while remaining a popular figure, was facing increasing criticism from wealthy conservatives on the one hand and destitute tenant farmers and peasants on the other. Civil conflict erupted as the military leadership split, resulting in the murders of five right-wing generals by an opposite faction of PKI sympathizers. General Suharto emerged as a powerful figure who, with American support, was able to crush the PKI in what was propagated as a counterinsurgency. Through the establishment of the New Order regime, Suharto instigated a plutocratic military dictatorship which eventually deposed Sukarno and conferred the presidency on Suharto. In the eighteen months that followed the attempted coup, around two million people may have been slaughtered, as Suharto purged all semblance of opposition or challenge to his authority.

Through this political genocide or "holocaust," civil order collapsed. The complex web of social ordering and historical infrastructure that had helped maintain peace and community governance was suddenly ripped away in a bloody and violent military revolution. In Bali, as in other provincial domains, community grievances became amplified through the rupture of this violence. A new class of warlords emerged through the vortex of this violence and immediately appended themselves and their local interests to the authority of the New Order regime and the global polemic of Cold War politics. Anyone in the villages with sufficient status and connection aligned themselves strategically with the warlords. In the blood and confusion, village feuds turned to murder. Gangs roamed the streets. Individuals were dragged from their homes, robbed, beaten, and slain. As with the arrival of the Dutch colonists, the Japanese, and the nationalists, the complex fusion of customary and modern modes of governance in Bali was strained to breaking. Only this time, the slaughter was unconstrained, as the Balinese turned viciously against one another. As public officials and village heads were killed or removed from office, a yawing vacuum of power revealed itself. The Suharto paracommandos and local nationalists moved to fill the vacancy, eliminating anyone or anything that encumbered the imposition of their authority. Whole villages were purged. In those areas that had splintered between leftist and nationalist sympathies during the last years of the Sukarno presidency, properties were seized, groups of men were arrested and summarily executed.[2]

The customary law or *adat*, which had evolved through a meticulous historical blending of Hindu ritual and complex modes of village and civil governance, was shattered.[3] Mass graves appeared but were quickly camouflaged by the authorities without the proper exercise of ritual and rites. Bodies were piled, flushed with oil, and burned. The highly detailed Balinese funereal ceremonies were deposed by the maddened rash of death. Relatives and communities were denied access or ownership of the corpses. Many individuals—fathers, sons, husbands, brothers—disappeared without a trace, leaving the spirits to wander uncleansed in the netherworld. The trauma of grieving families was thus intensified by the belief that their loved ones were condemned to an eternity of wandering—the fate of those who leave the world unrestored to their essential divinity and hence exposed to the eternal torment of *leyak* and demon spirits.

Even the holy men were unable to assist the bereaved families. In the midst of the chaos, the Hindu priests were subjected to stringent controls as the emerging New Order state quickly recognized the political potential of religion. This issue was particularly significant for Suharto's management of the Islamic political interests and power groups in Java, but it was also relevant for controlling the Hindu Balinese. Thus, while it is a mistake to identify the customary *adat* or community law as determinedly theological, there is no doubt that religion and ritual were deeply embedded in a Balinese culture, sense of identity, and modes of community governance. Through a very pragmatic understanding of cultural politics, the New Order leaders concluded that the "modern" state they were seeking to create could work successfully through religion and customary law, as long as the authority of the state was conditioned as the supreme authority of the mortal world. In order to maintain the legitimacy of his secular power, Suharto realized that he would need to assert control over the seditious potential of faith and theology, especially in Bali where the dominant Hindu religion already deviated from the national Muslim norm.

Thus, in the aftermath of the killings and with terrible grief smoldering across the Balinese communities, Suharto moved to quell the seditious potential of these emotions through a strategy of institutional management.

The New Order regime began to assert greater control over the nation's Hindu population and culture, most particularly in terms of neutralizing religiously inspired agitation over the Balinese holocaust. Social sanctions were instated against public mourning for the dead. Traditional cremation ceremonies were rendered impossible for many families due to the brutal manner in which the killings had been conducted, particularly the mutilation and dumping of corpses and the absence of actual bodies. The victims and their families were denied the purifying rituals that would restore the cosmic balance by releasing their loved one's spirit for reincarnation and return to the extended family. However, by the beginning of the 1970s, the practice of cremating the dirt and cloth effigies of massacre victims was becoming widespread in Bali. Parisada Hindu Dharma, the semigovernment organization established as the authority on Hinduism in Bali,[4] began to sponsor special *nyapuh* or purification "sweeping" rituals in lieu of actual bodies and cremation ceremonies. The Parisada leaders insisted that it was the cleansing of the soul which was critical to its restoration with the divine and not the presence of a material body. For many grieving Balinese the expression of these funereal rites was largely political. The New Order regime, and General Suharto, in particular, had imposed a profoundly violent and secular will over the metaphysical dimensions and political potential of Balinese culture.[5]

Many of the women who had survived the political genocide in Bali continued to resist the imposition of this power. Even into the present day, they refuse to recognize the efficacy of the substitution rituals and they engage in their own spiritual practices to assert the continuing absence of the dead. By denying that closure has been reached on the past, these women are marking their resistance to a vicious history and the impact of Bali's political modernization.[6]

To this extent, tradition, Balinese culture, and spiritual life are integrated into a much broader *cultural* politics, a politics which is not limited to parliaments or party polemics. Different social groups and political interests enlist culture and ritual elements into the service of their own specific desires, aspirations, and demands. Culture is neither neutral nor apolitical; it is the living dimension of any social group's capacity for meaning-making and the imposition of those meanings over the interests, aspirations, and meanings of others. In Bali today, this is particularly pertinent as the advocates of tourism and development, governments, business operators, community leaders, academics, writers, filmmakers, environmentalists, preservationists, priests, and tourists themselves continually use Balinese culture to promote their particular interests. In fact, and as we will discuss in detail below, these disputes over the meaning of Balinese culture, in all its complex manifestations, have become a critical, if not defining, component of the island's history. In our view, the Balinese political genocide is the fulcrum of these many perspectives and cultural claims, as it announces the beginnings of a new phase in the island's modernization and integration with the global community.

The 1965/1966 mass killings, in fact, bring the previous century of colonization, decolonization, and incipient modernization into a consummate moment. The cultural and psychological impact of these events, like the holocausts of Germany, Yugoslavia, Russia, and Cambodia, has left a terrible though generally unacknowledged legacy for the surviving generations. In the forty years since the genocide, Bali might seem to have evolved into something entirely unrecognizable, closing forever the horrors of a violent past. But there is an intractable force that seems, like the souls of the uncleansed dead, to rise perpetually to break the silence and blacken the lives of the Balinese. Ibu Sewitri speaks for the dead, and for the many secrets that lie hidden in the earth and in the private minds of the Balinese themselves. Behind the mask of pleasure, in the invisible spaces, these traumas continue to resonate. So, when Ibu Sewitri speaks, she gives voice to an excess of evil which neither her offerings nor the rejoicing of a tourist brochure can entirely erase.

HOUSE OF SPIRITS

As with the terrorist attacks in Kuta in 2002, many Balinese viewed the 1965/1966 killings as apocalyptic. For John Hughes, one of the few Westerners to witness the genocide, the incendiaries were prescient. Out of the black smoke and burning villages, the image of Bali's new tourism industry emerges with a powerful foreboding:

> Almost in view of the big new luxury hotel the government had built to woo tourists to Bali stand the charred and blackened ruins of one such village. For their Communist affiliations the menfolk were killed. The women and children fared better; they were driven screaming away. The village itself was put to the torch. Night after night the sky flared red over Bali as villages went up in flames and thousands of Communists, or people said to be Communists, were hunted down and killed.[7]

Notably, the "luxury hotel" around which the killings were taking place was the new Hotel Bali Beach at Sanur. The Hotel Bali Beach (later the Grand Bali Beach Hotel) was commissioned in 1964 and completed in 1966. The hotel had been viewed as an ensign of the new Indonesia and the grand potential of luxury tourism in Bali. With a growing interest from mass tourism markets in Europe and the United States, public authorities in Jakarta decided to establish a more lucrative form of tourism at Sanur, until then a largely undeveloped fishing village and port situated in the southeast corner of the island.

For John Hughes, however, the presence of the hotel amid the carnage was profoundly symbolic. Sanur had evolved as a major entry point for international visitors, including the invading armies of the Dutch and the Japanese. Between 1904 and 1908 the Dutch completed an invasion strategy which had begun almost sixty years earlier. The final onslaught was precipitated by the plundering of a Chinese-Borneo trading vessel which had run aground on the Sanur coral reef. The Dutch administration forwarded a compensation bill to the rulers of the Badung realm which incorporated Sanur. Supported by the rulers in Klungkung and Tabanan, the raja of Badung refused to pay. The symbolism of this refusal provided a perfect excuse for a military assault on the ruling family of Badung. Landing at Sanur, the Dutch forces, including cavalry and heavy artillery, marched to Denpasar, the capital and home of the ruling family of Badung. When the soldiers arrived, the palace was already in flames. The raja appeared in his palanquin borne by four attendants, bejeweled and clothed in traditional cremation garments. The raja was followed by the officials of the court—his priests, guards, wives, children, and retainers. At around a hundred paces from the Dutch soldiers, the raja stepped from the palanquin and signaled to the attendant priest who plunged a *keris* dagger deep into the ruler's chest. At this, the other members of the procession began to strike themselves and each other with their *keris*, committing ritual suicide before the bewildered gaze of the invaders. The carnage seemed to panic the Dutch soldiers who opened fire on the bloody pageant, filling the air with smoke and flames. Before the bodies were cold, they surged forward, stripping their jewels and sacking the remnants of the royal palace.[8]

This terrible *puputan* or finishing ritual was followed by several years of carnage in Bali. The Dutch forces continued to surge into the island, destroying any semblance of resistance or challenge to their authority. In the final campaign in 1908 four companies of the Netherlands Indies army disembarked and marched east to the island's capital at Klungkung, one of only two Balinese realms still independent of Dutch rule. Two weeks earlier a colonial lieutenant had been shot during a routine march through the streets of Gelgel. The attack had been ordered by the lord of Gelgel who opposed his king's policy of appeasement which maintained Balinese independence through regal collaboration. The Dutch responded by razing Gelgel and bombarding the capital with canon fire from their warships for nearly a week. The royal family at Klungkung were ordered to surrender, but the king's request for more time and for the repatriation of the women and children to a safer place were met with silence. According to their own records, the Dutch believed that the royal family had determined upon a fight to the death—another puputan—which left them with no alternative but all-out assault.

The ensuing attack on the royal residence at Klungkung has become legendary. The Dutch established their heavy artillery outside the high brick walls of the Semarapura palace, the home of the gods of love. Dressed in ritual white clothing, subsequent waves of men and young boys appeared outside the walls brandishing lances and the traditional *keris*. They faced the artillery and howitzers and were mercilessly slain. As one group of Balinese fell, another came to take their place. Women dressed in purple and gilded batik were murdered along with their children. In the final wave, the king and his remaining lords appeared and they too were slaughtered. The king's six wives knelt beside him and plunged the *keris* into their hearts. These events ended the 600-hundred-year rule of the Majapahit empire's descendants in Bali, taking with them a millennium of Balinese history. Nearly two hundred Balinese lay dead as testament to this great victory; modern Europe had taken another jewel for its imperial crown.

The puputan barely rated a mention in official dispatches. The conquest of Bali that began in 1849 had been finally accomplished without a Dutch casualty and "relatively few deaths" on the other side. While it is certainly true that the Dutch had inflicted much higher casualties in previous battles in Bali, these final two puputan represented a more complete occlusion for the Balinese world. Over the final four years, these and several other more minor puputan left around 1,400 Balinese dead. And while the events at Denpasar and Klungkung are often promoted in Bali tourist brochures as a symbol of national honor and courage, there remains considerable debate over their cultural value and meaning. Some scholars are quite dismissive of these events, arguing that Bali had already surrendered to its fate and that the royals were reacting to their situation with a historically typical predisposition to spontaneous acts of violence. Crazed by opium, the ruling family and their entourage merely acted out of a fantasy of divine heroism. Other scholars take this view further, arguing that the puputan were a final statement of aggrandizement from a social elite that for centuries had imposed itself and its privilege over the bent backs of laborers and slaves. In this sense, the Klungkung puputan, however majestic it might appear, was merely a changing of the guard, as one class of warlords was superseded by another. Facing the ultimate degradation and with their role in history passing, the royals presented themselves to their ancestor spirits. The dead beckoned and the royal family embraced their destiny. If nothing else, a heroic death would confirm the honor of their bloodline, caste, and the gods who had chosen them to rule.

Whatever the specific motivations of the royal families, the puputan laid the foundations for Bali's transformation and integration into the global economy and a global geopolitics which would lead ultimately, almost inevitably, to the holocaust of the mid-1960s. Symbolically and materially, the puputan constituted the self-immolation of the old regal structures, replacing them with a new institutional framework that had been created and exported by modern, industrialized Europe. Moreover, the puputan marked the moment when Bali's long history of resistance to Javanese Muslim expansionism was also at an end. The Dutch had not only brought Javanese into Bali through the Netherlands Indies army corps, they also brought a whole class of Javanese civil servants, one of whom was to spawn Indonesia's first national president, Sukarno. Surrender to the Dutch represented an accession to a new, though obviously inchoate, national integration—and a new contiguity with its powerful and populous Javanese neighbor. More broadly, however, the Dutch Residency conscripted Bali into an imperial framework which was shaped through the nascent but increasingly powerful ideology and imaginary of the nation-state. Thus, while Europe exposed Bali to this modern mode of thinking about social organization—the nation—this new consciousness would ultimately lead to a rejection of the Netherlands and the embrace of Java. Thus, the defeat at Klungkung seemed to ensure that Bali would become infused by a liberational cultural psychology which sought to supersede the integrated Dutch colony with the independent nation of Indonesia. Through the period of Dutch conquest and rule, that is, the Balinese sense of an autonomous self and culture had moved sufficiently to allow many Balinese to participate in the independence revolution (1945–1949), and accept, by and large, their place in the republic and the national state ideology (*Pancasila*).

LANGUAGE AND POWER IN BALI

By the early twentieth century, it was fashionable for European invaders to dignify colonialism with the language of a utilitarian Social Darwinism. That is, colonial powers would insist that their annexation of foreign territories was largely an exercise of social and cultural necessity. In return for resources and commercial profit, the "superior" nation was ethically bound to bring light to the darkness of inferior peoples: by and large, this light was cast through economic integration and administrative efficiency. In the Social Darwinist model, therefore, the "fittest" would not subsume or destroy the weaker peoples, but would aim to mobilize them through an ideology of mutual benefit (utilitarianism). Such an ideology would continually persuade and cajole the conquered peoples through the imperatives of language and institutional structure.[9] The conquered peoples, that is, would cooperate with the new ruling classes not only because the threat of actual force remained an observable possibility, but because the ideology of colonial administration was both logical and "naturalized" through various systems of institutional management—law and order, trade, technological and social advancement, and a hierarchy of cultural and social value: being Balinese was good, but being Balinese within the protection and care of the Netherlands was even better. Thus, even if it were not clearly the case, life must seem to be enhanced under colonial administration.

The Dutch administration of Bali, which effectively lasted from 1908 until the Japanese invasion in February 1942, is frequently treated by historians as a fairly benign period. This impression, however, falsifies the smoldering resentment and sense of humiliation which seems always to accompany invasion and occupation. Nor indeed does it clearly distinguish the psychological and cultural transformations which were occurring throughout the period. The Dutch experience in Java had taught them that the most efficient and inexpensive administrative strategy was to work through and then transform existing social and governmental structures. In Bali, the Dutch therefore decided to work through and modify the existing caste system, even though the system was already being challenged by many of the more politically sanguine members of the lowest castes; in fact, many Balinese, such as the mountain Aga people, had never actually adopted the system in the first place.

Nevertheless, in a deft move the colonists declared, without evidence, that the Majapahit invasion of Bali in 1343 essentially destroyed a preexisting system of village governance, which the Dutch intended to restore. The caste system, therefore, could be mobilized through a less visible system of village autonomy and royal patronage. After eliminating, purging, or banishing the more troublesome aristocrats on the island, the Dutch sanctioned the existence of eight districts within which a hierarchy of regal and village governance would operate. From the 1920s this mode of indirect rule would be exercised through a fusion of colonial patronage and the old feudal structures. The villages would have their own notional autonomy, but the Dutch were very careful to ensure obedience to their general tax and commercial framework. This hierarchical order suited the Dutch, and there is little doubt that a small group of Balinese elite benefited quite substantially from their adhesion to Dutch rule. The Dutch congratulated themselves on its relatively uncomplicated and invisible force, though for the vast majority of laborers and tenant farmers there was an absurd familiarity about it all. Their backs remained bent to the landholders, only now there was another class of overlords who expected some profit from their labors.

Of course, European and Chinese traders had been extracting profit from the East Indies for centuries. The aim of a direct administration was to expand trade through the military control of a region, and also to generate public profit through taxes and duties. For the colonial administrators a surplus could only be ensured by minimizing the costs of running the Residency—

military and legal administration, public buildings, water, roads, harbors, salaries of officials, and so on. While constrained by the principles of Social Darwinism, liberalism, and their own Ethical Policy, the Dutch administrators nevertheless were driven by a profit motive which had little moral concern for the living conditions of the majority of Balinese themselves. The trade in opium, for example, was the major cash component of the Balinese trading economy during the Dutch Residency. In 1910, two years after the puputan at Klungkung, the Dutch monopoly on opium trade in Bali netted taxation returns of around (guilders) f. 1,000,000, a substantial proportion of the Residency's total budget.[10]

More generally, however, the Dutch imposed an extraordinary array of taxes on the Balinese themselves. These included income tax, personal wealth tax, street light tax, export and import duties, firearms tax, bicycle tax, the deeply resented slaughter tax, and the extremely burdensome land tax. Local village life also involved the payment of duties and levies, including religious obligations paid to the local irrigation society. While these taxes might on the one hand seem vaguely absurd, they are part of the transformations being wrought by modernization and the integration of Bali into the world economy. For many Europeans, in fact, Bali represented a kind of agrarian cash-paradise; its rich soils and relatively well-established social structures provided considerable opportunities for exploitation and the production of wealth. On the other side, however, the Balinese peasants and tenant farmers were being crushed by the burden of these taxes. During the thirty years of Dutch rule the tax income for the Dutch Residency increased manifold, as though there were no limit to the bounty. Overall, it was estimated that the Dutch government extracted over f. 37,000,000 more than its cost to run the Residency. Even the government itself was bewildered by the surplus, noting in a 1935 report into the possibility of Balinese self-rule that "the surplus from Bali has been obtained through the imposition of an extremely heavy tax burden on the people."

But it was not only that the taxes were heavy, the mechanisms used to collect the tax further contributed to tensions within Balinese society and its increasing fragmentation. In this way, the Dutch strategy of invisible or indirect administration meant that local officials were responsible for the collection of the most significant of these taxes, the land tax. As they received in commission up to 10 percent of the monies collected, these local officials were often very forceful in their collection techniques. Moreover, tax regulation did not specify whether it was the tenant or the landowner who was responsible for paying the land tax. In situations of greatest social or economic stress, for example where land was scarce or newly appropriated into the tax regime, the responsibility usually fell to the tenant. As well as paying a yield levy to the landowner, the tenant would thus be faced with the additional burden of government tax.

The inequity of the system and the clear lines it drew around the collector and the payee were further exacerbated through the Dutch transformation of traditional corvée labor. Once again, the colonists identified an historical practice which they then invoked to their own fiscal advantage. Corvée labor had been part of a mutual obligation arrangement whereby peasants were obliged to donate a certain amount of their labors to the patron lord. While the corvée varied across the regions, reports from late-nineteenth-century Tabanan suggest that the total labor days were around twenty and tasks were largely associated with collective responsibilities such as irrigation management and the maintenance of royal gardens. It was also reported that peasants could remove themselves from a particular patron lord, if it were felt that his treatment was in any way unjust. For the Dutch, however, the corvée offered a no-cost labor force which they could employ for various heavy labor tasks, including the construction of roads, bridges, public buildings, and irrigation channels. Each village was required to present two hundred men for corvée duty, although the members of the high caste were exempt. Once again, the Dutch exploited and hence solidified social divisions in Bali, leaving much of the administration and overseeing of the corvée projects and workers to their Balinese higher caste collaborators.

In fact, the Dutch introduced the new, modernist language of tradition and preservation into Bali. Paradoxically, this language of tradition was an essential part of the European ideology of imperialism and colonial control. Less developed, that is "traditional" societies, could be controlled by a technologically and culturally superior nation, which would then "reserve" the customs and culture of the premodern subjects. The Dutch, in effect, adopted, modified, and then actually created traditions which were administratively expedient; at the same time, of course, they were busily "modernizing" the island's economy and social infrastructure. Tradition, in this sense, became entirely fused with modernization, especially as it proceeded through governance, labor, and trade. The Dutch strategically appropriated "tradition," claiming persistently that they were merely restoring Bali to an ancient mode of social governance and order. The Dutch, therefore, didn't just retreat behind a façade of ancient village autonomy; they meticulously manipulated the Balinese sense of self, tradition, and customary law in order to invest as few resources as possible into the ongoing management of the island. If the Balinese believed the propaganda, then the Dutch were relieved of the problem of excessive military interventions. Serendipitously, perhaps, this propagated image of a peaceful and harmonious Balinese society became the trademark of the island's cultural value, a value which would ultimately be transformed into a central commodity in Bali's international tourism trade. The language of preservation, that is, became a critical component, not only of social management, but of a new mode of commercialization and trade in human culture.

In either case, the preservation of rituals and relics on the island was a matter of priority for the Dutch. This led to an ossification of the caste system, as well as the preservation of relics and cultural landscapes which would normally have atrophied and been rejuvenated through new cultural forms and ideas. It had long been the practice in both Java and Bali to allow old temples and sacred sites to crumble over time and to reappropriate residues and surviving relics from the decay for reuse in other temples or sites. The Dutch employed modern architectural and preservation techniques to ensure the survival of the multitude of significant Balinese temples, which the Dutch themselves had marked for conservation. This approach was itself strange as it denied the Balinese the opportunity for renewal and rebuilding, which are critical components of the Hindu notion of cyclical decay, downward flow, and rebirth. But for the Dutch the temples represented a demonstrable symbol of their own success as colonizers, most particularly within the framework of Social Darwinism, and their Ethical Policy and responsibilities. The Dutch seemed to deceive themselves into believing that their preservation of Balinese culture was something more than pragmatic—an ethical gesture which glorified the Balinese aesthetic under the protection of Dutch administration.

It was precisely this aesthetic which lured many scholars, artists, and writers to the island during the period of Dutch control. The European imaginary of an exotic and spiritually transcendent Orient was clearly engaged by the island's traditional elements. Not surprisingly, the European artists who came to the island to "discover" its unique and authentic Hindu culture were entranced by its pantheon of spirits and sacred manifestations. The romantic imagination was stirred by the island's "otherness," most particularly as it was expressed by the people's artistry, sensuality, and primitivism. The redemptive qualities of nature were personified for a European imaginary that had been so savaged by industrialization and the collapse of provincial lifestyles and morality. For the casual visitor, Bali represented the purity of the Garden of Eden: its clean waters, rice paddies, and bare-breasted women symbolized a life before the Fall, a world of pure nature untouched by the prurient and repressive moral constraints of Christian Europe and the dehumanizing of industrial work and decay.

As in Gauguin's Tahitian idyll, the Balinese "maiden" became iconicized as "pure native," a conflation of sexual innocence and availability. She was pure and visible, untainted by Christian values and unencumbered by the encroachment of civility and cold weather. One of the early European photographers of Bali, Gregor Krause, captured the Balinese women in informal poses exhibiting very little self-consciousness or stylization.[11] Krause, a German doctor employed by the Dutch administration, presented an image of the women and the cultural landscape of Bali which corroborated the perspective being generated through early tourist brochures and journalists like

Otto Jan Nieuwenkamp, who had witnessed the 1906 puputan at Denpasar. While it was not until 1914 that Bali first appeared in Dutch tourist brochures, these early images clearly contributed to the increasing interest in the island as a part of the new eastern grand tour. The Netherlands Indies administration in Batavia (Jakarta) began to invest in the nascent Balinese tourist industry, welcoming Dutch passenger ships to the port of Singaraja in 1923 and later upgrading the government guesthouse in Denpasar to a more comfortable hotel status. Still operating today, the Bali Hotel signaled the arrival of a new industry which was to accelerate during the 1930s when a significant number of artists began arriving as cultural colonists, especially around the area of Ubud.

Walter Spies is often regarded as the spearhead of this new band of artists. Born in Russia of wealthy German parents, Spies first became interested in Indonesian music and art during the 1920s when he was employed as a bandmaster by the Sultan of Jogjakarta. Spies moved to Ubud in Bali in 1927 where he experimented with hybrid forms of painting and music. His interest in indigenous gamelan orchestra and local crafts clearly influenced his own work, which he then shared with his Balinese hosts. Spies, and a number of other painters who arrived to form a small but highly influential bohemian community around Ubud, are seen as pivotal in the Balinese adaptation of European painting styles and practices. This confluence of Eastern and Western artistic practices is often viewed as a high point in the globalization-modernization process in Bali.[12] Spies's artistic community, along with scholars and writers like Miguel Covarrubias and Clifford Geertz contributed enormously to the West's understanding and appreciation of Bali specifically and "the East" more generally.

This scholarly and artistic image of Bali, however, somehow contributed to the overwriting of its difficult and often violent cultural-political history. Indeed, as one very important scholar, Edward Said, has noted, the external phrasing of the Orient is most responsible for the formation of the Western imperial imaginary.[13] While the tourist brochures spoke glowingly of a harmonious idyll in Bali, the artists and scholars seemed somehow to generate a more legitimate perception of a mysterious and spiritually ascendant world. Thus, while the artists and scholars liked to conceive of themselves and their work as far more enlightened and hence more valid than the discourses of tourism brochures, government, and the popular media, their voices merely added legitimacy to the Residency which facilitated their presence and perspective. The guilt that might otherwise have overwhelmed their colonial excursions was somehow redeemed, if not entirely erased, by the image of scholarly and aesthetic mission that this imperial access facilitated. Scholars and artists were neither travel agents nor military campaigners; their view was not compromised by greed or brutal self-interest. As Edward Said has noted, the mere presence of these artists and scholars in the colonies served merely to justify the right of any outsider to occupy and represent the space and culture of other peoples.

In fact, the Romantic yearning for pure nature—spontaneous, sensual, beautiful—is constructed out of, and in reaction to, modern Europe's own hierarchical rationalism. The manifesto of protection and preservation was largely generated through the Europeans' conflation of control and desire. Bali provided for the colonists a new resource to administer and exploit within the schema of global economics and international militarism. The whole of the East Indies had become, at this point, the keystone of the Netherlands' prosperity and strategic influence. The Netherlands' control of the Straits of Malacca, Western Europe's primary trading route to South East and East Asia, ensured that the Dutch exerted considerable influence in the region. Moreover, the rising importance of oil during the twentieth century reaffirmed the serendipity of centuries of colonial administration. In this context, the annexation of Bali was quickly identified as an important supplement to the colonial economy, adding a new income stream to the colonial coffers. Of growing significance, the aesthetic of the island created the potential for a tourism trade which marshaled an equally important component of imperialism—the sexuality and libidinal power of the conquerors over the conquered. While this quality is often sublimated in discussions of colonialism, it is very clear that the administration of Bali was infused by a profound sexual imperative which was linked to Romanticism, Social Darwinism, and the invocation of desire in pure nature.

While this issue will be discussed in detail in chapter 3, we need to note that the Dutch administration of Bali created pathways for the sexual engagement of the occupation officials, as well as the scholars, artists, and tourists whom the Residency lured to the island. Thus, the representation of the island as pure nature, most particularly in terms of a premodern erotic naturalism, served both to stimulate and satisfy the Romantic yearning. This yearning is itself paradoxical as Romanticism's rejection of industrialism and embrace of nature is constituted through a thoroughly modernist philosophical and artistic grounding—a celebration of imagination, reason, form, and aesthetic originality seeks its inspiration from nature and the primitive. The art and scholarship of the 1930s in Bali was very much generated by an antimodern modernism, a desire by wealthy Europeans to cast off their rationalist legacy and assume the persona of acolyte, student, and devotee of the traditions of Hindu, Balinese culture, and its sensual aesthetic. Thus, for all their undoubted value, the writings and art of people like Miguel Covarrubias and Walter Spies have been queried as a form of cultural imperialism, a mechanism by which the underlying conflict, extreme poverty, and violence that continued throughout the Dutch occupation are falsified or distorted by the Orientalist romanticization of beauty, provincial lifestyle, and sexuality. In this light, Spies's bohemian and permissive lifestyle is also being reexamined as it so directly transgressed the customary law and sexual practices of the Balinese themselves. Spies's sexual dalliance with Balinese boys, in particular, is being reconfigured today as a dangerous and exploitative form of pedophilia.

In some respects, these new sexual practices in which Walter Spies and many others engaged during the colonial period constitute a basic metaphor describing the "prostitution" of Balinese culture. On the other side of the violence experienced by many Balinese, sexual engagement with the new Western overlords defines the exchange of dignity, honor, and bodily pleasures for material returns. This refers not only to the boys and women who still give Westerners access to their sexuality and bodies in exchange for money, food, gifts, or employment; it refers also to a community and culture which exchanges its artifacts, values, and image for the more sublimated desires that are exercised through tourism. During the colonial Residency, the bottom line was that the Balinese peasantry was extremely poor and the burden of new taxes merely exacerbated their misery. Whatever the cost in personal dignity, tradition, or social cohesion, the tourism trade presented real opportunities for additional income. To this end, the Balinese adapted many of their traditional arts, crafts, and dance into hybrid forms. Whether this was tourist consumer preference or a normal part of cultural experimentation is largely a matter of perspective. The more benign view of tourism notes that the Balinese adopted these changes with considerable enthusiasm and that the Balinese culture had always been adaptable and dynamic. Those with a less favorable view of tourism argue that the presence of foreigners created a new commercial imperative for the expressive arts in Bali. While both perspectives are partly correct, it is more important to recognize that these changes to the expressive forms were integrally associated with the reimaging of the island's culture, a reimaging that would ultimately drive Bali's immersion in a global modernization project.

BEHIND THE MASK

While the Dutch occupation is frequently treated by historians as an unexceptional phase of Balinese history, there is no doubt it contributed to the construction of cultural and political pathways that would eventually lead Bali into a condition of deep crisis. The cruelty of the Dutch occupation was not always extant, but would frequently present itself through a mask of ethical responsibility and cultural approbation. But it would do so through a grand and often misleading invocation of often quite fanciful traditions. The caste system and modes of village authority, in particular, were deftly manipulated, enabling the Dutch to hide behind their puppets while ensuring an efficient and inexpensive framework of social control and economic exploitation. Through the exercise of ideology, the Dutch seemed to be creating a cohesive and largely harmonious society, which they were able to market to European and American travelers.

This image of unity, however, is largely false. Through the progress of modernization a new class-consciousness was being stirred by poverty, social fragmentation, and humiliation. While there were clearly a number of Balinese who had found advantage in the Dutch occupation, or may even have developed a sense of friendship or imperial loyalty, for the great majority of the Balinese, people of low-caste birth, life became increasingly more difficult under the Dutch. To this extent, the strategy of indirect rule meant simply that the resentment for excessive taxation was often directed at other Balinese, especially the landholders and officials who worked on behalf of the Dutch. This social fragmentation, while nascent and amorphous, nevertheless inspired many Balinese to join the nationalist revolution (1945–1949) when the Dutch tried to reoccupy Indonesia after the defeat of Japan. This exceptionally modern sensibility of "belonging to a nation" was actually forged by the Dutch themselves, not merely as their colonial boundaries created the cartography for a national state, but because they fostered a collective hatred for themselves which, at least temporarily, united many of the archipelago's diverse peoples and cultures.

Bali's participation in the nationalist revolution does not disprove the fragmentary nature of its people at the end of the Dutch occupation. Rather it demonstrates how a common enemy might parenthesize difference. The power of these differences would again reveal itself during the Sukarno period when the social lesions created by the Dutch occupation would ultimately break the surface and expose themselves as teeming sores. To this end, Sukarno, who would become the first president of Indonesia, personifies the deep contradictions which characterize Balinese modernization. Sukarno's Javanese father had been conscripted by the Dutch to work as a public official in Bali. He married a Balinese woman, and the couple's son, Sukarno, very much represented a reconciliation of the ancient hostility between Muslim Java and Hindu Bali. Equally, Sukarno might have been expected to be an acolyte of the benevolent Dutch colony, having benefited from Dutch patronage, a reasonably comfortable family income, and a European education.

In reality, however, Sukarno became disillusioned with the Dutch as he grew to understand the despotic nature of colonial rule. Sukarno's vision, like Nehru's in India, was formed around a fusion of modern sensibilities with a modern national consciousness, and a deep regard for the ancient traditions of Islam and Balinese Hinduism. Thus, the Dutch had facilitated a psychological and cultural framework for a sense of nation, but they had not reckoned on this consciousness being formed around a revolution which excluded the colonial master. Had they not insisted on the restoration of their colonial rule after the defeat of the Japanese in 1945, Sukarno and other Indonesians may have regarded them more kindly. The so-called Police Wars, however, incited a bloody and violent nationalist revolution, which served to spread the consciousness across the archipelago. Bali's own participation in the formation of nation, as in Aceh (Northern Sumatra), was fortified by the intensity of armed struggle and the ousting of a common enemy.

Even so, Bali was far from a cohesive province, and the national revolution seemed to fan many of the old tensions and disputes that had been smoldering throughout the Dutch occupation. Of the nearly 2,000 Balinese killed in the revolution at least one-third were fighting on the side of the Dutch.[14] The defeat of the Dutch, however, failed to restore social harmony, as both the administrative structure they had established and the resistance and social fragmentation it had precipitated fell away into a vortex of institutional and civil disorder. After the departure of the Japanese and the Dutch, modernizing Bali became a vista of roaming gangs and armed vigilantes; hundreds more Balinese and Javanese were left dead as vengeance was wreaked upon the remnant Dutch loyalists.

Even up to the national elections of 1955 the island was besieged by a violence that was increasingly influenced by, and integrated with, national political issues that were embedded in the ideological polemics of the Cold War. Throughout the period of the Sukarno presidency, in fact, these polemics were reforming and reshaping many of the older political contentions through an emerging sense of class-consciousness. The political landscape in Bali was no longer set exclusively within village rivalries or the regal template. The Dutch had brought new ideologies and ideas into play and the politically active minds of the Balinese wanted to understand their poverty and the hierarchical structures within which they labored. Political parties and loyalties began to appear in Bali during the 1950s and while they do not entirely equate with the polemic of Right and Left ideologies, they nevertheless constituted a new awareness of social ideals which reached beyond the village boundary.

This somewhat nascent form of class-consciousness became more clearly defined during the 1960s when the Sukarno government embarked on an ambitious land reform plan.[15] These measures, which were designed to produce more equitable land ownership, appear to have catalyzed the transformation of these complex political elements into a more clearly defined and modern mode of class-based social conflict. This is not to say that the older grievances of caste, tradition, and religion were extinguished by a new political consciousness. On the contrary, it is to suggest that these older tensions were supplemented through the accretion of new political issues, ways of thinking, and modes of power. While there is some debate about the extent of these changes, it is nevertheless clear that the political modernization of Indonesia was being accompanied by new forms of political expression. The somewhat amorphous and cross-class political interests and party allegiances of the 1950s were maturing into a more modern style of political bifurcation. By 1965 the two major parties, the nationalist PNI (*Partai Nationalis Indonesia*) and the communist PKI (*Partai Komunis Indonesia*), had evolved relatively distinct class characteristics and followings. The poorer tenant farmers and rural workers, along with a number of intellectuals and progressive high-caste members, were developing a strong interest in the ideals of socialism, while major landowners, public officials, and a growing group of Balinese entrepreneurs were becoming increasingly active in the PNI. These entrepreneurs, in particular, were benefiting from a system of patronage which granted lucrative government contracts and licenses to those select people who could return favors to the governing elites.[16]

The lines separating these parties, however, were not absolute, and there were certainly a number of poor tenant farmers who remained loyal to the political interests of their landlords. To some extent, this loyalty is partly an expression of traditionalism and caste duty; it is, however, more significantly linked to the insecurities associated with the Sukarno land reforms by which the tenant farmers feared the loss of tenancy on redistributed holdings. Land, of course, was the principal economic resource in this period with almost 90 percent of all economic activity at the time being derived from primary production, most of which was subsistence agriculture. Within a context of severe economic shortages and accelerating inflation, the Sukarno land reforms were designed to increase agricultural productivity through a more equitable distribution of land. As large holdings were divided and redistributed, the new landowners would engage in more productive, higher-yield farming. A similar reform plan had been undertaken in Bali during the 1950s whereby local legislation ensured that a fixed percentage of a crop yield would be returned to the tenant farmers. The idea was to liberate the tenant farmers from uncertainty and a somewhat unreliable dependence on the generosity of specific landowners.

This legislation, in fact, directly cut across the traditional lines of social management and the control of land. In standardizing yield distribution and protecting the interests of the tenant farmers *as rights* rather than as an expression of social dependency, the legislation brought old and new ways into clear conflict. While the resource of land had always been the single most contested social resource, it was becoming even scarcer during the course of the twentieth century. The Dutch had brought modern medicines into the Netherlands Indies, and increasing infant survival rates had produced a population boom. Without modern industries to absorb the labor, the increasing population was forced to survive on a diminishing per capita land resource and hence agricultural yield. Not surprisingly, the landholders were reluctant to surrender any economic advantage to the growing peasant hordes. The situation was rendered even more severe in 1963 when Gunung Agung erupted, killing over 1,500 people and destroying 63,000 hectares of prime, arable land.

The incendiary, death, and deep despair that the eruption delivered seemed somewhat prescient, as the Sukarno land reforms began to take hold across Bali. Irritation over the yield guarantees exploded into fury and hostility as landholdings were confiscated and distributed to the peasant farmers. In the midst of the reform process, however, simmering divisions within the army elite in Jakarta suddenly cascaded into violence and an attempted coup d'état by a pro-leftist faction. Calling themselves the September 30 Movement, these pro-leftist generals assassinated five rival generals and attempted to seize power. Major General Suharto managed to evade interest from the revolutionaries and was able to recover support for the conservative faction of generals, eventually mounting a successful counterrevolution against the leftists. In Suharto's version of these events, the PKI were intricately involved in the coup, but it has become increasingly clear that this perspective was merely a political ruse which could be used to justify the horrific campaign of bloodshed which followed his ascent to power. In a sense, the real revolution in Indonesia was perpetrated by Suharto and other right wing generals who opposed the September 30 Movement. In this version, the September 30 generals were forced to act against their rivals who, supported by the American CIA, were preparing to "eliminate" the leftists and President Sukarno.[17] The CIA and the right-wing generals had been deeply opposed to the land reforms and to Sukarno's increasing interest in the socialist strategies of the PKI and China.

While the events of September 30, 1965, remain shrouded in mystery, the impact of these events is staggeringly clear. In Bali, in particular, the outrage felt by landholders over the compulsory acquisition of their lands articulated itself in the post-coup purges. In fact, in those areas where the land reforms were completed by 1965, the revenge murders were most extensive. In Jembrana and Buleleng, for example, where the reforms had been largely completed, the killings were extreme. Similarly, in Karangasem, where there had been some quite violent disputes over the reforms in 1964, the PNI, with the backing of the Suharto paracommandos, had been especially vengeful, killing swathes of villagers who were to benefit from the land reforms. Conversely, in those areas where the land reforms were more nascent, the violence was far less severe. In either case, the class-consciousness and newer forms of social fragmentation which had been evolving over decades found its grizzly expression in the holocaust. This was not simply a purge of potential political opposition; it was an attempt to redirect the consciousness of the Balinese people. The PNI, military paracommandos, landholders, and new entrepreneurs in Bali formed a cruel and blood-hungry vigilante whose principal aim was their own social ascent and the restoration of elite interests over the bent back of the peasants. It was no longer caste that was the critical dividing line, but class—a consciousness which was driven by historical grievances and a deep fear of the poverty that surrounded all Balinese.

NEW ORDER: NEW VISION

The United Kingdom and Australia were quite explicit supporters of the Suharto "counterinsurgency," confirming by their inaction the right of vigilantes and Suharto paracommandos to slaughter unarmed civilians across Java and Bali.[18] This is a particular note of shame for Australia where the trade union movement had actively supported the Indonesian independence movement. The Australian wharf laborers, in particular, had refused to reload and service the Dutch vessels which were returning to Indonesia in order to reclaim their colonial territories. Sukarno himself had paid tribute to the Australian union movement and Australian people more generally, praising them for their strong anticolonial stand. During the 1960s, however, the Australian government had grown increasingly nervous about Sukarno's land reform policies—also a major issue for the American Central Intelligence Agency, which appears to have contributed significantly to the destabilization of the Sukarno presidency and the eventual rise of Suharto to power. This nervousness certainly lies behind the brutal indifference expressed by Australia's prime minister of the time, Harold Holt. In response to the killings, Holt reputedly joked to a colleague: "With 500,000 to a million communist sympathizers knocked off, I think it's safe to assume a reorientation has taken place."[19]

Just as the United States, United Kingdom, and Australia recently comprised the core of the Coalition of the Willing, they also constituted in the 1960s a primary triad in South East Asia's Cold War. To this extent, the "reorientation" to which Holt refers might be represented in the Hotel Bali Beach and the light it cast across the killings of 1965/1966. That is, the island's first five-star hotel located at Sanur may be understood as a sentinel to Bali's modernization—a peculiar and deadly conflux of desire and terror. The hotel represents the constellation of all the horrors and violence of Bali's past—from the mass suicides of the puputan and the brutal rationalism of the Dutch colonization through to the Japanese occupation, the Police Wars, the national revolution, the land reforms, and finally the political genocide which raged around its doors. But woven through these horrors was an accretion of human grace, a beauty which itself becomes transfigured as desire. This aggregation of opposite intensities finds its expression in the Hotel Bali Beach where desire is contained within a propagated commercial ideal that can be packaged and corporealized as pleasure beyond the reach of the horror from which it has been created.

In a strange way this packaging becomes directed toward the Anglophones who are drawn like moths to the Bali Beach beacon. We have already noted that tourism was becoming an established proto-industry during the Dutch Residency, fueled largely by a European Romantic yearning for an authentic Oriental experience and pure nature. By the 1960s this yearning had percolated through to a rising youth culture in the West. With relatively high disposable incomes, this generation was taking advantage of cheaper and faster air travel in their pursuit of new social knowledge and experiences. Thus, while the Hotel Bali Beach was designed to capture the high end of the market, a more formidable and numerous class of younger tourists were already discovering Bali and its cultural pleasures. Dissatisfied with the sorts of Western values that had produced two world wars, nuclear crisis, and continuing belligerence in Indochina, these young travelers began to focus on places like India and Bali as sources of a new kind of enlightenment, a form of spiritual and sensual elevation intimated in European art and Romantic literature and the popular music of bands like the Beatles. Even before the establishment of the Hotel Bali Beach, new forms of low-cost accommodation were appearing in the art village of Ubud and the fishing village of Kuta. While the Jakartan authorities viewed these sorts of tourists with indifference or even disdain, they at least indicated that there was significant and growing international interest in Indonesia's physical and cultural resources—especially Bali.

As noted, Sukarno himself had developed a particular affection for the Hindu island. As a scholar with a highly sophisticated worldview, Sukarno saw Bali as a vibrant and extraordinarily resilient cultural frieze, an historical pathway to Indonesia's Hindu heritage. This same delight in Balinese culture was expressed by India's first president Nehru who, in the company of Sukarno, described the island as "the morning of the world." This image of paradisiacal purity clearly accords with European scholarship and imagery which, by the 1960s, was being transformed into a marketing vehicle for international tourism. Sukarno's profound affection for the island and its culture did not, of itself, preclude the possibility of commercial exploitation. The deep poverty of the island's people—and indeed of the broader populace itself—was the cause of considerable consternation for the Indonesian president. Clearly, while land reform was a priority, the potential of international tourism to facilitate development and the acquisition of foreign capital could not be ignored. The establishment of the first five-star hotel was not merely a symbolic gesture, therefore, but the harbinger of a new industry which would provide a boost for a nation that was perpetually at risk of total bankruptcy.

Thus, while Sukarno had been astute enough to recognize the potential of "mass" tourism for Bali, it was the New Order regime under Suharto that centralized the industry as a platform of economic development. Suharto seems to have been preoccupied during the later 1960s and 1970s with the fortification of his power through both public and clandestine means. But while potential opposition was either eliminated or controlled through a rigorous campaign of terror, Suharto was also sensible enough to realize that he needed to court a statesmanlike international profile. To this end, Suharto elevated his authority through the propagated image of international tourism. In particular, the "Bali harmony" motif became a useful vehicle for the promotion of Indonesia as a welcoming and orderly nation. Of course, the New Order was broadly recognized as an oppressive and vicious totalitarian regime, but the Bali tourist narrative seemed somehow to evade contamination by association. In the eyes of many of the increasing numbers of tourists who were visiting Bali, the Hindu island was not really a part of the Indonesian state. Bali was different. The Balinese were special.

Rather than feel offended by this perception, the New Order plutocracy turned it to their advantage, pouring billions of dollars into tourism development on the island,[20] especially at the higher resort end of the market. And while these development surges mobilized Bali's natural and cultural resources to generate huge returns for the investors, there was virtually no regard shown toward the cultural and natural environments which were sacrificed to the torrent of development activity. The template of cultural synthesis and harmony that had been created by the early tourism industry was amplified and proliferated by the New Order developers. There could be no challenge to the mantra of growth. The airport was expanded, and new hotels, restaurants, and shops were constructed in the more established tourist zones of Kuta and Sanur. Entirely new and increasingly more extravagant resorts were constructed on the Bukit Peninsula and Nusa Dua. Farms were wiped away; sacred areas were plundered, entire villages were destroyed and replaced with five-star condominiums, golf courses, gyms, shopping malls, and theme parks.

Bali was a cheap and exotic idyll, a paradise that could release desire and liberate the pleasure-seeker from the cold constraints of Western life. In a marketing brochure for the Oberoi, one of the first luxury hotels constructed on the Kuta side, Bali is an unself-conscious miracle of the authentic East:

People knows that Bali has been described by many different great names *"The Hidden Paradise," "The Last Paradise on Earth," "Morning of The World," "Island of God,"* and *"Island of Thousand Temples."* This Island of Gods is situated approximately on latitude 8° South and longitude 115° East. . . . For centuries Bali has attracted visitors from all over the world for its colorful ceremonies, natural scenery, and its genuine ever-smiling and friendly people. The Balinese people are predominantly Hindu and their traditional and religious beliefs are as strong today as they ever were. The colorful festivals and ceremonies of the Hindu, the traditional music and dances have always been a way of life, and have unwittingly contributed much to the success of Bali tourism.

Built in 1981, the Oberoi marked the expansion of luxury accommodation on Bali. The "success" to which the text refers is the colonization, occupation, and transformation of villages and rice fields into "beaches" and modern luxury accommodation for international tourists.

   More telling, however, the Oberoi is also frequently cited by many commentators as a site of historical fusion. In many respects, it is the first major resort project in Bali in which the Suharto family rechanneled international development funds for their own private gain—a practice which was to flourish and multiply across the Badung district for the following two decades. In some ways, the Oberoi was an ideal site for this sort of infamy as it was also a key killing zone during the period of the Suharto genocide. That is, the Oberoi represents the pernicious fusion of horror and desire that more broadly characterizes Bali's modernization. Both metaphorically and literally, the Oberoi appears to have been constructed on the misery of

1.1.   Guard at the entrance to the exclusive Oberoi Hotel (2007).
Courtesy of Belinda Lewis.

1.2.   The remains of the original cemetery wedged between the Oberoi Hotel and the exclusive and ironically named restaurant Ku De Ta (2008).
Courtesy of Belinda Lewis.

those "friendly and ever-smiling people" to whom its promotions brochure refers. Rumors that have persisted since the opening of the Oberoi at Semi-nyak claim that it was built on one of the genocide's mass gravesites.[21]

According to these rumors, the Suharto government strategically located its hotel developments in order to seal forever the evidence of their atrocities. This strategy served several purposes. First, it helped erase the nearly 50,000 corpses that were never returned to their families as a result of the holocaust. The killing fields were rapidly excavated by the public authorities, but there was always a chance that over time these mass graves would be discovered and used as evidence against the perpetrators. Secondly, the escalation of international tourism in Bali was increasing the demand for development. Any significant evidence of these atrocities would have surely disrupted the growth in tourism, while seriously damaging the island's reputation. It was far better, in these circumstances, for the government to choose specific development sites, rather than allow a dangerous and haphazard excavation program. Thirdly, the sealing of the mass graves beneath these new and impressive structures created a form of political synthesis. Modernization and the New Order vision coalesced in the diction of the tourism brochures. The new Bali, with its five-star resorts, swimming pools, and swaddling opulence, would reign supreme over a grubby past. The fresh lawns and puppet shows have encased the future. And while the ghosts might continue to wander the pathways and gardens at night, nobody, not even the new generation of smiling Balinese waiters, ever really see them. They are cast out and forgotten, sealed beneath a thousand tons of concrete and steel.

THE REASONS FOR SILENCE

There has been a great deal of debate about the relative condition of silence that has surrounded the Balinese political genocide. A number of commentators argue that the genocide is simply part of the tyranny of silence imposed by the Suharto dictatorship. Others claim that the Balinese themselves have suppressed discussion of their violent past, fearing that any acknowledgment of the genocide and the psychological damage it has caused would simply endanger the island's fragile tourist economy. Still others, such as one of Bali's leading intellectuals, I Nyoman Darma Putra, argue that the Balinese are culturally predisposed toward recovery and resilience. According to this view Balinese ritual life and the acceptance of the binary interdependence of good and evil enable the Balinese to manage crisis and create new opportunities for the pursuit of spiritual ecstasy. In this context, Balinese cultural life is a conduit to the future and the transcendence of horrors which are an inevitable part of living in a mortal world.[22]

While each of these explanations is credible to some extent, it is the third that is perhaps the most contentious. Of course, social groups throughout history have been forced to deal with social trauma. As with individuals, social groups deal with trauma in a range of ways, including various forms of acknowledgment, expiation, retribution, forgetfulness, deflection, and even forgiveness. As a social group, the Balinese have tended to ritualize and suppress the trauma, forcing it back into the darker channels of their collective psyche. Unacknowledged and constantly threatened by Suharto's violence, the grief and horror has integrated itself into a range of psychocultural symptoms, including a somewhat disjunctive obedience to authority, ritual, and externally imposed order. It may be, in fact, that the Balinese's capitulation to the tourism development orgy and reluctance to participate in civil and legislative processes are further symptoms of an unacknowledged and forbidden crisis.

Our argument in this book is fundamentally that the confluence of the genocide trauma and the new style of economy have created a crisis which is difficult to estimate or define. The Balinese feel overwhelmed by the recent decades. The ways in which the trauma has been treated and not

1.3. Ceremony in front of the Oberoi Hotel (2007).
Courtesy of Belinda Lewis.

treated leaves them in a state of complex uncertainty, a condition clearly exacerbated by the velocity of social change. Thus, while Balinese intellectuals such as Darma Putra ask legitimate questions about the value of "opening old wounds," there is an equally forceful argument which insists that a people take account of their past in order to move forward with more confidence and autonomy.

REVEL WITH THE DEVIL

In many of the traditional Balinese dances, performance conjures the mythical beings of all-time for the rendering and comprehension of a mortal world. Through various local permutations, the *Barong* and *Ramayana* dances, for example, tell of eternal and irresolvable battle involving love, war, death, and honor. These cosmological contentions are restored to the mortal world of ethics and social management through the guiding principle of *rwa bhineda* (two-in-one). According to this principle, good and evil are locked in a perpetual and contiguous conflict which, like the wearing of masks and makeup, frequently involves the blurring of identity. Unlike the major Christian and Islamic traditions, where good is destined to conquer evil, Hindu cultures often regard good and evil as interdependent and conterminous: good and evil are poised within a single boundary which blends the material and spiritual domains of the cosmos. In this sense, good can neither conquer nor expunge evil, but must work within and through its extant manifestations. The responsibility of the living, therefore, is to manage the worldly and spiritual dialectic in order to limit the harm that evil might inflict upon the living and the dead. Within this context, the *bhuta kala* demons are not considered entirely evil, nor are their deeds necessarily predisposed toward destructive or calamitous outcomes. Reciprocally, protective spirits must be continually appeased and cajoled in order to ensure the best possible conditions for human life; the hideous appearance of these kindly spirits warns us, therefore, that nothing in the cosmos can be taken for granted.

In this sense, the ideal of synthesis which has been propagated by the Indonesian political elite and the tourism industry is entirely illusory. The deep emotional and psychological wounds that have been inflicted on the people and culture of Bali have not been redeemed or erased, but rather absorbed into the realm of myths and mask. A whole generation and their children have been scarred by the genocide. These people are now the leaders of a society that has cast its crisis by necessity into the realm of silence. But the Hotel Bali Beach and the Oberoi are still standing, and the memories of terror still haunt the smiles of the "smiling Balinese." These are a people who have endured a terrible and bewildering event, which has somehow been caught in a torrent of rapid and seemingly implacable social change. Not only has the landscape of their country so radically altered, but the surge of new social practices has left them bewildered and strangely inert—even though many of these changes have offended their ethics and values and brutalized the environmental beauty of their island.

But it is not, as some commentators believe, that the Balinese are incapable of political response, nor is the grace and warmth they exhibit fallacious. It is rather that they are embattled within the extremes of hideous political violence on the one hand, and a hyperbole of propagated and impossible beauty on the other. Within the blended borders of these extremes is a level of economic activity and radical social change that is producing cultural catastrophe. As with the holocausts in Europe, Russia, and Cambodia, the genocide in Bali has left its victims in a state of profound confusion and anxiety. As we will explore in the following chapters, it is precisely this emotional and psychological condition which constitutes the underpinning of a crisis which cannot be spoken for fear of exacerbating its effects. The speaking, thereby, must be left to the *nenek gila*, the mad women or mediums who continue to consort with the dead—women like Ibu Sewitri, who persistently rejects the erasure of the past and a synthesis which perpetually offends her right to justice.

NOTES

1. This story is based on primary research conducted by the authors. Each of the stories in this book has been constructed from our analysis of a combination of historical documents, contemporary texts, and personal accounts gathered through in-depth interviews and more informal conversations with a range of respondents. As the principal characters in this story are still living, all names have been changed to protect privacy. Stories like these, however, are numerous. We have conducted interviews and primary field research between 1991 and 2008. However, most of the material for this book has been drawn from research conducted since the 2002 bombings. For a more complete account of the violence perpetrated against women, in particular, see Leslie Dwyer, "The Intimacy of Terror: Gender and the Violence of 1965–66 in Bali," *Intersections: Gender, History and Culture in the Asian Context* 10 (2003).

2. See Geoffrey Robinson, *The Dark Side of Paradise: Political Violence in Bali* (Ithaca, N.Y.: Cornell University Press, 1995), 297–303. See also Robert Cribb, ed., *The Indonesian Killings of 1965–1966* (Clayton, Australia: Monash University Centre for South East Asian Studies, 1990); Katherine McGregor, *History in Uniform: Military Ideology and the Construction of Indonesia's Past* (Singapore: University of Singapore Press, 2007).

3. Thousands were rounded up and transported by trucks to the notorious "killing centers" where they were shot, beheaded, or stabbed. Others were marched in procession through the streets to village "execution places" where they were murdered and either burned or thrown into mass graves by Suharto's military commandos and their co-opted Balinese village officials. Citing community knowledge and his own experiences as a child, Dr. I Nyoman Darma Putra, a leading Balinese scholar, claims that although some of the killings were conducted in "proper places," many suspected PKI members and their families were mutilated and brutally murdered at random, on roadsides and in full view of the public with brutal indifference to rites and ritual lore. See also Robinson, *Dark Side of Paradise*, 297–303.

4. Parisada Hindu Dharma was the semigovernment organization of Hindu intellectuals and Balinese religious leaders established during the late 1950s to campaign for the Hindu religion to be acknowledged as one of the state religions, equal to Islam and Christianity. Later, in the 1980s, as Parisada Hindu Dharma Indonesia, the organization became the bureaucratic authority on Hinduism at a national level. Since then, Parisada and its factions have been engaged in ongoing debates and tensions about caste hierarchies, religion, and custom in modern Bali. For a more detailed discussion, see Henk Schulte Nordholt, *Bali an Open Fortress, 1995–2005: Regional Autonomy, Electoral Democracy and Entrenched Identities* (Singapore: NUS Press, 2007), 22–24.

5. For more analysis of discourses of cremation, Hindu "identity," and modernist reform, see Linda Connor, "Contestation and Transformation of Balinese Ritual: The

Case of 'ngaben ngirit,'" in *Being Modern in Bali: Image and Change*, ed. Adrian Vickers (New Haven, Conn.: Yale Southeast Asia Studies Monographs, 1996).

6. Leslie Dwyer, "The Intimacy of Terror: Gender and the Violence of 1965–66 in Bali," *Intersections: Gender, History and Culture in the Asian Context* 10 (August 2004).

7. John Hughes, *The End of Sukarno* (Sydney: Angus and Robertson, 1968), 175.

8. There are many interesting and vibrant accounts of the *puputan*. For a systematic analysis of this period of Balinese history see Margaret Wiener, *Visible and Invisible Realities: Power, Magic, and Colonial Conquest in Bali* (Chicago: University of Chicago Press, 1994).

9. Mike Hawkins, *Social Darwinism in European and American Thought 1860–1945* (Cambridge: Cambridge University Press, 1997). See also Edward W. Said, *Orientalism* (New York: Pantheon Books, 1978); Edward W. Said, *Culture and Imperialism* (London: Chatto and Windus, 1993). Said's canonical studies distinguish between the colonial administration of conquered territories, and the reforming and reshaping of the culture of those territories (imperialism). Imperialism is essentially an ideology: the imposition of language and ideas which effectively recast the ways in which conquered peoples constructed meanings about themselves and their relationship with the colonizing power.

10. Robinson, *Dark Side of Paradise*, 273–303.

11. Gregor Krause, *Bali 1912* (Republished) (Singapore: Pepper Books, 2001).

12. See Michael Hitchcock, *Bali the Imaginary Museum: The Photographs of Walter Spies and Beryl de Zoete* (Oxford: Oxford University Press, 1996).

13. See Said, *Culture and Imperialism*, 1993.

14. Robinson, *Dark Side of Paradise*, 273–303.

15. See Adrian Vickers, *A History of Modern Indonesia* (Cambidge: Cambridge University Press, 2006).

16. There were, of course, a number of smaller and less significant political parties operating in Bali during this period. Most notable was the BTI (*Barisan Tani Indonesia*), which also had a leadership drawn from commoners. The PSI (*Partai Socialis Indonesia*) was banned in 1963 after enjoying considerable influence during the early years of the revolutionary national government. The party had a number of clandestine but loyal followers in Bali even after it was banned.

17. Evidence of CIA involvement in the assassination attempt has been growing. An extensive analysis of American involvement in the coup can be found in George Kahin and Audrey Kahin, *Subversion as Foreign Policy: The Secret Eisenhower and Dulles Debacle in Indonesia* (Washington, D.C.: University of Washington Press, 1997). See also Victor M. Fic, *Anatomy of the Jakarta Coup* (New Delhi: Abhinav Publications, 2004).

18. See John Pilger, "John Pilger on Australia's Collusion with State Terror," *The New Statesman* (24 October 2002).

19. See Richard Tanter, "Witness Denied: Australian Media Responses to the Indonesian Killings of 1965–66," *Inside Indonesia* 71 (July–September 2002).

20. See Michael Hitchcock and I Nyoman Darma Putra, *Tourism, Development and Terrorism in Bali* (London: Ashgate, 2007), 5–39; Shinji Yamashita, *Bali and Beyond: Explorations in the Anthropology of Tourism* (Oxford: Berghahn, 2003).

21. These rumors are reported in many places and from many different and unrelated sources. It is virtually impossible to confirm or deny them, as public officials and private property owners will not give permission for systematic research or excavation. The temple and cemetery that are adjacent to the Oberoi are, of course, sacred sites for the repurification of the human soul. Given the unbordered nature of Balinese cemeteries, it is almost certain that there are graves of some kind in the Oberoi grounds. The critical question is whether or not these graves involve mass interments that are related to the 1965/1966 murders.

22. For a broad discussion on this silence see Degung Santikarma, "Monuments, Documents and Mass Graves: The Politics of Representing Violence in Bali," in *Beginning to Remember the Past in the Indonesian Present,* ed. Mary Zurbuchen (Seattle: University of Washington Press, 2005). This edited collection contains a range of essays that discuss the Suharto killings in Indonesia.

2

Development and Destruction

The Consequences of Change

You know the bombs may not be so bad thing. Before the bomb, everything is crazy in Bali. There is no time. No time for friends, for the ceremony. The kids going crazy. The streets, you know. Midnight in Legian Street is peak hour. Trucks, buses, cars, all trying to get somewhere. Now there's nothing, and we can take a good look at where we are. We can think about what is Bali now.

—Gede Narmada, 2006

This is Tommy's territory. Tommy Suharto pushed all these people off their land. No choice. Look at "Dreamlands." Roads. Building sites. Golf course. Always a golf course. But you know, Tommy loved to gamble, but this one just did not pay off [Laughs]. He comes in, ruins the Bali coast and now he's counting his chips in a Jakarta prison cell.

—Wayan, hotel worker at Dreamlands Beach, 2004

My grandfather is a veteran of the Nationalist struggle. When the Turtle Island Development Corporation began to fill the land that separated the island from the mainland at Serangan, they killed the sea beds and the marine life. They also killed my grandfather because he had no way to live any more. I am living in Holland, but by the time I found this out, my grandfather had already starved to death. He was frail, but very proud. The Turtle Island company just came in and removed the villagers and their livelihood. There were no titles in Bali, and the government in Jakarta says it has the right to use the 100-meter strip of the coast. That is where the villages are. My grandfather was killed by the nation he helped to build. That is not right.

—Paripan Lobeng discussing the development of Nusa Dua, 2004

WHILE THE TYRANT SLEEPS

In May 2005 the former Indonesian president, Suharto, was officially excused from charges of corruption. On the grounds that the aging tyrant was
too sick to stand trial, the Indonesian government and judiciary excused
Suharto from his crimes of embezzlement and, more importantly, his
crimes against humanity. During the thirty-two years of his reign of terror,
Suharto amassed a personal fortune of nearly 25 billion dollars, while the
majority of the country's population lived in squalor. And despite remark-
ably high growth rates during the 1980s and early 1990s, Suharto's presidency ended with a resistant 16 percent poverty rate, 12–15 percent unem-
ployment and much higher rates of underemployment, and a per capita
GDP which had barely moved beyond US$3,000. With foreign debt now
running at around 120 percent of GDP, Indonesia remains the weakest and
most vulnerable of the former "tiger" economies of the South East Asian region. According to the American CIA International Factbook, Suharto has
left Indonesia's economy with significant problems of "high unemploy-
ment, a fragile banking sector, endemic corruption, inadequate infrastructure, a poor investment climate, and uneven distribution of resources
among regions."[1] Until his death on 27 January 2008, Suharto himself continued to live the life of a retired sovereign, leaving a trail of murder, plunder, oppression, and squalor in the wake of his aged dozing.

The weaknesses of the New Order's economic and social management
were dramatically exposed in the 1997 Asian monetary crisis. Suharto's corrupt practices and failure to establish autonomous and effective institutions
unraveled much of the country's potential, leaving subsequent governments
to deal with the legacy of these severe economic and social problems. Of
course, the New Order plutocrats who surrounded and supported Suharto
shared in the spoils. Senior army officials, businessmen, public servants,
and members of the judiciary were rewarded for their loyalty with lucrative
government posts and contracts. Development money acquired through the
World Bank, the International Monetary Fund (IMF), Asian Development
Bank, and major international development organizations such as the
United Nations Development Program (UNDP) and USAID was marshaled
into projects which maximized profit for the Suharto plutocracy. Billions of
development dollars were siphoned into the favored investment interests of
the elite, particularly for natural resource exploitation (oil, gas, timber) and
tourism development. The Suharto family found Bali particularly appealing
as it provided a grand international stage for displays of statesmanship, national cultural treasures, and the opulence of their own grotesque wealth.

Whatever we may think of the tourism developments in Bali, there is little doubt that they have radically altered the Balinese social, cultural, and
physical landscape. Indeed, much of the analysis of Bali's modernization

struggles with the question of whether the economic benefits derived from development have been worth the sacrifice of cultural and ecological integrity.[2] Those commentators who treasure the "authentic" or "traditional" Balinese culture, in particular, seem most aggrieved by the Balinese adoption of modernist social and economic practices, arguing that the force of Suharto's New Order regime entirely deprived the Balinese of political choice and political will. Beginning with the 1965/1966 genocide and continuing through the "development invasion," the New Order truncated the Balinese's potential for self-determination and resistance. According to this view, the genocide successfully neutered Balinese political consciousness, leading the people into a listless and capitulative silence.[3] This silence manifests itself in two quite distinct ways: first, it is expressed in the uncritical adoption of Western practices and consumerist lifestyles, especially by Balinese youth; and secondly, it is expressed through the widespread "reassertion" of traditional Hindu rituals and customary law (*adat*). While these alternative responses may seem to contend with one another, they are in fact equally bound to the tourism culture that has been so broadly imposed on the island. Even the reinvigoration of ritual has commercial value and it has been widely integrated into hotel and tourist entertainment.

The *adat* has evolved through a meticulous historical blending of Hindu ritual and complex modes of village and civil governance. Its rituals and religious practices serve to maintain cosmological and social integrity as well as sustain rigidly structured modes of community management and civic decision-making. The rituals and religious practices of the *adat* further complicate the processes of development, exacerbating tensions between modernization and tradition.[4] Paradoxically, while the *adat* has been a central platform for the island's tourist promotion it has also continued as a critical site of resistance, a site in which the Hindu-Balinese confront modernization and the power and influence of international economic interests.[5]

In this chapter we will explore the impacts of development in greater detail, including the responses of the Balinese. While it is clear that the political genocide and oppressive tyranny of the New Order have influenced the Balinese response to development on the island, the arguments outlined above fail to adequately describe the complex and diffuse character of Bali's modernization. As we will contend in this chapter and throughout the book, the Balinese have been exposed to extraordinary transformational conditions that have themselves been formed through a collusion of powerful and often clandestine political, social, and economic agencies. Against the perpetual threat of violence and privation, the Balinese have been forced to accommodate a very particular form of modernization that has been largely constituted around the power and avarice of the New Order military and political plutocracy. The structural and environmental changes that modernization has brought to Bali have been shaped by a moral and ideological order which has clearly cast itself over the customs and ethical integrity of the island culture. Indeed, while many Balinese have experienced some level of financial improvement through the process of modernization, this prosperity has been achieved through a radical compromise of their sense of personal and social well-being. Inside the concrete superstructure of modern Bali, the Balinese themselves seem to be shadowed by the past, vaguely bewildered, at times even despairing, within a profoundly shifting social perspective and personal consciousness. Thus, the state of "being Balinese" has been challenged, not just by the changes associated with modernization itself—but by a *particular* modernization that is replete with violence, severe cultural dislocation, and the incursion of an alien and entirely disjunctive moral order.

Not surprisingly, the Balinese accommodation of change has been characterized by contradiction, double-coding, and a deft manipulation of externally created ideas and images. "Peace," "paradise," "harmony"—these are epithets that have been frequently invoked to describe Balinese culture and lifestyle. Travelogues, tourist brochures, cultural texts, and the Balinese themselves have used these descriptors in order to promote the culture and its attractions. Yet these epithets are as illusory as they are authentic since they are constructed around an historical narrative which consciously emphasizes the cultural elements that will attract tourists against those elements that may not. Indeed, the tourism allure and prosperity that are inscribed into these descriptors demand the obfuscation of Bali's own violent and egregious history of modernization; the Balinese must themselves parenthesize their past in order to secure their financial future. This form of social denial or silence seems to have further deepened a sense of crisis in Bali. The fullness of the island's future, thereby, is perpetually destabilized as it is falsified through an unresolved social and cultural trauma. Thus, modern tourism is not merely the bearer of prosperity for Bali: it is also the source of a continual state of social and psychological deferral for a people who have been snared in the rising dust of change and the political economy of pleasure. This chapter examines the processes of development in terms of these central problems and the cultural politics we are calling "forbidden crisis."

GLOBAL INTEGRATION: THE NEW TOURISM

As discussed in the previous chapter, the grand projects and buildings which are the legacy of the New Order's project of transformation now stand like tombstones above the ruined lives of those many millions of people whom Suharto slaughtered and plundered in the exercise of his own obscene and insatiable greed. In Bali these monuments dominate the southern tourist zones from Kuta to Sanur and Nusa Dua (the Badung district). We have spoken in chapter 1 about the significance of the Hotel Bali Beach and the Oberoi in Seminyak. While these buildings have a clear connection to the 1965/1966 political genocide, Suharto and his family have also been directly involved in the rapid expansion of tourism development which occurred after 1980. Until that time, growth had been relatively measured. The establishment of the Hotel Bali Beach in the mid-1960s and the new Ngurah Rai international airport in 1969 were designed to attract higher-paying tourists who could now come directly into Bali without having to travel via Jakarta. In 1972 the United Nations Development Program sponsored a development plan to be funded through the World Bank. Preferring, it would seem, Suharto's human rights abuses to the dangers posed by communism, the World Bank poured millions of dollars into the New Order. This development scheme was designed to reshape the low-level tourism industry in Bali into a model which the whole nation could emulate. Following the principles of cultural preservation promoted during the Dutch Residency (1908–1942), a French consulting company SCETO urged the Indonesian government to ensure that the island's cultural integrity was protected from excessive development: any degradation of the Balinese culture was both morally and economically indefensible as the island's culture was its primary attraction for tourists.

However, while the Master Plan for Development of Tourism in Bali focused primarily on the higher-paying international visitor, Bali became increasingly appealing to young Westerners—backpackers, hippies, and surfers—who were seeking some authentic experience of "the East." Inspired, perhaps, by the writings of Covarrubias or films like Albert Falzon's *Morning of the Earth* (1972), these youthful travelers were part of a generation that had become somewhat disillusioned by Cold War politics and the excessive materialism of their home cultures. In the late 1960s and early 1970s, these antiestablishment and often middle-class youth were seeking new expressive spaces in which they could explore new ideas and moralities that were not bound to the ossified social structures of the West. Bali, which had already been iconicized in Hollywood films like *Road to Bali* and *Honeymoon in Bali*, was seeping into a Western imaginary that was becoming increasingly entranced by Eastern music, sensuality, and the euphoric potential of drugs like marijuana. Through bands like the Beatles and the Mahivishu Orchestra the mysticism and esoteric splendor of Eastern culture were being revivified into a Romanticism which symbolized the antiestablishment aesthetic of Western youth culture. This imaginary was not merely a fantasy, but was a confluence of imagining, emotional engagement, and a rationalism which was constituted around genuine and deeply felt political and social judgments. That is, the imaginary which created the young Westerners' experience of Bali was forged through a hybrid knowledge, one which didn't falsify the island and its culture, but which necessarily privileged particular qualities and amplified them through experience and perception. In this sense, the imaginary—or cultural imaginary—is the foundation of our meaning-making, our capacity to comprehend and translate experiences through the ordering processes of language. For the young visitors, the totality of their knowing of Bali was created through books, films, music, anecdotes, and their direct interactions with the island and its people. To this end, Bali was not simply a "created paradise," but an imagined culture which was a hybrid of home-based (Western) and travel (Eastern) aestheticizations.[6]

During the 1970s, most of these young people stayed at Kuta Beach, at that time a small coastal village with very few facilities or services. A single lane of tarred road ran from the airport to Bemo Corner and a hundred meters to the beach. There were a few small guesthouses or *losmen* around the village and along the unmade road to Legian. Local village entrepreneurs had constructed the *losmen* in traditional grass and bamboo. Some used masonry excavated from the coral reefs that began at the south end of the beach and stretched around toward the Bukit Peninsula. A few restaurants had begun to appear around Bemo Corner and down toward the beach along Poppies Lane. Made, a widow from an adjacent village, had established a small *warung* (café) out of driftwood and grass at the spot where surfers paddled out to Kuta Reef. This small, shabby building blew away each rainy season and miraculously reappeared in the dry. Made's warung provided a gritty banana jaffles and Coke to ravenous surfers and the few European beachcombers who would swim naked in the still waters that lay inside the reef.

Entranced, perhaps, by their own imagination of a Romantic primitivism, the Continental visitors would lie about the sand dunes on the eastern fringe of the village, often smoking joints and marveling at the intense majesty of the setting sun. Nude and topless bathing at this time was commonplace and it was as though the Westerners, Europeans in particular, had found in the premodern lifestyles of Bali an access to their own essential nature, which modernization had effectively obscured. This typically Romantic essentialism was a primary focus of the conversations for visitors, particularly as it was coupled with the ideals and practices of a distinctly Western sexual liberationism. Perfumed by the tropical gardens and warm night air, the island seemed to intensify the languor and lawlessness of desiring bodies. Bali, that is, became the locus for an expressive freedom which had much more to do with the Western imaginary than the actualities of Balinese culture and the Balinese themselves. Like many of the early colonial visitors and writers such as Julius Jacobs, the young Westerners of the 1970s projected into Bali a primitivism that had been created through their own culture's fetishization of nudity and in particular female breasts. To this end, the Westerners imagined in Bali their own libidinal ideals and a morality which was itself quite disjunctive, bearing little resemblance to the strictures of Balinese social and sexual codes.

Young Westerners also assumed that the smoking of Indian hemp (marijuana) was a common cultural practice in Bali. However, while beetlenut and even opium were used in various Balinese communities, marijuana smoking was less common. The production, processing, and distribution of marijuana and other hallucinogenics, including "magic" mushrooms, were largely constituted around a Western youth market which had adopted the practice from a combination of American jazz culture and the modeling of popular musicians like the Beatles, the Grateful Dead, and Jefferson Airplane. For the young visitors, Balinese dope was cheap, highly accessible, and largely unpoliced. Until 1997, in fact, drug laws in Indonesia were moderate and only sporadically enforced. If a young Westerner was detained by the military-based police and in possession of illicit narcotics, there was a standard bribe which would ensure exoneration. As the 1970s progressed, in fact, the military in Bali became increasingly active in the sale of narcotics and in protection rackets for local drug traffickers. But for the most part, the young travelers were left alone to huddle in Poppies Lane, contract the full raft of intestinal disorders, and watch the milky sunsets and shimmering blue seas which were yet to be contaminated by the onslaught of five-star hotels and mass development.

By the end of the decade, however, Kuta was attracting investors, petty entrepreneurs, and workers from across the island. As the tourist numbers continued to swell, much of the coastal strip between Kuta and Legian had been divided and developed. While in 1970 there were only two guesthouses in Kuta, by 1980 there were around two hundred, along with forty-five restaurants and a broad class of *tokos* (small shops) selling cheap clothing, wood carvings, and other tourist paraphernalia.[7] Several large hotels were planned for the area, including the Oberoi and a new strip of luxury hotels on the new beachfront road connecting Kuta and Legian: the end of the village lifestyle was nigh. A large proportion of tourist visitors were younger travelers who barely ventured beyond Kuta, with the occasional sojourn to Uluwatu, Tanah Lot temple, or the Immigration Office in Denpasar. And indeed, while Kuta had not been targeted in the Tourism Development Plan, table 2.1 demonstrates that the young travelers themselves had brought a particular kind of growth to the area.

Kuta very quickly established itself as a hangout for surfers and beachgoers who satisfied their cultural appetite with visits to adjacent villages or through the community rituals frequently performed along Kuta beach. Young travelers who ventured a hundred meters inland from Kuta Reef could, for example, attend cremations and cleansing ceremonies at a small village cemetery which was nestled secretively among the palm groves. While well camouflaged from outsiders, the cemetery was a final resting

Table 2.1.   Tourist Visitors to Bali in the Early Years

1972	1973	1974	1976	1979	1980
6,096	14,532	18,010	14,832	36,052	60,325

Note: The Indonesian government began to take official figures after 1966. While accurate early statistics are difficult to obtain, see more detail in G. Francillon "Tourism in Bali—Its Economic and Social Impact: Three Points of View," *International Social Science Review 12* (1975): 723–752. See also I Nyoman Darma Putra and Michael Hitchcock, "The Bali Bombs and the Tourism Development Cycle," *Progress in Development Studies*, no. 2 (2006): 6.

place of a number of victims of the 1965/1966 massacres. It too was obliterated in the development surge of the 1980s.

It has certainly been suggested that the Kuta crowds were perhaps the most hedonistic of the early mass tourism period. Oblivious, perhaps, to the extent of the Suharto genocide, or simply distracted by the ideal of a pure and beautiful paradise, the young Australians and Americans who came to Kuta in those days seemed entirely comfortable in their own fantasy of freedom. Without seeing the horror of recent history, the Kuta visitors seemed entirely convinced that they were welcomed, even loved, by their Balinese hosts, and that this low-level incursion was of mutual benefit, an ecstasy of cultural exchange. And indeed, it is true that that the young Westerners, by and large, learned an enormous amount about being non-Western and about the many things that their home cultures had surrendered through the progress of modern rationalism and technological or-

2.1.   Tourist crowds on Kuta Beach (1984).
Courtesy of Belinda Lewis.

ganization. But these new learnings were constituted in a relatively safe, if somewhat naïve, context: a comfort zone of vaguely familiar foods, lodgings, and language which ensured interaction with their own kind, and an emergency escape to Australia or Singapore was only a several-hour flight away.

This, of course, was not a luxury afforded the people of Bali, who in 1980 remained extremely poor with poverty rates at equivalent levels to the rest of Indonesia. In fact, villages in the drier parts of the northeast and the southern hinterland from Kuta to the Bukit Peninsula were frequently subject to the worst conditions of drought, malnutrition, and famine. Even around Kuta, which was an economic boomtown, the tourists represented unimaginable wealth and a lifestyle which inevitably dislodged the security and confidence of their hosts. Appended to the visitors' wealth and privilege were new clothing styles, ideas, sexual and cultural practices which inevitably attracted the interest of the younger Balinese. While recognizing that the tourists were confirming the value of traditional Balinese culture through their presence and interest, many young Balinese began to aspire to the lifestyle and cultural practices of their visitors. Even the surf, which had always threatened the Balinese and which perpetually required cosmological appeasement, was transformed into a play space for leisure and sexual display. The horrors of the massacres which had occurred barely a decade before were somehow recast by this hedonism. In order to survive their catastrophe, many young Balinese were ready to absorb these new practices and adopt an economic framework which had been entirely alien for the vast majority of the Balinese barely a generation before. New bonds were being forged; new attitudes and practices were being adopted.

The more culturally inquisitive traveler, however, found this form of Western cultural appropriation unpalatable, a contamination of the purer and more authentic Bali created in the writings of Miguel Covarrubias and Clifford Geertz. Seeking a less contaminated cultural experience, many of these young visitors ventured to the idyllic and less densely trammeled village of Ubud. Still staying in low-cost and locally owned guesthouses, they sought to immerse themselves in the spiritual aesthetic of local ritual, dance, and craft. More particularly, they wanted to know the Bali which painters like Walter Spies had represented and which had inspired Bali's own new generation of painters and sculptors. Many of these young visitors sought to emulate the earlier Western aesthetes, residing for considerable periods in the village in order to create their own art and their own sense of an exotic, creative community. These pilgrim artists, in fact, wanted to reenliven the Western aesthetic through an immersion in ancient Vedic spiritualism and the Balinese unique sensibilities which, for the imaginary of the visitors at least, were deeply esoteric and nonmaterial. Bali, and Ubud in particular, offered a new and hybrid form of freedom and expressivity which was not constrained by the sexual and gender structures of Western rationalism and Judeo-Christian moralities.

The art community in Ubud, which remains vibrant today, abhorred the tawdriness of Kuta and Sanur, retreating into a primitivism which was perpetually elevated by spiritual and ritual enlightenment. Ironically, however, the Ubud community landscape was far from a pure example of Balinese tradition. Rather, it became a creation of modernist preservationism, a hybrid of "Eastern" and "Western" aesthetic ideals and expressive forms which (re)created the past through its own highly positioned perspective. While Ubud has become a central locale on the Balinese tourism map, its painting forms are strongly influenced by western art styles and its ongoing "success" as an arts community is supported by Western interests, perspectives, and occupation. Moreover, the tawdriness and clichéd lifestyles which the Ubud expatriate community found abhorrent in Kuta and Sanur are not entirely absent from Ubud itself, most particularly in terms of its anachronistic claims to authenticity and tradition. Many of the paintings that are produced in Ubud merely mass-produce the motifs that iconicize (and stereotype) Bali and Balinese identity. The Balinese art and craft industry, in fact, has been largely geared to a Western market that is narrowly fixed on the imaginary of Eastern primitivism.

In a sense, this line between original expression and mass production marks the broader history of tourism in Bali. From 1980 the line is crossed as an increasing number of major developments begin to change radically the landscape of the Badung district. In fact, the low-level and locally constituted tourism development which had been established around Kuta and Ubud was somewhat discomforting to the major planners in Jakarta. By 1980 Kuta was already regarded by the Indonesian government and its tourism agencies as shabby, dirty, and decadent. For many in the government and Jakarta social elite, the Kuta side of the island had deteriorated, bringing into Indonesia the worst excesses of modern, Western culture. In a sense, Kuta was a social blight which threatened the sanctity and moral security of Indonesia's youth. These attitudes fortified Suharto's personal financial ambitions which he was able to mobilize through the broad range of developments supported by the World Bank. The collapse of oil prices in the early 1980s hastened a tourism investment boom which saw billions of dollars of development funds directed into large and expensive resort projects. While Sanur continued to grow, large hotel complexes such as the Oberoi, the Bali Intan, and Legian Beach Hotel were being established along the Kuta beachfront. Perhaps the most ambitious resorts, however, were being constructed at Nusa Dua. These "two islands" had been separated by shallow seas and a mangrove swamp that was critical to the ecology of the whole southern region. As we will discuss later, estuarine areas like the mangrove wetlands at Nusa Dua are essential for the repurification of river waters, as well as shellfish and marine breeding. The Suharto family became directly involved in land "reclamation" which connected the islands to the mainland, a process which obliterated long-standing village settlements and their estuarine economy.

RESHAPING THE SOUTH: THE SUHARTO EMPIRE

The most recent phase of Bali's growth cycle correlates with the final decade of Suharto's rule (1988–1998). During this period, three distinct tourist zones had been formed in the south, each with their own distinct historical and geospatial characteristics—Kuta, Sanur, and Nusa Dua. However, even the spaces in-between have been largely drawn into a tourism consciousness and economy, leaving barely a hectare unaffected by the transformations and modernization project. Exponential growth in visitor numbers continued from the 1970s through to the Kuta bombing attacks in 2002. In 1980 there were less than 100,000 direct foreign tourist arrivals per year in Bali. By 1990 this figure had grown to around 400,000 and by the turn of the century it had increased to around 1.3 million.[8]

The International Monetary Fund (IMF) and World Bank who were the primary sponsors of Indonesian development had asserted their own fiscal interests over the Suharto government, insisting that the country adopt a strong deregulatory and "neoliberalist" monetary policy. Until 1987, when Indonesia established a more robust deregulation policy, development had been focused around a "feed all" notion of agricultural consolidation and intensification, textiles, and handicrafts. However, in the twelve months following 1987 international and domestic investment in Balinese tourism increased from US$17 million to US$170 million, a tenfold increase. This figure nearly doubled again by 1990. With no effective planning process or mechanisms for managing investment and growth, the total figure for new investments in the southern Badung area of Bali accelerated to a total of US$7.5 billion, virtually all of which was for five-star hotels and integrated resorts.

At the center of it all was the Suharto family and a centralized development process, which was based on a private profit motive that entirely subsumed the interests, customs, culture, and ecology of Bali and the Balinese. In a replay of the political genocide of the 1960s, the Suharto elite embarked on a form of social annihilation which once again subjected the humanity of the Balinese to a modernization "surge" that was based upon the privilege, power, and wealth of the military elite. Through a combination of corrupt planning processes, manipulative real estate deals, compulsory acquisition, and of course the perpetual threat of quasi-legal military interventions, the Suhartos and their allies colonized substantial tracts of land across the south, establishing a series of high-end hotel complexes and exclusive resorts. In particular, the three Suharto sons and daughter— Trihatmodjo, Hutomo Mandal Putra (Tommy), Sigitharjoyudanto, and Siti Hardiyanti Rukmana—have dominated the exploitation. Their interests included the Sheraton Laguna Nusa Dua, Bali International Convention Center, Four Seasons Resort Hotel Sayan, Four Seasons Resort Hotel Jimbaran, Lor in Bali Resort Gianyar, Bali Cliff Resort, Nikko Bali Resort, Westin Nusa Dua, Amanusa Nusa Dua, and Uluwatu Ocean Resort. While other members of the Suharto dynasty, including grandchildren, nephews, and cousins, have been equally active in the Bali resort industry, the core sibling group also owned significant portions of the real estate, development, and tourism service sector. These have included the Turtle Island Development Corporation, the Lombok ferry, most of the white-water rafting companies around Ubud, water purification companies, major restaurants, the Benoa Marina, and innumerable golf courses. The Suhartos were also behind a major development plan which would have established a casino near the island of Nusa Penida.[9] The casino was to be constructed as an offshore structure in order to evade Indonesia's Muslim-related gambling laws as well as the intense opposition and protests from local Muslim communities on adjacent Penida Island.

WATER AND THE NEXUS OF HUMAN COMMUNITY

From the 1990s the development patterns established by the Suharto family led to a dramatic geographical transformation in Bali. Around 1,000 hectares of arable land per year has been surrendered to tourism development, contributing to the even more dramatic transformation of Balinese culture and cultural practices. Such a radical reorganization of space, economy, and social structure inevitably affected the less visible dimensions of community interaction, meaning-making, as well as individual and collective sense of self (identity). The corruption and nepotism that has imposed itself as legitimate economic development and "rule of law" has contributed to an intensification of Balinese cultural disjuncture. Undoubtedly, the Balinese have become deeply suspicious of a law and legal system which presents itself as economy, progress, and civilization, but which bears the mark of a new wave of colonization. In particular, the colonizers showed little respect for the complex relationship between Balinese spiritualism and the agricultural and natural environments. Even at the time of Suharto's death in 2008, the new empire had left deep scars in the physical and psycho-spiritual landscape of the Balinese people.

While cultural disjunction is a common entry in the chronicle of modernization, for the Balinese in particular the incursion of alien practices into the "lifeworld" of the island people critically unbalanced the nexus between nature, religion, and society. Thus, the technological rationalism and system of social knowledge (epistemology) that support modernism and the global economy have proven profoundly disruptive for communities which have shaped their lifestyle, belief system, and cultural codes through centuries of social experience.[10] The fracturing of spatial integrity necessarily threatens the complex network of community relationships and highly ordered modes of communication and interaction. The Western and modern paradigm of individual autonomy and ownership ruptures the social as well as physical landscape, as land-use begins to switch from collective and collaborative action toward a more emphatic individualism, individual ownership, employment, and capital-based service. In this sense, the raw materials of meaning and ritual which provide stability, durability, and order for the Balinese communities have been substantially destabilized through these formidable incursions into the physical landscape.

Thus, while Western rationalism has created its own taxonomies of knowledge, the Balinese knowledge system insists on the complete interdependence of the natural and human spheres. This compound is constituted through the transcendent power of the spirit. The customary Balinese conception of spiritualism, however, is unlike the Christian or Hegelian idea that the body is a material and subordinate manifestation of the inner being; it is also clearly antithetical to modernist and secular notions which regard spiritualism as irrational, superstitious, and historically atavistic. In fact, the Balinese see the mind, body, and spirit as contingencies within a more encompassing cosmological order that is populated and controlled by the gods. Society and nature, therefore, are creations of the pantheon of spirit beings who are neither entirely benevolent nor entirely malevolent but who exist within and through all dimensions of the human and natural worlds. Thus, the gods, as with all human impulses, are locked in the eternity and entirety of cosmological condition, an "equanimity" which is itself the outcome of a potent and finely structured hierarchy of order. The distinguishing characteristic of this order is represented in the universal processes by which all nature moves from the purity of supreme being to a state of chaos and pollution, rendering itself available for renewal and rebirth.

Water is both the central element and motif representing this universal process of downward flow and renewal. While we will discuss the different types of water defined by Balinese custom in chapter 3, we should note here that irrigation water, in particular, is generally viewed as the *life source* of Bali's economic and material society as well as a key feature of its ritual and belief system. Thus, water represents the "confluence" of spiritual and material being for the Balinese. Just as the cosmological order flows from purity to pollution, water too must flow unimpeded from its source to its lowest point of return and renewal. To this end, the Balinese have constructed

an extraordinarily complex reticulation and farming system which is replicated in ritual and the social network that supports and surrounds their economic survival. Thus, the terracing designed to harness nature for human
agriculture is entirely confluent with the natural processes of gravitational
flow.

Moreover, since all the plots and fields which draw on the water rely on
its presence and flow, these reticulation networks have traditionally been
managed through highly collaborative forms of social interaction and order. Thus, while the Hindu caste system has been adopted into many areas
of premodern Balinese community life, there is also a very strong tradition
of communal decision-making and interdependence. In this sense, the rigid
social hierarchy associated with caste is perpetually mediated through a
more complex *homo aequalis* or system of equality which parallels the participatory and civil democracy frequently identified with ancient Greece.
Community farming in Bali, in fact, is characterized by two types of collaborative forum both of which are typically conducted on a monthly cycle.
The first is a form of community council where villagers congregate in order to discuss important local issues, including matters of infrastructure,
law, and ritual. The second is generally referred to as the *subak*, which is a
council of community farmers.[11] While farms vary in size and farmers vary
in social power and wealth, all farmers depend for their livelihoods on the
critical resources of water and gravitational flow. To this end, all farmers are
responsible for ensuring the health and well-being of all other farms, including the management of fertility, levees, biological pests, weeds, and ritual order. The *subak* is thus an organizational superstructure whose collective integrity is greater and more important than the individual parts. To
this end, individual farmers have traditionally had to address the *subak* in
the honorific codes of high Balinese, just as they would address a Brahmin
priest or other member of the highest caste. The use of these codes demonstrates that the farmer recognizes and respects the status of the *subak* and its
importance in ritual, as well as social and economic life.

The well-known American anthropologist Clifford Geertz was sensitive to
these complexities, arguing that the Balinese society he observed in the
1960s and 1970s was still largely organized around a seemingly paradoxical balance between hierarchy and equality. This complex and quite delicate
network of interdependence and hierarchical order, however, was severely
disrupted by the onslaught of development in the 1980s and 1990s. Yet as
early as the 1960s the Indonesian and Balinese governments had introduced a modernization program which was designed to reform the island's
agricultural system and its outmoded production capacity. Thus, through a
series of Five Year Plans, the Indonesian government and relying largely on
Western "expert systems" introduced higher-yielding hybrid varieties of rice
crops into Bali. While the failures of this Green Revolution are now leg-

endary, it was extremely telling that these innovations were accompanied by a powerful nationalist discourse which accused resistant farmers of anti-Indonesian or seditious intent. The project of modernization, that is, was introduced to the farmers through a fundamental ideological assault, one that directly challenged Balinese identity and the integrity of community intelligence and collective self-management.

The high-yielding introduced seed varieties were susceptible to pestilence and disease, and before long the Balinese farmers resumed their use of traditional seeds which had over centuries developed patterns of disease resistance. Undeterred, however, the Indonesian government and its Western expert systems introduced further modifications against the collective wisdom and highly evolved community practices. One innovation, in particular, represented a significant disjuncture in consciousness between the Western-style modernists in Jakarta and that of the Balinese farmers. With around US$55 million from the World Bank, the innovators introduced the Romijn gate which was installed at the head of the major canals feeding the terraced reticulation systems across Bali. These gates enabled a single "expert" or system manager to control the major flows of water that supplied the downstream wet rice fields. Until this point, farmers had used a highly sensitive system of observation to ensure that there was exactly the correct level of water and flow for the specific growth requirements in a specific paddy. A complex series of dividers were deployed to manage this flow and the whole system relied on each farmer participating in a collective duty of observation and adjustment. The Romijn system, however, relied on a hierarchy of expertise where an appointed individual would read the calibration gauge on the gate and release water accordingly.

Once again, the system proved a disaster. Not only were the gauges ineffective or simply not supplied with the gate, a high water level would make the calibrations impossible to see. In order to deal with the alien system, many Balinese simply raised the gate permanently or removed it altogether. While we will have more to say a little later about the impact of chemical fertilizers and pesticides, our point here is that the tourism boom was accompanied by a broader shift in thinking about agriculture and traditional societies. The Indonesian and Balinese governments seemed to view agriculture and agricultural communities as both anachronistic and dispensable, premodern relics in a rapidly changing world. Of course, the picturesque terraces and even the image of the peasant farmer himself were valuable postcard motifs, but the rapidly growing urban areas and cosmopolitan resorts required much more food than Balinese subsistence farming could provide. The new world demanded higher-yielding crops and different crops, but more importantly it required entirely different forms of land-use and labor. To this end, many young people from the villages embarked on a wealth pilgrimage to Kuta and other parts of the island in search of cash-yielding jobs or opportunities in the tourism industry. Those who were successful and who could deal with the cultural and psychological rupture that accompanied the radical change in lifestyle were able to remit surpluses of their salaries or profits back to the village. While these remittances have proven extremely important for the family income, they also represented the significant disruption to agricultural labor, inheritance, and knowledge transfer. Deprived of much of its youth and ongoing vitality, many rural communities have become fragmented and in some cases entirely exhausted. As the senior generation of farmers become infirm or too old to work, fields in some areas are lying fallow and gaps are appearing in the nexus between community, nature, and the spirit.

Thus, while young people are frequently summoned back to the village to ensure piety and religious observance, there is no doubt that the spiritual energy of many villages has been severely drained by their general absence. This problem is further exacerbated as land is increasingly occupied by outsiders. With serious shortages in agricultural labor and expertise, landowners are appointing tenants from other parts of Indonesia to farm their plots. Having no knowledge or particular interest in the local rituals or customary law, these farmers often engage in practices that seriously transgress community directives and sensibilities. Often, for example, these outsiders build shelters or small houses on the rice fields, a practice strictly prohibited by customary law (*adat*) and a profound offense to the many gods who preside over the crops and irrigation waters. Furthermore, these sensitivities are barely registered within the much broader panorama of change occurring as a result of tourism and real estate development. In these instances, the land is entirely transformed as the fine balance of nature and culture are subsumed within a universalizing monotone of meaning that is generated by the global economy.

THE ENVIRONMENT: CRITICAL CONTENTIONS

The Balinese, of course, had confronted such challenges since the *puputan* and the final conquest by the Dutch in 1908. The valorous but hopeless resistance to the Dutch invasion has been invoked in the more recent struggles against the injustices of current spatial and cultural incursions. Perhaps the most dramatic and telling examples of this new resistance occurred during the 1990s when a major integrated resort development was to be established around the sacred Tanah Lot temple. *Tanah* (land) and *Lot* (sea) are represented as an essential and integrated feature of the spectacular temple which sits on a rock knoll separated from the landmass by high tides and wild ocean swells. As well as its profound spiritual significance, Tanah Lot is located within a lush and extremely fertile farming area often regarded as the food bowl of the island. At a time when all political criticism or opposition was still violently crushed by the Suharto government, the development proposal provoked an intense and powerful response from the Balinese. While a malevolent and silent capitulation had become the prototypical Balinese response to compulsory land acquisitions and other government directives, Tanah Lot marked a significant deviation from this pattern. Indeed, while the alien occupation of their lands had always disturbed the religious and social sensibilities of the Balinese, it appears to be the sheer extravagance of the proposed development and its commensurate transgression of spiritual integrity which most provoked the local community. The amplitude of the offense, that is, seemed finally to have cracked the silence and complex political torpor that had settled over the Balinese since the 1965/1966 massacres.

Not surprisingly, the source of this political return was "the environment" (*lingkungan*), itself a critical component within the nexus of nature, society, and the divine. However, rather than invoke a simple traditionalism or preservationism that would be articulated through this nexus, the political resistance which formed around the Tanah Lot development was charged by a very modern and globalist response to a modernizing socioeconomic project. As with environmental politics across the globe, the Balinese protests against the Tanah Lot development were constituted around a range of grievances and modes of strategic response. Just as the developers invoke tradition to sell their products, the protestors mobilized community and tradition (including the *subak*) in order to challenge the development discourses. The debates between these contending invocations of history were communicated through the most modern channels of the mass media, public opinion, and ultimately the platform of the national political stage. The protestors replicated strategies of the global environmental movement and other forms of international advocacy and activism.

In a sense, and as we have intimated, the foundations of this battle were laid during the land battles of the 1960s. However, unlike the earlier expropriations of land that had been sponsored by the nascent New Order regime, the forcible acquisitions that were occurring during the tourism boom were often insidiously subtle and enforced by a far less visible exertion of power. Even the processes of expropriation of the rice lands surrounding Tanah Lot were unclear at the time. While the original 1971 Master Plan for Balinese Tourism had specifically promoted the protection of Balinese culture and sought to restrict development to three relatively contained zones, the later incarnations of the plan dropped any pretence to preservationism and by 1993 had expanded the number of development zones to twenty-one. By decree, the Balinese governor opened a quarter of the island's landmass for tourism development, permitting as many as one in five villages to be appropriated for the tourism industry. Once again, the

higher-end tourism developments were to be favored, as the governor responded to the interests of the Suharto plutocracy. In particular, the investment boom parenthesized culture in favor of the new leisure-oriented developments that would separate tourists from the more squalid or even
dangerous elements of Balinese society. The logic behind this model, while
patently thin, argues that higher-end tourists will stay for briefer periods,
spend more money, and create less impact.

In fact, these high-end developments have proved only partially successful and occupancy rates have fallen well short of supply. While we have
more to say about this below, there is clear evidence to suggest that the developments are part of a locally constituted cultural politics which was, in
part, designed to provide a leisure space for the Jakartan elite which had no
interest in Balinese culture at all but sought relief from the constrained and
bustling lifestyle of the capital. In either case, the integrated resorts began
to multiply across Badung, creating increasing anxieties among the Balinese
themselves about the sanctity and integrity of the *adat* and their own environment. In 1990, as a result of some local and international agitation, a
moratorium on new developments was imposed, allowing the UNDP to examine the environmental and cultural impact of this rapid expansion of
tourism development. However, before the report was even released, the
moratorium was lifted and the pace of development accelerated even further in order to make up for lost time.

The Tanah Lot project was at the apex of these developments. Like a number of the resorts appearing on the Bukit Peninsula, the Bali Nirwana Resort
(BNR) was proposed as a fully integrated hotel complex, providing five-star
accommodation, shops, restaurants, pools, a medical center and health stu-
dios, as well as a range of recreational facilities crowned by an eighteen-hole
golf course with views to the Tanah Lot temple.[12] Sited around forty-five
minutes from the airport, tourists could be transported directly to the resort
where they would experience luxury accommodation without encountering
the hassle of Balinese street life. Dance, music, handicrafts, art, and theater
performances would be delivered to the resort. Guests staying at the resort
would not have to encounter the polluted beaches, vendors, and degraded
urban and natural environments which had become the distinctive side-
effects of Bali's modernization and economic transition.

However, in 1993, the arrival of the bulldozers at Tanah Lot was greeted
with profound consternation. While agitation over the proposed erection of
a massive gilded *garuda* (mythical bird) and a Balinese museum park had
stirred some environmental agitation in the months prior to the com-
mencement of work on the BNR site, the bulldozers seemed somehow to
draw out some of the deeper angers and sorrows that many Balinese had experienced over previous decades. But whatever incited this return to direct
political activism, it was both politically pointed and direct. Much of this

agitation was reported through the *Bali Post*, which had assumed a key role in the protests:

> I keep asking why the conglomerates find it so easy to get permits to scoop up the area around Tanah Lot which is so sacred to us. To those in Bali who hold power, don't be seduced by the money that you have been offered to give permits to these conglomerates who would take over our sacred land. . . . The government . . . opens the door to the conglomerates. Haven't you measured how small our island is? (*Bali Post*, 21 December 1993)

As with other parts of the island, the farmers who had surrendered their lands appear to have had little choice. However, encouraged by the strength of the protests, the farmers actually sought to reclaim ownership of their land, arguing that they were deceived in the original contract. In fact, many reported that their irrigation waters had been truncated from upstream, an act that not only deprives the land of waters necessary for production, but which desecrates the spiritual essence of the island and the protective *adat*. As we have outlined, the downward and continuous flow of water is a central cosmological force in the Bali-Hindu belief system. The interruption of flow causes a divine imbalance and the contamination of environment and spirit. Once confronted with the BNR's ultimatum on water flow, these farmers no longer had a livelihood and were forced to acquiesce, believing that their lands were to be used for a public project and might therefore be saved from spiritual as well as ecological pollution. In the end, those who refused to sell were entirely deprived of water and had their lands impounded by the court.

The arrival of the bulldozers and the strength of public protest brought the farmers back into the fray. While the protesters appealed to their governor and to the Brahmin priests who preside over Bali's divine culture, the developers appealed to the national government. Around 5,000 Balinese attended a rally in January 1994, forcing the regional government in Bali to suspend construction of the resort until the religious, cultural, and social issues had been resolved. Parisada Hindu Dharma, the national Hindu organization established by Balinese religious leaders and intellectuals, issued a *Bhisama* (religious proclamation) on the sacred space of temples. The Bhisama stated that no development should take place within two kilometers of a sacred temple site for risk of pollution. While the edict applied to the Tanah Lot site, it was entirely ignored by the national and provincial governments and the law enforcement agencies of the TNI (Indonesian Army). In fact, the national government, keen to encourage the specific development and repress the political potential of the *adat* and a distinct Balinese identity, made two dramatic strategic moves. First, they replaced the military commander in Bali who, despite his substantial role in controlling the civil unrest, was seen as excessively sympathetic to the protesters' cause.

And secondly, they withdrew publishing licenses from three Indonesian news publications that had been supporting the Balinese protests: *Tempo, Editor,* and *DeTJK.* [13]

The result of these moves was profound. The police moved in with a brutal crackdown on the protesters. Student activists were assaulted and many sustained injuries requiring hospitalization. The physical attacks on protesters were matched by serious threats to the protest leaders and to those publications which evinced any form of criticism of government or support for the protesters or their ideals. Even the outspoken *Bali Post* became conspicuously silent. To the dismay of many Balinese, the Tanah Lot development resumed. Paradoxically, the Bali Nirwana Resort continues to deploy the language of culture and religion to promote its products, claiming to have enhanced the beauty and divine spectacle of the island and its people. The cliff-top vision of Tanah Lot temple is now the exclusive property of the Bali Nirwana Resort.

GERMINAL OUTRAGE

The failure of the BNR protest movement has not, however, destroyed the resolve of many Balinese who continue to be angered by excessive development and various forms of environmental degradation. The appalling effects of development can be seen throughout the island, most especially around the Badung coastal fringe. Balinese anger and frustration are clearly evinced in the rise of a new concern for the environment which, as noted, is a critical component of the *adat* and Hindu religious system. In 1997 a major resort development was planned for a site around a kilometer north of the Bali Beach Hotel at Sanur. The resort was to be built at the mouth of the Ayung River at Padang Galak, an important purification site for many of the Balinese living in the district. As we have noted above, the downward flow of water is a primary motif for the Hindu-Balinese cosmology; waters flow from their source of purity downward to greater impurity and hence spiritual danger. Purification and renewal rituals frequently occur around the mouths of rivers where the waters represent the confluence between land and sea.

According to the customary law, the coastal fringe remains critically bound to the collective interests and ownership of the community. Indonesian law, however, denies title ownership across a 100-meter coastal strip, regarding this zone as the property of the state. In this and the broader context of Indonesia's ambiguous property title laws, the governor of Bali permitted a development which would clearly transgress the *adat* and its cosmological reference. With the disappointment of the Tanah Lot protests still resonant but inspired by the fall of Suharto, a number of community leaders began to agitate against the development. Local villager Anak Agung Kusuma Wardana led the resistance, boldly calling for the resignation of Governor Ida Bagus Oka because of his support for the development. The case was particularly pertinent as both Wardana and the governor hailed from the village of Kesiman, one of several villages with responsibility for the purification ritual at Padang Galak. Moreover, Wardana was also prominent in community affairs as he was a descendant of the Kesiman ruling family, which was a powerful court at the time of the Dutch invasion. He had also been recently elected to a seat in the regional parliament as a member of the ruling Golkar party. Two days after Wardana's pronouncement, the Kesiman community council which protected and enforced the *adat* threatened to ostracize the governor from the village. This situation would have profoundly disrupted the governor's Balinese identity and his own ritual life. The loss of funeral rites, in particular, would prove a terrible prospect for any Hindu Balinese who sought the divine grace of spiritual purification.

Clearly, the threat was a significant influence on the governor's decision to withdraw the development permit.[14] It is also possible that the end of Suharto and his authoritarian regime had contributed to a rethinking of the imperative of obedience. The success of the protests and grassroots resistance of villagers was a powerful expression of new opportunities for political participation. That is, the possibility of a more democratic mode of state governance may have elicited some greater optimism about the management of civil process and the relationship between public and private interests. While these questions continue to circulate through various levels of public and community discussion, the Islamic attacks of 2002 and 2005 and the subsequent downturn in tourism have circumscribed their urgency.

TRANSFORMING CULTURAL SPACES

Contentions over the ownership and use of space in Bali are clearly connected to contentions over culture. It is nevertheless wrong to think of the Balinese politicism (or *a*politicism, as some conceive it) as a rejection of modernization or a simple retreat into the *adat*, ritual, and tradition. Rather, the complex issues around change center principally on the speed, character, and control of the modernization the Balinese are experiencing. The environmental movement in Bali is constituted around a genuine desire for regaining control and freedom of expression. Most Balinese understand very well that they are caught within a difficult transition and that there are costs and benefits associated with change. The major concern for most Balinese is that other people and other forces appear to have driven these changes, and that the economic benefits have been achieved without due regard for history, divinity, community, and the environment.

Tourism scholars, in fact, have identified Bali as a paradigm in the development cycle. In what has been called the "Bali syndrome," scholars refer to a mode of tourism evolution in poorer countries which follows a quite distinctive pattern.[15] Tourism emerges at a very low level, often through the interest of younger international travelers; there is a period of accelerating investment and growth in which the market extends to higher-paying tourists; there is a phase of deceleration and environmental degradation accompanied by a retreat to resort-style developments which are separated from the broader host context; and finally the locale begins to atrophy with decreasing visitor numbers and returns, contributing to a severe economic crisis for the host.[16]

Within Bali itself, the Bali syndrome is evident through the broad division of tourism spaces. While there are twenty-one nominated tourism districts on the island, these can be generically defined in terms of four dominant types. The first is the old Kuta-Legian area which we discussed in the early part of this chapter. These tourism spaces have been formed in an ad hoc manner with a mixture of low- and medium-level hotels and guesthouses, mostly owned and operated by Balinese families. Popular with surfers and backpackers, the Kuta-Legian area is sprinkled with higher-end hotels which, in many cases, have lost their markets over time to the newer and more luxuriously appointed developments at Sanur and on the Bukit Peninsula. The Kuta area is open and untidy, derelict in places, and a key locale for youth entertainment and various forms of drug-related crime. In many respects, Kuta is the key space for cultural interbreeding and hybridization, a site where Western and Asian tourists mingle with the Balinese, exchanging money, ideas, beliefs, and cultural practices. Since the 2005 bombings and the brief but significant economic downturn, Kuta has been deserted by a number of surfers and beachgoers who now prefer the more urbane setting of Seminyak, or who travel directly to the surf centers of Uluwatu, Changu, and the eastern islands of Lombok, Sumbawa, or Roti. Moreover, while tourism numbers have accelerated again since 2006, many of the newer tourists from Java, Taiwan, China, and Korea are avoiding Kuta altogether and staying in the well-guarded resorts where they feel safe and comfortable.[17]

The second key location is the Sanur area, which was the site of the original five-star development. While surrendering some of its luster, the area has also become an important place for expatriate Westerners. The third key cultural space is rather more open and less impervious than Sanur. It includes the recreational art and craft villages that have evolved to service the specific interests and consumer practices of international visitors—places like Ubud, Gianyar, and a myriad of craft villages like Celuk, specializing in silver jewelry, and Batubulan, noted for its stone engravings. While also servicing larger-scale and bulk international commercial markets, these villages have become part of the tourist circuit, satisfying the interests of individual visitors who are seeking authentic craft products and experiences.

The fourth and most recent permutation of the cultural tourist space—the integrated resorts—has evolved out of Sanur's luxury retreat model. While situated principally on the Bukit Peninsula and the reclamation zones of Nusa Dua, integrated resorts are also evident in places like Tanah Lot. These leisure resorts have been designed to capture and represent the symbolic essence of Bali: its nature, culture, and spiritual aesthetic. As a highly dynamic and rapidly mutating industry, tourism—especially "developing world" tourism—is designed around the market's need for constant change and refurbishment. This taste for the perpetually exotic or perpetually new, however, is constituted through an equally formidable desire for leisure, comfort, and pleasure. The integrated resort, therefore, significantly retreats from the details and unpleasantness associated with developing world conditions, isolating the symbology of the exotic location within its walled and secure perimeters.

It seems somewhat paradoxical that the 2007 International Climate Change Conference was conducted within the resort citadels of Nusa Dua. Beyond the walled comfort of the resort village, where delegates railed against the excesses of (Western) economic development, Balinese ecology continues to crumble. It is certainly evident that the Bali syndrome is largely constituted around a cultural space that has exhausted itself and left in its wake severe social and environmental problems. The cultural experience of the Bali holiday is crowned by good-natured and smiling attendants who have come to epitomize Bali harmony and a paradise that is free of pollution, contention, or chaos. It is represented in the luxurious lawns which overlook Jimbaran Bay, Benoa Harbor, or the temple at Tanah Lot. In this locale, the high-end tourist is not only emancipated from the grubby streets of Kuta and Denpasar, but is also free of the contaminating effects of thieves, local contempt, and the peculiarities of Bali's new cultural conditions. Here, the tourist is free to sample the authentic but digestible cuisine of the East without risk, discomfort, or personal challenge. At Jimbaran there is now a cosmetic surgery clinic in which mostly Australian cosmeticians and surgeons rejuvenate the faces of the international visitor—just in case the relaxation, indulgence, and pampering are not quite enough to produce eternal youth.

GROWING RICE

The sanitized social experiences that are created through cosmopolitan cuisine, clichéd modifications of traditional dance, and parodies of authentic art are necessarily part of a new history and cultural reality—the walls that surround the resorts cannot entirely isolate these spaces from the social mutations that are taking place across Bali. Indeed, the resorts are themselves part of these mutations, forming their meanings, values, and practices around various cultural contentions and contingencies associated with modernization. Like the perpetual battles between good and evil that characterize the Balinese cosmology, the struggle between traditional and modernizing values continues to evolve and emanate around the resort spaces. These struggles of meaning and value are themselves implicated in considerable economic as well as ecological and cultural dangers for the Balinese. As many development economists have noted, the financial benefits of tourism for the Balinese have often been overstated by those non-Balinese elites who have reaped the greatest rewards. As the minnows or "sweepers" of the major tourism developments, the Balinese have received very little social or fiscal recompense for the significant sacrifice of economic autonomy and self-determination. The loss of land and the agricultural economy in the south has not been balanced by the rise of a new form of Balinese commercial entrepreneurialism. Rather, the Balinese economy has been swallowed by the alien forces of wealthy developers who have demonstrated little interest in the culture, community, and economic well-being of their hosts except perhaps as salable commodities.

Indeed, even the guests who visit the segregated resorts seem almost entirely oblivious to the fate and conditions of their hosts. They were the first to retreat and slowest to return following the 2002 and 2005 bombings, and it is very clear that these resorts themselves contribute far less to the local economy than the medium- and lower-level tourism businesses. As the larger resorts are owned by Jakartans and international consortia, profits are repatriated to Java or elsewhere, leaving little for the locals other than meager wages for their low-level occupations. Even the food and other products consumed by the segregation tourist are purchased through the owners' related businesses, most often companies based in Java. On the other hand, tourism economists have pointed out that it is the lower- and medium-level hotels and guest houses which are owned by Balinese families who employ Balinese staff and buy local foodstuffs from local suppliers and growers. This multiplier effect means that the tourist dollars are proportionately more likely to stay in Bali itself.[18]

Perhaps the most threatening aspect of the newer forms of higher-end tourism is linked more generally to the dilution of the indigenous culture. From a tourism point of view the quality and integrity of "Bali," the brand, is being challenged by its *over*representation in highly consumable expressive forms which ultimately render the "original" Bali a mere parody of itself. The investment in the higher-end products has generated an equally formidable Bali discourse: that is, representations, images, and advertising narratives which incessantly repeat the "essential" qualities or attractions of Bali in highly simplified and easily digestible forms. In a consumer society, where markets are perpetually seeking an original product or experience, the representation itself becomes the product. Bali is now reduced to a simple and simplistic set of motifs and stereotypes. Its richness and diversity are trimmed to become a repeatable and easily recognizable message or iconography. Like the images of Tanah Lot sunsets, the celebrated complexity of the Hindu-Balinese rituals is reduced to generic tropes where the meanings are little more than memorabilia, a photographic boast.

This overexposed and exhausted rarefaction of the island's rich culture and history is also an attribute of the Bali syndrome. Tired, dishonored, divided, and damaged—Bali is being forced to confront the immensity of its own crisis, even in the continuing context of denial and a fear that the riches of the tourism boom may be entirely illusory. While it has only been temporary, the radical disruption to the tourism economy after the 2002 and 2005 bombings has impelled the Balinese to reconsider the damage that a homogeneous and stratified development process has wreaked upon the island. In particular, a new wave of environmentalism, cultural revivalism, and economic revisionism is emerging in Bali. Notably, the Balinese are seeking to broaden their economic base and revive the customs and social values associated with communal life, the *adat*, and the growing of rice.[19] As the tourism economy returns to boom conditions, particularly with the influx of new tourists from East Asia, it is difficult to know whether the Balinese will maintain their energy and interest in cultural revivalism, or simply satisfy themselves with the "blessing" of this new incarnation of global integration.

THE EXTENT OF DEGRADATION: CASE STUDIES

It is clearly the "massification" of tourism—the sheer volume of high consuming visitors—which is most responsible for the degradation of Bali's cultural, social, and natural spaces. However, the absence of an effective legal and social framework for managing development and tourism has produced a level of damage that is utterly incommensurate with the benefits it has provided. Violence, corruption, and pillaging by the Jakartan plutocracy have clearly contributed to inept governance and the almost total neglect of public works and public infrastructure. As we have noted above, the avarice of the Suhartos and their allies was designed merely to produce rapid returns on investments with virtually no regard for effective social and public planning. Roads, drainage, public utilities, regulations to protect natural environments, cultural artifacts, and sites—all were subsumed to the interests of the developers. While the fall of Suharto in 1998 and the move to a more

democratic and decentralized system of government have created new conditions for planning and development, the Balinese and their landscapes
bear the scars of this long period of unimpeded tourism growth.

As early as 1985, for example, the pristine beaches at Kuta-Legian were severely polluted. Overpopulated by tourists and Indonesian transmigrants
seeking work in Bali, the beaches had become littered and thick with raw
sewage. The new hotels were pumping raw effluent into rivers or directly
into the sea; rubbish was being dumped on the beaches and in lane-ways,
and open drains festered and spilled across the streets. A range of new manufacturing industries had been established to support the growth, and they
too were releasing their noxious wastes into streams and rivers around Denpasar and the tourist zones. As recently as 2007, environmental reports
demonstrate that untreated effluent and toxic waste are still being flushed
into waterways and marine areas, including those beaches between Kuta
and Seminyak. High levels of chemical and agricultural toxins have been
found, for example, near the Oberoi Hotel, a favored locale for bathing and
surfing. A 2007 report on the textile industry argues that clothes-dyeing
practices in inland villages are now utilizing more resistant and toxic chemicals but maintaining traditional practices whereby villagers rinse excess
chemicals out of the fabric in nearby rivers. Toxic industrial wastes are being discharged directly into the river system and ultimately to the beaches
in Kuta and Sanur.

Of course, the problem of waste management and sewerage is a critical issue for all forms of urbanization. The rapidly increasing population that
has been stimulated by development in the south has not been effectively
managed. While the net value of privately owned tourism assets in Bali is
estimated at around US$8 billion, there has been relatively little money in-
vested in the public infrastructure necessary for managing these assets, including the immense waste that the industry generates. In Denpasar, where
some attempts have been made to remove and treat effluent, at least 20 percent of solid wastes are still deposited onto the general household waste
sites or dumped directly into drains where, eventually, it will contribute to
the thick pollution already choking the beaches on the island's southern
coast.

As we have noted, however, the territory of "the beach" has already been
largely expropriated by the developers and hoteliers. The sandy strip of land
from Seminyak to the airport and beyond from Jimbaran Bay to Uluwatu
has been redefined as private space, the property of an alien elite. The whole
face of the coastline has been transformed by often appallingly designed
and very often grotesquely imposing hotel infrastructure. Thus, while the
adat seeks to preserve the coastal strip as a community and ritual resource,
developers have appropriated the beachfront areas, creating extraordinarily
ugly seascapes that impose geometric blocks of architecture over the "na-

ture" and cosmological beauty of the ocean. Indeed, even where the development has been set back from the beach, serious beach erosion has brought developments virtually to the edge of the water. The 2002 and 2005 bombings have led to a mass evacuation of the Kuta area, leaving many of these buildings deserted and parodic monuments to bad planning and bad taste. The new bleach-white *Discovery* shopping mall and hotel at Kuta Reef, for example, is perhaps the most absurd and abominable of these developments, glaring down from its tiered steps toward a beach that is now eroded and filthy with plastics and pollutants, its unattended facades already peeling and weathered, its appalling edifice a blight on the extraordinary beauty that it has replaced.

In fact, Kuta Reef itself is a monument of exploitation and overdevelopment. Once rich with marine life and living coral, the reef has been heavily excavated, most particularly for the construction of the international airport and highway to Sanur in the late 1960s. These excavations and the high level of water pollution have left many parts of the reef bleached and dying. The destruction of the reef has created new current and tidal effects which have caused such serious erosion that seawalls and artificial reefs are now being constructed in order to protect the developers' precious beachfront

2.2. Empty: The Discovery Shopping Mall, Kuta Reef (2007).
Courtesy of Belinda Lewis.

assets. Thus, the exploitation of Kuta, Sanur, and other coral reefs for roads and building materials is now threatening one of the island's most valuable tourism resources—the beaches and reefs themselves. At Candi Dasa on the northeast side of the island, developers imagined that they could build a hotel complex that would provide tourists with an alternative to the grubby ecological degradation of Kuta. Again, however, the protective reef was exploited in order to build hotels, restaurants, and roads. The damage to the reef was so severe that the beach began almost immediately to degrade and erode. A protective seawall was constructed, but this merely exacerbated the problem and the beach has now all but disappeared. The reef damage has clearly impacted on the diving and other recreational activities which were part of the original tourism design for the area.

While traffic, air pollution, and waste management have become the public bane of development, the most formidable and destructive environmental issue for the Balinese centers on the use and management of water. As we have emphasized, water and water flow are primary elements in the social and cosmological life of the Balinese. While agriculture has maintained a coextensive relationship between land, water, and human settlement, the rise of modern tourism has cleaved them apart. The surrender of 1,000 hectares of arable land to tourism development each year during the 1990s has had a commensurate effect on the island's reticulation system. Dams and other forms of upstream water extraction have deprived the lower waters of flushing volumes, contributing further to the high levels of river and coastal pollution. The purified water market, which has been constructed around mass tourism, is also placing enormous pressure on the whole water system. The extraction of water out of the system for tourist water consumption is contributing to increasing incidences of water shortage, low production, and rice shortages in one of the world's most productive and fertile food production areas.

Equally, interference in the reticulation system has led to a far greater volume of water extraction from the artesian (subsurface) water system. Artesian water has been a critical resource in village lifestyles where wells are the primary source of drinking water. Water is replenished by rainfall and reticulation seepage, but the resource which is formed over thousands of years is fragile and finite. The resort boom has critically endangered the resource, not merely through the reduction in seepage, but through the astonishingly high levels of groundwater use for gardens, lawns, and cleaning. The average water use per room in a five-star hotel is around 2,000 liters a year; this contrasts with an average 400 liters in non-star accommodation. But by far the greatest source of artesian depletion is through the watering of golf courses. The golf course at Tanah Lot, for example, occupies around two-thirds of the total development area, and the water demand for greens and fairways is enormous. Since the 1990s boom, there has been a steady increase in reporting of water shortages and increasing levels of salination caused by artesian depletion. A summary of environmental issues in Bali is provided below in table 2.2.

Benoa Harbor

In many respects the foundation for these changes were laid during the Asian monetary crisis of 1997. The collapse of credit and fiscal value which accompanied the crisis clearly contributed to a pause in development projects, and importantly raised the profile of alternative political perspectives— including Balinese environmentalism.[20] Thus, the fall of Suharto and the New

Table 2.2. Environmental Damage in Bali

Environmental Problem	Evidence
Forest destruction	Bali total 130,000 ha of forest. Almost 20% is critically damaged or 'empty' (cleared). Land clearing and illegal logging is still increasing.
Flora and fauna	41 species of plants, 47 species of animals are now endangered.
Land degradation	Almost 20% of Bali has heavy soil erosion.
Air pollution	Lead, nitrous oxide, carbon monoxide in urban areas are at unsafe levels for human health.
Seawater pollution	Ammonia, lead, and other heavy metals are above safe levels in the seawater at the beaches of Sanur, Kuta, Lovina.
Water pollution (rivers)	Rivers in Badung and Buleleng have unsafe levels of E-coli and phosphates.
Rubbish/waste	1,000 tonnes produced per day. 25% is inorganic. Major problems are due to open dumping of rubbish, waste is untreated, landfill is contmainated. Beach erosion and intrusion of seawater (rising levels). Seawater intrusion over land is 50m at Sanur and up to 100m in other coastal areas in the south of the island.
Coral reef damage	25% of the reefs are critically damaged. Only 35% are in healthy condition.
Mangrove degradation	Most damage in tourist areas of Sanur, Nusa Dua, Serangan. Indonesia is losing up to 50% of mangrove area per/year.

Note: Adapted with permission from data presented by I Nyoman Sunarta, Center for Environmental Studies, Udayana University, Bali, 2007.

Order dictatorship which followed the crisis have contributed to a more thoroughgoing reconsideration of the Balinese development program. The impact of these changes is dramatically represented in the development projects at Serangan (Turtle) Island and Benoa Harbor, which are located at the northeast side of the Bukit Peninsula near Nusa Dua. A major resort and real estate development was planned for Serangan Island which sits three kilometers off the mainland in the middle of Benoa Bay. Despite protests and the destruction of several villages and their livelihoods, the estuarine area was covered with landfill and a three-kilometer causeway constructed linking the island to the mainland. All but a small enclave of villagers on the 120-hectare island were reappropriated and the developers were in the middle of dredging a further 300-hectare reclamation rim when the Asian monetary crisis struck. As with the Tommy Suharto real estate project at Dreamlands on the west side of the Bukit, the development rapidly ran out of credit and was forced to close down. Despite the liquidation of the development company, the completed works have left a continuing legacy of appalling environmental damage. The island is now scarred and largely deserted, a haven for surfers and the café girls who emerge in the ghostly evenings to serve the pleasures of Denpasar businessmen.

2.3.   Serangan Island: Decimated mangrove forests, erosion, and neglect (2008).
Courtesy of Belinda Lewis.

As an estuarine area, Benoa Bay is a significant part of the water reticulation system of southern Bali.[21] The mangrove swamps are essential for filtering and repurifying the complex river systems which rise in the mountains in the north and flow through the estuarine area before emptying into the sea. Until the construction of the causeway and related port facilities, the area was pristine, supporting a rich marine life, which in turn supported a moderate level of village-style, aquatic economy. The causeway, however, has created a solid structure across the bay, forming a significant obstruction to tidal and reticulation flush-out. Moreover, the tourism and harbor developments have destroyed around 50 percent of the mangrove forest, seriously impeding the capacity of the ecosystem to filter and purify the estuarine waters.

Rising in the agricultural regions of the north, these waters have become increasingly laden with high-level nutrients, *E. coli* bacteria, and fertilizer residues, including phosphates, potassium chloride, and the growth hormone ZA. While some of these pollutants are associated with animal husbandry, they are more clearly linked to high levels of chemical fertilizers and human sewage accumulated through the rivers' excursions through the densely populated areas of Denpasar. These high levels of nutrient remain trapped inside Benoa Bay, creating vast beds of algae and other more toxic blooms. Chemical pesticides are also evident in the Benoa waters, creating considerable dangers for marine and human health. Mixed with the fertilizers and fecal nutrients, these pesticides constitute a toxic cocktail which accumulates in the fish stocks consumed both by villagers and international tourists.

Equally troubling, a freshwater dam has been constructed close to the mouth of the Badung River in order to alleviate the increasing acute water shortages in the southern area of Bali. The construction of the dam has further limited the flush-out capacity of the estuary while at the same time feeding highly polluted waters back to settlement areas. A United Nations Development Program report has encouraged the Bali government to build filtration and chlorination facilities to purify the water; however, even if the water were cleansed of nutrients and *E. coli*, highly toxic pesticides would remain. Local government plans to build a second stage reservoir will further exacerbate the problems, leading to further destruction of mangrove forests and reduction in flush-out volumes.

The mangrove swamps are also being destroyed by tourism waste and landfill. While efforts have been made to clean up rubbish from the tourist beaches and streets, the burden of waste has now shifted to Suwung, which is at the northern end of Benoa Bay. Along with the solid wastes from Denpasar, the site receives much of the high-volume wastes from the southern tourist hotels. Raw sewage pumped from septic tanks is dumped directly into the site. Less formal and legal sewage and rubbish dumpings occur in

2.4.   Serangan mangrove wetlands choked by waste (2008).
Courtesy of Belinda Lewis.

the estuarine creeks, contaminating waters which flow through villages and across the solid waste piles. Wastes of various kinds are frequently incinerated, exacerbating conditions for the spread of respiratory illness and other airborne diseases which are carried by the dense population of flies and mosquitoes that inhabit the Suwung swamp. The contaminated smoke and insect plagues constitute a particular health danger for workers, villagers, and the army of human scavengers who live in makeshift huts around the fringe of the site and who spend their evenings picking through the rubbish in search of something valuable they may be able to use or sell.

Sewage from Suwung, the river systems, and several villages on the Benoa Peninsula and Serangan has created an effluent fringe around the entire bay and island areas into the ocean. Surfers and other tourists who frequent the Serangan area are sometimes deceived by the narrow vision of the coral beach. Tests in the beach area show that the island waters are heavily polluted, with Chemical Oxygen Demand (COD) at levels well above international standards for safe aquatic recreation. Many of the resorts on Nusa Dua, however, are oblivious to the problems, focusing their recreational activities toward the southern seas away from Benoa and Serangan. Nusa Dua's sewage treatment plant, however, while out-of-sight of the high-

2.5. Scavengers make a meager living from selling reclaimed rubbish outside Suwung waste facility (2008).
Courtesy of Belinda Lewis.

paying guests, adds further to the effluent spillages in the Benoa region. Situated in the southwestern corner of the mangrove forest, the plant frequently overflows, and sewage again runs into the reticulation system and into the bay.

NEW RESOLVE

The environmental and cultural damage associated with rapid development and modernization represents another dimension of the crisis in Bali. Very clearly, tourism has brought major benefits to the island, most particularly in terms of increased incomes and interaction with new cultural forms. These interactions have themselves produced a new kind of cosmopolitanism, particularly in areas like Kuta and Ubud where the Balinese (and their guests) have evolved new and more internationalized cultural perspectives. For many Balinese, these interactions have widened their choices and experiences, allowing them to participate in the more productive and generative dimensions of globalization. As we have noted, the Balinese have paid a heavy price for their modernization, a price which most Balinese understand and now contemplate. In most cases, the Balinese have borne this burden in relative silence, recognizing that any form of social or political disturbance would have immediate and direct effects on the fragile tourist economy.

Thus, the image of harmony and ease is propagated over the smoldering anger and resentment which many Balinese feel about the loss of autonomy and the degradation of their environment. In the post-Suharto context and against the background of the Islamic militant attacks, which have damaged the reputation of the island as a safe holiday destination, the Balinese now seem more prepared to articulate these emotions. Thus, while environmental and other political movements remain somewhat fragmented and underdeveloped, there has been a strong reinvigoration of customary law (*adat*) and ritual community activities. The traditional community protectors of ritual, the *pecalang*, have become increasingly extant in civil and community affairs, including the management of transmigrants and other forms of community policing. While we will investigate these and other law enforcement agencies in chapter 4, it is worth noting here that the *pecalang* have become a central mechanism for the control and management of the beach spaces around Kuta and Legian, most particularly since the fall of Suharto. As the army has been forced to surrender its rather lucrative control of the beaches, communities themselves, including the various groups of Balinese beach-vendors, have assumed greater responsibility for the care, cleanliness, and social management of the beach areas.

Modest as these changes may appear, they represent an increasing chauvinism among the Balinese: the beaches, and other territories on the island, are not merely their livelihood, but their birthright and inheritance of a deep history. Thus, while nearly 80 percent of the total US$8 billion in tourist assets in Bali are owned by outsiders, the Balinese are seeking to reassert their interests and recover control of spaces which, for many, were illegally appropriated. The Balinese know that they are vulnerable to the whims of tourists and the tourism industry. They bear many scars that history has delivered. But they also recognize the significance of power and the possibilities associated with new, more participatory forms of democratic decision-making. To this end, the reassertion of the *adat* and ritual expression is not simply an expression of apoliticism or retreat from the agonisms of modern social and political circumstances. It is actually a mobilization of an imagined and more heroic history in order to fight the battles of the present. In a move that is common in indigenous and environmental activism across the world, the Balinese are invoking a sense of deep history as a shield against the excesses of development and the subsumation of their own distinctive sense of culture and identity. This mode of cultural politics, therefore, is a powerful gesture in the complex and often contradictory advance of modernization.

NOTES

1. *CIA Report on Nation Factbook 2006*, www.cia.gov/ciapublications/factbook/geos/id.html.

2. See I Nyoman Darma Putra and Michael Hitchcock, *Tourism, Development and Terrorism in Bali* (Aldershot, UK: Ashgate, 2007).

3. Graeme MacRae, "Art and Peace in the Safest Place in the World: A Culture of Apoliticism in Bali," in *Inequality, Crisis and Social Change in Indonesia*, ed. Thomas Reuter (London: Routledge-Curzon, 2003); Carol Warren, "Whose Tourism? Balinese Fightback," *Inside Indonesia* 54 (April 1998).

4. Linda Connor and Adrian Vickers, "Crisis, Citizenship and Cosmopolitanism: Living in a Local and Global Risk Society in Bali," *Indonesia* 75 (April 2003). See also Belinda Lewis and Jeff Lewis, "After the Glow: Challenges and Opportunities for Community Sustainability in the Context of the Bali Bombings" (Paper presented at the First International Sources of Insecurity Conference, Melbourne, Vic., Australia, November 2004), ed. Damien Grenfell (Melbourne: RMIT Publishing, 2004), search.informit.com.au/documentsummary;dn=876201933383235;res=E-LIBRARY (accessed 15 May 2008); Jeff Lewis and Belinda Lewis, "The Crisis of Contiguity: Communities and Contention in the Wake of the Bali Bombings" (Paper presented at the First International Sources of Insecurity Conference Melbourne, Vic., Australia, November 2004), ed. Damien Grenfell (Melbourne: RMIT Publishing, 2004), search.informit.com.au/documentSummary;dn=876183300411977; res=E-LIBRARY (accessed 15 May 2008).

5. Thus, while the "Bali harmony" discourse has mobilized the *adat* in order to distinguish Bali as a domain of the exotic East which is comfortable for international visitors, the *adat* is also deployed by the Balinese in order to assert social integrity. Over the last two decades, Bali's population has been increasing rapidly as transmigrants from other Indonesian provinces relocate to the island in search of the relative security and economic opportunities associated with tourism and related industries. Within this latter context, the *adat* traditions have become available for a cultural politics of self-assertion—and at times aggression—against outsiders, particularly Muslim labor migrants, arriving in Bali. See also Jeff Lewis and Belinda Lewis, "Transforming the Bhuta Kala: The Bali Bombings and Indonesian Civil Society," in *Interrogating the War on Terror: Interdsiciplinary Perspectives*, ed. Deborah Staines (Newcastle-on-Tyne, UK: Cambridge Scholars Publishing, 2007).

6. This notion of Bali as a "created" paradise derives from Adrian Vickers's book *Bali: A Paradise Created* (Ringwood, Australia: Penguin, 1989). While excellent in many ways, the book tends to overstate the falsity of this created image of Bali. Our view is that there is no single, authentic, and complete truth about Bali and what it means. The view of these young travelers, therefore, is not simply "false," but it is true within the circumstances of the travelers' own culture and experiences. Clearly, their image fails to see or understand many details of the island people, their culture and history. Even so, it is a legitimate version of the island, which has contributed ultimately to its transformation.

7. I Nyoman Darma Putra and Michael Hitchcock, "The Bali Bombs and the Tourism Development Cycle," *Progress in Development Studies*, no. 2 (2006): 6.

8. Source: Bali Provincial Government 2008, *Statistik Pariwisata:* "Direct Foreign Tourist Arrivals to Bali by Month," www.baliprov.go.id/informasi/stat_par/index .php?op=stat_2 (accessed 20 August 2008).

9. See Michel Picard, "Touristification and Balinization in a time of Reformasi," *Indonesia and the Malay World* 31, no. 89 (2003): 108–18 (11).

10. See Thomas Reuter, ed., *Sharing the Earth, Dividing the Land* (Canberra, Australia: ANU E-Press, 2006).

11. For an excellent discussion of the *subak* and the Balinese agricultural water systems see J. Stephen Lansing, *Perfect Order: Recognizing Complexity in Bali* (Princeton, N.J.: Princeton University Press, 2006).

12. As we will discuss, the *Bali Post* actively opposed the development. It became a major agenda-setter for the event and rallied much of the agitation against the development proposal. For an excellent discussion of the *Tanah Lot* (and more recent) environmental disputes in Bali see Carol Warren, "Community Mapping, Local Planning and Alternative Land Use Strategies in Bali," *Dutch Journal of Geography* 105, no. 1 (2006).

13. According to I Nyoman Darma Putra, who was a journalist for *Editor* at the time, Suharto's decision to ban these publications was also strongly connected with the papers' critical coverage of the government's decision to buy a secondhand warship from Germany.

14. For a more detailed discussion, see Henk Schulte Nordholt, *Bali an Open Fortress, 1995–2005: Regional Autonomy, Electoral Democracy and Entrenched Identities* (Singapore: NUS Press, 2007).

15. Claudio Minca, "The Bali Syndrome: The Explosion and Implosion of 'Exotic' Tourism Spaces," *Tourism Geographies* 2, no. 4 (2000): 389–403.

16. See Richard W. Butler, ed., *The Tourism Area Life Cycle: Applications and Modifications* (London: Channel View Publication, 2006).

17. There has been a significant change in the national mix of tourists in Bali, particularly since the two bombing attacks. Notably, there has been a significant increase in the numbers of domestic tourists from Java and international tourists from China and Taiwan. See chapter 5. Also see I Nyoman Darma Putra and Michael Hitchcock, "The Bali Bombs."

18. See *Bali Post* (22 November 2004) for a more complete discussion of these issues. The *Post* cites an Indonesian economist who claimed that Bali has become a "waste basket" and that 85 percent of its tourism assets are owned by non-Balinese. See also Nyoman Erawan, *Pariwisata dan Pembangunan Ekonomi: Bali Sebagai Kasus* (Denpasar, Indonesia: Upada Sastra, 1994).

19. See Graeme MacRae, "Growing Rice after the Bomb: Where Is Balinese Agriculture Going?" *Critical Asian Studies* 37, no. 2 (January 2005): 209–32.

20. Lewis and Lewis, "After the Glow."

21. This discussion is based on research conducted by the authors, Carol Warren, and I Nyoman Sunarta (M. Hum), Center for Environmental Studies, Udayana University, Bali. See also Carol Warren, "Unfinished Business: Environmental Impact Assessment and New Order Legacies in the Bali Turtle Island (Serangan) Development Case," in *Environmental Regulation in Indonesia*, ed. A. Bedner and J. McCarthy (Leiden, Ger.: Kluwer Press, 2007).

3

Bodies in Motion

Love and Desire in Contemporary Bali

In 1939 I became a Gandrung [erotic male dancer]. I was young then and very handsome. I had the dukun write the attraction magic on my body. I was still 14 and not thinking about women or marriage. With the attraction magic, I had the soul of a woman and the men in the audience want to touch me and kiss me because they see me as a woman. For these many years I only wanted to be with men because I have the *jiwa perempuan*, the soul and heart of a woman. Then I only think of men. I only want men to kiss and sleep with. It is only when I become older that I ask for the magic to be removed. Then I can think of women. And men no longer want to kiss me. I can no longer dance in the Gandrung but I can marry and have children.

—I Ketut Sudiarta, 2004

I like the older women because they have more money. The young ones just want to party. The old ones are nice. They takes care of me and gives me massage. I'm not care if her body's old . . . I tell her that she's the only one, so it is not sounding cheap. I tell the one in Japan, Sweden, Australia, and Germany—she's the only one!

—Montana, twenty-one, resident of Kuta Beach, 2007

The Bali chicks are pretty frigid, really. Don't get me wrong, they're as cute as. But you can't get 'em away from their little shops or restaurants. The Javanese hookers are the go. They all have Euro names like Annie or Lucy. One of 'em I met at Paddy's called herself Madonna. They're all pretty cool. Gorgeous, some of 'em. But you have to watch the diseases—and your wallet! I heard one bloke took a Javo back to his hotel, flaked out and when he woke up, she'd taken everything. Money, passport, some jewellery he was taking home for his wife. How low is that! [Laughs]

—Matt, Australian tourist, 2007

3.1.   European tourists on Kuta Beach (1994).
Courtesy of Belinda Lewis.

I likes the porn, you know. I likes the sex scene and the things it show me.
I not know these things before. I come from a small village and we don't
talk about these things. My mama she never talks about these things to
me. So now the porn tells me and my friends what to do. Is good for me
when I marry. But I have boyfriend now and he touch me sometimes, you
know. It's OK. But I must be virgin when I marry.

—Iluh, nineteen, female, *pembantu* (domestic staff), Seminyak, 2008

DANGEROUS SEX: POLITICS AND SEXUALITY

For many people, Bali is sex. Sensual, fecund, liberated—a lush and un-
bounded garden of mystical pleasures. From their earliest encounters, European visitors imagined a people who were not encumbered by the austere
and prohibitive mores of Christian culture. The natives' brown skin and
dark eyes evinced a sensuality that could release the colonial visitor to the
intoxicating delights of tropical evenings, the gamelan, and the delicious
plenitude of guiltless and unrestrained desire. In this strange and enchanted
place the Europeans found themselves peeling back, drifting through the
milky warm nights into new bodily forms. Here, where they were master,
this beauty would do its bidding. The conjured motifs of bare-breasted
women and languid, nut-brown youths inscribed themselves on the visitors' consciousness, creating a new site of conquest for the imperial imagination. And into the present, this fantasy is articulated through the beaches
and the bars, in the rustle of the palm leaves and the pulsing bass of the
nightclubs. Indeed, rather than being diminished by the modernization

process, this fantasy of Balinese sexuality has been intensified, captured, and commodified through the ubiquitous sexual imagery of the global tourist economy.

In *The History of Sexuality*, the French philosopher and historian Michel Foucault claimed that sex and desire are fundamentally linked to culture and language.[1] Thus, while the biological operations of a body may be driven by chemical and organic processes, the body itself is stimulated by a "mind" that is absolutely integrated with its external environment. For Foucault, this means that sex and desire are largely shaped by the culture in which a given body functions. Language, social relationships, power, meanings, ideas, beliefs, and, above all, the imagination, therefore, are the primary drivers of sex. According to this view, biological urges, sensations, desires, and needs are actually the predicate of culture, rather than the other way around. In either case, the social relationships and language which shape sex and sexuality are critically bound to the complexities of culture and power. Desire is not "natural" in this sense; it is an important part of the way a society constructs itself and determines its meanings, values, character, and structure. Sex and desire, in fact, constitute the most personal of human conditions in which the individual body and society coalesce. Sex is not merely a sensation or an action done to oneself or another: it is part of the complex chain of being which is engaged in the equally complex associations of reproduction, pleasure, and power. In all its visible and invisible diversity, sex is perhaps the most intriguing and ecstatic of human capacities—as well as the most dangerous and mysterious.

Thus, as forms of social and cultural expression, desire and libido are implicated in the radical transformations that have been taking place in Bali over the past century. Adrian Vickers has argued that Western perceptions of Bali are largely formed around the visitors' own libidinal fantasies. According to Vickers, there is a hiatus between this imagining of Bali's sexuality and the anthropological-historical reality.[2] Along these lines, numerous commentators have argued that the transformation of the Balinese and their sexuality is a direct outcome of European and Western colonization. Balinese culture, including indigenous sexuality, has been changed by the incursion of modern values and sexual practices, especially during the period of mass tourism. While there is clearly plenty of evidence to support this proposition, our own view is that the processes of change have been far more complex and interactive than this deterministic model acknowledges. In particular, we would suggest that there is no single and all-encompassing Balinese sexuality; even in premodern Bali there was a range of quite diverse sexualities and "realities." The interaction between Western and Balinese sexualities over the past century, in particular, has led to an even greater diversification and hybridization of sexual expressivity. In this context, it is perhaps better to think of these libidinal and sociosexual modes as part of an eclectic sexual imaginary, one which ranges from various forms of customary practice to the more recent relationship transformations associated with Western culture.

Of course, as with all other forms of human relationships, sexual interaction and expression (sexuality) are subject to considerable social and personal dispute, especially through the assertion of power and self-interest. In both premodern and modernizing Bali, specific social groups have sought to assert their particular interests as preeminent—and hence normal (normative) and "natural." Sex, in this sense, is a critical social and political tool which particular economic, ethnic, religious, or gender groups may seek to deploy over others. The use of reproduction and kinship (bloodlines) in the management of property and land was a key strategy for premodern elites. In Bali, the whole caste system, for example, has been structured around the maintenance and management of bloodlines and property. Colonial authorities, as we noted in chapter 1, used sexuality as a strategy for maintaining their own power and control over their conquered subjects. Thus, we need to understand the concept of "sex" or "sexuality" in the following terms—

1. Sex is an act of bodily stimulation and engagement. We will be using the concept of "sex" as a general descriptor of this form of human stimulus.
2. Sex is formed through the mind and imagining of individuals and social groups. Hence, bodily functions are subject to the conditions of desire, imagining, and expressivity.
3. These conditions are formed in relation to the ways in which social groups prohibit, legitimate, and stimulate sexual activity through complex laws, values, attitudes, collective imagining, texts, and practices. All human societies and their meaning systems (culture) construct laws and moral codes around sex, sexual behaviors, reproduction, and kinship. However, these laws, moral codes, and meanings around sex are not static; they change over time through the adoption of new cultural influences, attitudes, and practices. Often these new elements are introduced through interaction with other, external social groups. Sometimes they change through the internal reorganization of social forces and practices.
4. These prohibitive and permissive laws are shaped by, and help to shape, social norms around "sexuality," including the nature of gender, sexual identity, and sexual orientation. *Sexuality*, therefore, is the social and cultural expression of sex. Sexuality, as the public expression of one's sex, is subject to the full range of social, cultural, and political interventions. As we have claimed above, however, we cannot draw a simple divide between the "natural" feelings of sex, and the

imposed social ordering of sexuality. The two interact through social knowledge, meanings, and imagination such that feelings can be stimulated by sexuality, and sexuality can be formed in relation to feelings.

5. Sex and sexuality, therefore, are not simply modes of personal expression, but are generally related to various forms of social practice, values, and codes. However, a social group's culture is neither uniform nor universal, and social groups often experience considerable disagreement and "battles" over the meaning of sex and sexual practices. Elite groups, in particular, often assert their own interests and power through the imposition of particular sexual codes as the social "norm." Other groups and individuals may resist the imposition of a generalized sexual ideology through direct confrontation or by maintaining clandestine sexual practices.

THE SEXUAL POLITICS OF EMPIRE

The Dutch colonists used sex and sexuality as part of their general schema of social management. Early in the colonial period, as we have noted, Balinese bodies and culture were absorbed into the sexual imagination and libido of the Dutch, providing a rich, though often sublimated, resource for the colonists' own sexual aesthetic. More broadly, and in apparent contradiction to this aesthetic, the Dutch imposed a system of management which was designed to constrain the sexual practices, sexuality, and diversity of the Balinese. This process of normalization and standardization, as Michel Foucault argues, was largely an exercise of controlling populations through the administration of kinship, marriage, gender, labor, and fertility. Indeed, while the authorities might have built the colonial administration upon the rationalized order of economy, militarism, and law, the less orderly and potentially subversive power of sex represented both a problem and a solution for the Dutch Residency.

As outlined in chapter 1, the Residency recognized that in order to impose a cost-effective administration, they would have to assert themselves over all dimensions of culture, including sexuality. To this end, the Dutch instated the caste system as a legally protected institution, thereby creating an administrative hierarchy through which they could control the island's people, economy, and social practices.[3] As we also noted in chapter 1, at the time of the final Dutch invasion, the caste system was under considerable internal pressure in Bali, with many commoners and their communities challenging its authority and status; other groups, such as the Bali Aga people,[4] had never adopted this social structure at all. Nevertheless, the Dutch invoked the ideal of tradition or historical origin in order to use the caste system as a vehicle for their colonial administration.

The Dutch grounded their sanctification of the caste system through the work of the German philologist, Rudolph Friederich, and a field researcher named Frans Adam Liefrinck.[5] Friederich's analysis of esoteric palm leaf manuscripts (*lontar*) provided an extraordinary image of Bali's ancient ritual and courtly life. The palm leaf manuscripts are religious writings inscribed onto the leaves of the lontar palm and rubbed with a mixture of lamp soot and oil as a preservative. Because they rarely survive more than 100 years, many have been copied and reproduced several times since the original ancient writings. Each leaf is bound to the next by strings to form a "book" which can be unrolled and read at temple ceremonies. Most are written in the ancient *Kawi* language, so public readings are often followed by a translation in Balinese.

Liefrinck's studies of ancient Balinese history were conducted many years after Friederich's and were far less focused on regal culture. They were, however, confined to the northern region of the island, and were not meant to represent the variations that occurred across the Balinese kingdoms. Undeterred by this variability, the Dutch declared that the work of these scholars should be adopted as a universal rendering of the island's people, history, and culture. Dutch modernization, therefore, imposed a sense of social stability, order, and destiny which had its origins in deep history. This origin was clearly an invention of the Dutch overlords who used it to explain and determine the social character of the people whom they administered. In essence, the Dutch created a belief system around caste and social hierarchy that served their own administrative and political interests. Sex, through the articulation of parentage and birth, became the servant of the empire.

To this end, the Dutch created a new social hierarchy, including a class of loyalist elite, out of the old and decaying caste system. Of course, those members of royal families who had resisted the invasion or who represented some potential threat were eliminated from the local leadership group, leaving only the more compliant and grateful regents to perform the colonists' bidding.[6] Through this deft political move, the Dutch were able to exercise their administrative will with minimum visibility, external policing, and direct intervention. The assertion of colonial control and imperial values through a putatively "traditional" framework tended to redirect local grievances and criticisms away from the Dutch themselves and toward the Balinese (higher caste) administrators. Anger over increasing social inequity, unjust taxes, and new forms of cultural fragmentation was largely absorbed into the broader lexicon of local politics and communal dispute, thus truncating the potential for dissent or resistance to colonial rule. A propagated ideology of "tradition," that is, seemed to camouflage, as it neutralized, the negative and transformative effects of modernization.

Breasts and Blouses

The legal sanctification of caste, in particular, was most powerfully expressed in the 1910 edict prohibiting intercaste marriage. This restriction not only solidified the elite status of the high-caste trilogy (Brahmana, Kesatria, Wesia), it also ensured that the potentially disruptive sexualities of women, in particular, could be constrained within the borders of tradition and the legal system. Indeed, while it had not been uncommon for high-caste women to marry below their status (notably to the nouveau riche of the commoner castes), the 1910 edict ensured that any transgression would result in exile from Balinese society and the loss of property and privilege. Women's bodies, sexuality, and fertility, thereby, were inscribed with a new double fidelity, firstly to the caste of their birth and secondly to the legislative and administrative power of the Dutch Residency. So, at both the symbolic and legislative levels, women's sex became institutionalized, as they were marked with a responsibility to history, social reproduction, and the maintenance of privilege.[7]

Bali's pre-Dutch kinship system was constituted around patriarchal privilege. It was very common for nobles to have numerous wives and consorts, a form of polygamy that was also practiced (though less extensively) among commoner communities. The social role of women was generally constructed, therefore, around a femininity which was available for male sexual stimulation, but which could be transformed into a reproductive duty as determined by the politics of male-privileged kinship and property management. To this end, feminist analysis of Balinese sexuality and gender politics argues that the Dutch colonists simply mobilized the preexisting patriarchal system in order to serve their own economic, administrative, and sexual interests. A "modern" European patriarchal model was thus imposed over the premodern system, inscribing it with an alien and Orientalist mode of political oppression.

In this context, the 1910 edict preventing intercaste marriage further restricted women's choices. In particular, the Dutch law sought to close down the sociosexual fissures that had sometimes allowed women (and men) to seek love and fulfillment outside the borders of their birth caste. This strategy not only solidified the power of the colonists' puppet elite, it also sought to constrain the unruly and disruptive potential of women's sexuality more broadly. The great fear of the Dutch Residency was that their own people might be distracted from the economic and managerial objectives of the colonial rule by the *sexualis natura* and obvious permissiveness of the Balinese women. The nakedness and primitive sex drives of the women, the governors feared, might readily contaminate the moral and civilizational integrity of the Europeans. As early as 1848, when the Dutch had control of the north of the island, they introduced a local edict in Buleleng which insisted that Balinese women wear blouses when in public. Clearly, the Dutch had invoked their own contradictory fetishistic-prohibitive attitudes toward the most observable dimension of human sexuality, the skin, deeming that female breasts constituted an erotic obscenity. Subscribing to a Christian-European moral conception of the body and nudity, the prurient Dutch attitude toward exposure of the skin differed significantly from the Balinese and many other tropical premodern cultures. As will be discussed later in the chapter, the Balinese had developed a very elaborate cultural coding around the body and skin. Indeed, skin was not a simple expression of sexual permissiveness or ritualized modes of sexual arousal, as many colonists seemed to assume.

The Balinese body, in fact, represents the interface of spiritual, social, and natural forces; rather than constituting a vehicle of unconstrained lust and sexual availability, the body was regarded as a complex union of transcendent and pollutant impulses. Skin was used in many cultural practices as a form of "writing space" over which esoteric script, iconography, and spells could be cast. In most instances, the colonists failed adequately to appreciate or comprehend these practices, viewing them through their own Eurocentric ideological and moral lens. Thus, the Balinese and their practices were collapses into the Orientalist and Romantic imagery of the noble savage—innocent, childlike, but intrinsically dangerous. Thus, many European artists created a vision of Balinese life and sexuality that was both idealized and strangely pejorative, attributing to these mysterious Eastern people a primitivism which was beautiful, free, and uncivilized. In this sense, Balinese men and women were regarded as irrational, sensual, natural, feminine, and hence situated on a lower sociosexual and civilizational level than their more rational and masculine conquerors.[8]

THE IDEALIZATION OF BALINESE SEXUALITY

It is quite typical of colonial conquerors to typologize the conquered people in this way. Modern states, in fact, create an oscillating effect between sexual prohibition and stimulation since both are required for the ongoing management, order, and fertility of the social body. While contending with the disruptive potential of sexual desire, the state nevertheless requires sex for gratification and reproduction. In a more sublimated form, desire is also an essential part of human social progress within a modernizing context, most particularly as it is expressed through global consumer capitalism, economic growth, and market-based commerce. Thus, the desire for sexual gratification becomes symbolically translated through various forms of commodity, display, and deployment. While self-adornment has always been a part of human sexual interaction, consumer culture and modernization have broadened the repertoire for pleasure through products and modes of social self-expression and presentation. As the modern practice of advertising so clearly demonstrates, sexual desire can be modulated through the symbolic value of any consumable product—clothing, car, hairstyle, or holiday.[9]

A modern consciousness is characterized, therefore, by a largely unspecified state of arousal and desire. Modernization appears to have amplified the human propensity for self-adornment through a more intricate and complex wending of desire, aesthetics, and materialism. This amplification is further complicated by a highly unstable compound of rationality, the Enlightenment force which separates body, mind, and spirit while seeking their miraculous reconciliation. In a sense, modern consumer capitalism has evolved around this prayer of reconciliation, juxtaposing an extreme materialism and rational order with the social and psychological expansion of desire and libido. In the nineteenth and early twentieth centuries, European colonialists laid the foundation for a consumer-based capitalism as they created a more acute symbolic value around the "mystical Orient." The products which were exported out of the East, and Bali in particular, were largely constituted around bodily pleasure and self-adornment. These included textiles, spices, gemstones, silver, jewelry, and opium. Such products were marketed in the West through a conjured mood of Oriental exoticism and a subliminal sexuality that was evoked through travel writings, advertising, and quasi-anthropological accounts of *sexualis natura*. The consumers of these products did not necessarily or consciously link them to the images of bare-breasted native girls, but their intrinsic pleasures were stamped by the exotic motifs of the mysterious and primitive East.

To this end, the colonial project is profoundly implicated in the reshaping of the modern "Western" mind, Western sexuality, and the rise of consumer culture. The need for consumer capitalism to continually expand through the creation of new products, markets, and consumer practices is an important dimension of the sexual rendering of "the East." The European philosophy and aesthetic of Romanticism, therefore, is as much a contingency of global politics and economy as it is a mode of artistic and intellectual expression. While it may seem to contradict the rational and prohibitive impulses of colonial conquest and authority, Romanticism actually represents a cultural project designed to reconcile the competing psychological and social elements that were fragmenting through the process of modernization. The German philosopher Immanuel Kant was quite explicit about his desire to reconcile the sensory and imaginative components of human life through the assertion of a cosmically determined power of reason. Other Romantics employed their art and philosophy in order to elevate the human soul out of the degrading effects of industrialization and the destruction of nature. Romanticism raises the body and desire beyond its base corporeality to become a heightened condition of pure nature, the union of the actual and the divine. Thus, poets like Samuel Coleridge celebrated the Orient as a dominion of liberated sense, a site in which this pure nature could be freely expressed and experienced.

As we noted in chapter 1, the European imaginary of a sexual and aesthetic liberation was both invisibly and overtly inscribed into the Romantic ideal, invoking a sexual expressivity that was not constrained by the austerity of Christian morality. As we have noted, many of the early European visitors associated the relatively unselfconscious bodily displays of the Balinese with a liberated sexuality which clearly, in their view, subscribed to the pure nature celebrated in Romanticism.[10] Travelers, artists, and photographers like Julius Jacobs created an imagery which presented Balinese women as free-loving nymphs, merrily consorting with one another in a verdant "Eden before the Fall." Whether by design or error, Julius Jacobs, in particular, transposed his experiences of the Balinese courts to the general Balinese populace. Jacobs wrote extravagantly of "the Balinese woman," who not only engaged in licentious heterosexual practices but also lesbianism and a form of onanism which involved wax phalluses and various exotic fruits. Invoking the eugenics that underscored much of the colonial

3.2.   Classical motif of traditional Balinese life (Anon), Lusa Inn Hotel, Legian.
Courtesy of Belinda Lewis.

scholarship of the nineteenth century, Jacobs discusses the breasts of Balinese women in order to explain their racial derivation. This obsessive attention to comparative physiognomy and languages (philology) was constantly used by the Europeans to validate their colonial conquest and occupation of non-Western territories. Jacobs's fascination with the breast, however, was also motivated by "desire," a libidinal momentum which eroticized the colonists' interactions and authority in the East.

COVARRUBIAS AND THE ANTHROPOLOGICAL VISION

To this end, Jacobs's fascination with Balinese women's breasts and sexuality merely reflects the European fetishization of nudity and the body's transformation into new kinds of language. Naked breasts, that is, may be discussed in scientific or medical literature, depicted in high art representations, or identified as prohibitive sexuality in religious confessionals or law. In any case, as Balinese sexuality becomes translated into various forms of European language (including the language of art, photography, and film), it becomes subject to the interests of Western power. In other words, the process of modernization not only exposes the Balinese to colonial administration and direct interaction, it also conscripts the culture into new forms of representation. The immanent diversity of Balinese sexuality, therefore, becomes even more broadly diffuse through the knowledge and meaning formations of the West.

However, the prohibitive regime that the Dutch Residency tried to establish seemed paradoxically to intensify the more popular impression of Balinese licentiousness. The popular science and travel writings of people like Julius Jacobs and Geoffrey Gorer, who described Balinese sexual behavior as being "as natural as eating,"[11] stimulated the creative and economic interests of the most powerful image maker of the twentieth century—Hollywood. While anthropologically obtuse, films like *Goona-goona*, *Honeymoon in Bali*, and *Road to Bali* flattened the European romantic ideal into a form of comic romance in which Bali was a peculiar and delightful refuge from the rationality, prohibitions, and material orderliness of modern society. Thus, while *Goona-goona* (Balinese, literally "magic") emphasizes Bali's mysterious and amusing rituals, the island was represented as a form of sexual paradise in the later movies. In *Road to Bali*, Bob Hope and Bing Crosby find themselves entranced by the island people's easy attitude to love, sex, and polygamy. As symbolic products, these films extend the exotic quality of the commodities which the early colonists had exploited and exported to the West.

A dramatically different impression of Bali was represented in the writings of anthropologists like Miguel Covarrubias. In *The Island of Bali*, first published in 1937, Covarrubias argues that films like *Goona-goona* seriously misrepresent the Balinese, who are neither "romantic" nor sexually licentious. In

this context, Covarrubias is referring to the dilute and relatively uncomplicated ideal of "romanticism" which sentimentalizes the durable love which
is fostered in Hollywood films and popular magazines. According to Covarrubias, the absence of romanticism in Balinese kinship and marriage
arrangements derives from economic imperatives and the disinclination of
Balinese men to idolize women. More generally, Covarrubias claims, "romanticism flourishes where traditional barriers for the free and natural relations between men and women are strongest."[12] In other words, the Balinese
tend not to idealize sexual relationships and have a relatively pragmatic approach to sex and kinship. Covarrubias confirms his view by pointing to the
Balinese words for "love" (demen, suka, nyak) which, when attached to people, are more literally translated as "desire": that is, there is no literal equivalent to the English notion of a durable, sexual-romantic love. According to
Covarrubias, even stronger words like lulut have a more illicit or prurient
connotation.

Within its own cultural context, however, this naturalness seems to con-
found Covarrubias's own perceptions, which presumably are forged around
his own "romantic" heritage. Covarrubias recognizes certain differences in
the Balinese sexuality to his own culture, but he must rely on his own cultural framework to explain these differences. To this end, Covarrubias insists
that the Balinese are not "promiscuous," but rather approach their love with
a distinctive instrumentality which excludes intense emotions in either direction. Customary law and the careful management of property and marriage, therefore, underscore sexual interactions. While marriages were frequently arranged through families and the village banjar (council), on
occasions intimacies evolved through direct interactions between young
men and women. While premarital sex was (and still is) generally im-
pugned, customary law provides for certain sanctions and responsibilities.
Citing the customary laws of the village of Lumbuan in the Bangli mountains, Covarrubias explains this instrumentality in terms of basic economics:

> The desa [village] orders a man who is guilty of intimacy to take her as wife,
> making the offerings and ceremonies mentioned above. Should the man refuse
> to marry her, he has to pay the penyeheb (a roast pig) and tumbakan (a cow)
> while the woman will only have to pay the tumbakan to clear her impurity and
> the pollution of the village. Should there result a child, it belongs to the
> woman. If it is not known who the man was, the woman is responsible and
> must pay the penyeheb and tumbakan within an allotted time.[13]

This customary law, which provides such clear and precise sanctions for sexual transgression, might seem to disprove the notion of sexual naturalness
propagated by Jacobs and many others. The highly influential twentieth
century anthropologist, Margaret Mead, certainly came to this conclusion in
her study of Balinese sexuality, noting that "there was not an ounce of free

. . . libido in the whole culture."[14] Libido, that is, was largely locked into the complex network of customary law, ritual practices, and the micromanagement instigated by the new Dutch overlords.

The gulf between these two views—of sexual license and sexual constraint—can only be understood in terms of the context and focus of the contending claims. Sex, in fact, is perhaps the most difficult of human practices and imaginaries to describe precisely, if only because its very nature is often private and subliminal. Individuals and social groups, as we have noted, carry extraordinarily contradictory ideas and impulses over sex. To this end, the interactions between the Europeans and Balinese created a new regime of influence and sexual transformation. Covarrubias himself notes that such changes were compromising the traditions he had observed in Bali, most particularly in those areas where the Europeans tended to congregate. According to Covarrubias, prostitution had been largely unknown before the Dutch invasion, but tourism and the propagation of the sexual allure had created considerable temptation for young women and boys to participate in new sexual transactions. Even in this instance, however, Covarrubias is overlooking the practices of the courts where prostitution (payment for sex) was institutionalized through the concubine system and other practices in which regents provided economic security for widows and other destitute women. In a sense, the adoption of a transcultural prostitution model merely extended the pragmatism which characterized community marriage as well as nonmarital sexual practices. Covarrubias notes, with some regret, that the Balinese distinguished between those women who engaged in nonmarital sex for its intrinsic pleasure and those who were seeking financial return—"a type that is rapidly increasing in centers where there are foreigners."[15]

Recent studies of customary sexual practices in Bali have questioned the conclusions drawn by writers like Mead and Covarrubias. Megan Jennaway,[16] in particular, argues that the views of these earlier anthropological studies are shaped by distinctly masculine assumptions about the connections between sex, property, and kinship. Jennaway offers an alternative perspective based on her insights into the lives and desires of Balinese women. She argues that male views about the instrumentality of sex and marriage

coexist alongside alternative female discourses . . . in which their desire for connubial bliss, erotic pleasure and maternal fulfilment figure prominently. Women place a different construction upon marriage than men, one which is less concerned with the enhancement of kinship imperatives, clan alliances and political competition and more with personal destiny and emotional fulfilment.[17]

While some observers have accused the Balinese of being "unromantic" and without a word to precisely express the notion of romantic love, Jennaway shows that there is a rich tradition of Balinese folklore in which ideals of romantic love are powerfully evoked. Cultural representations of romantic love exist in Balinese songs and stories as well as in literature, and there is abundant recent ethnographic evidence that cultural beliefs in romantic love inform contemporary Balinese people's choices and thoughts about relationships.[18]

NATIONALISM AND NEW ORDER SEX

Our principal point here is that the colonial administrators, artists, writers, and scholars were all seeking to capture and represent Balinese sexuality according to the Europeans' own ideological, sexual, aesthetic, and cultural background and interests. These representations, however, rarefy the complexity and diversity of Balinese sexuality. Even in colonial times, this diversity was expressed through a range of practices, including arranged and love marriage, homosexual marriage, transgender and transsexual expressivities, "third-gender" identity, extramarital affairs, premarital sex, de facto heterosexual relationships, monogamy, polygamy, drug- and trance-based sex, and so on. Indeed, even the simple matter of gender is formed around a diversity that merges customary and more recent sexual practices and identities. Mark Hobart, who has studied the gender mix in Bali, argues that the fluidity of Balinese sexuality and gender cannot be treated as a simple man-woman dichotomy:

> There is, in short, no essential way of reading gender. Ascriptions of difference are recursive, situational and underdetermined by facts. . . . The nature of relations between males, females, *bancih* [trans or third gender], divinity and other beings is argued about and its significance rethought in public meetings, theater, the market, coffee stalls. . . . To subsume this diversity under some universal construct of gender or kinship, before inquiring whether Balinese actually talk in these terms, or need to presuppose them in order to talk, is hegemonic. . . . All too often it is a strange, truncated Bali that western investigators serve up, *severed* from Balinese commentary on their own motives and practices.[19]

That is, Balinese sexuality is not easily reduced to a single or monadic conception; rather, it is diverse, dynamic, and subject to multiple interests, debates, politics, and modes of representation within the Balinese community itself. While we will return to the question of gender and sexual identity later in the chapter, it is also worth noting that Hobart himself overlooks the important point that modernization and global integration have actually extended this Balinese sexual diversity, bringing new language, practices, and influences into a changing cultural context. Balinese sexuality cannot, therefore, be as easily isolated from the "West" and Western conceptions, as Hobart seems to suggest.

Thus, while the Dutch authorities sought to impose a standardized, homogenized, and highly prescriptive version of tradition over Balinese communities, diverse sexual modes continued to be practiced, albeit in the somewhat fragmented or less visible spaces of Balinese culture. These alternative or diverse sexualities were not necessarily regarded by the Balinese as aberrant or abnormal; rather, they were incorporated within the general lexicon of Balinese cultural practices and community life. The Dutch attempts to standardize cultural practices in order to control them created a dichotomy of legal and illegal sexuality and a notion of sexual deviance which was typically "modern" as it was based on a fabricated notion of tradition and historical legitimacy.

Even after the Indonesian independence war and defeat of the Dutch in 1949, this notion of tradition remained a central feature of political debate across the archipelago, including Bali. The repeal in 1951 of the Dutch colonial laws, which prohibited cross-caste marriage, exposed the concept of tradition to a more intense and highly charged political dispute. The Balinese scholar and journalist, Darma Putra, has argued that the modernization of Balinese society contributed to new forms of intergenerational tension, with younger people adopting new clothing styles, moral perspectives, and political positions. Sexuality was central to these debates, as younger and better educated women began to explore the possibilities of work and love that lay beyond the moral order imposed by high-caste public officials and the custodians of tradition.

With the Dutch retreat, these new cultural forms became more broadly embedded within the nascent constellations of class and "division of labor." So, while many middle-class youths were experimenting with a more modern social style, especially in Bali and urban Java, the Indonesian state itself became caught in a complicated oscillation of history and change. During the 1950s, as the Indonesian state sought to establish itself as the sovereign and overriding political authority, older and newer social divisions, including divisions of gender, were being swept together in a tempest of transition and realigning values. While Muslim Indonesia did not have an official caste system as such, it did have a clearly defined institutional division between the most and least powerful people in the society. As Benedict Anderson has pointed out in his extremely insightful book *Language and Power*, the old feudal divisions remained extremely powerful in Javanese society, even into the 1950s and 1960s. Anderson points out that the use of honorific codes in high Javanese, for example, remained a cornerstone of the Javanese legal system well into the period of Sukarno's presidency. An accused person who did not use the high Javanese address in court could be punished for failing to express appropriate respect for the judge and the court.

Within this context, considerable social changes were taking place and modernization emerged as a central objective for the new Republic of Indonesia. As in modern Western states, the Indonesian state sought to assert itself and its managerial authority over its population. Women's bodies were critical to this objective, most particularly through their primary role in reproduction, child rearing, sex, and family maintenance. To this end, once again, the modernization project strategically deployed the stabilizing and ordering motifs of history and tradition when it suited the specific interests of the state. The bodies of women, as a particular category within the population, could be strategically marshaled in order to support the state and its patriarchal foundations. Women's bodies, therefore, were an essential part of the cultural economy of the nation: as part of an unskilled labor sink, female bodies could be deployed for agriculture, fertility, domestic service (paid or family), and sex (paid or family).

New Order Power, Gender, and Transgender

The tactical deployment of tradition was also a key political strategy for the Suharto New Order government. Suharto sought constantly to impose an official national culture over all the regions of the archipelago, equating any deviation from the centralist perspective with seditious intent. To this end, regional arts and dance troupes were conscripted into the national project through regional authorities and arts colleges appointed by the New Order government. Thus, a standardized notion of tradition replaced much of the more community-driven creative activities, squeezing the grassroots artistic bodies and new trends into the cultural margins. This is particularly evident in the dance forms of East Javanese *Ludruk* and Balinese *Arja*, which had both presented a fluid impression of gender in the pre–New Order period. Various anthropological studies have argued that these forms were directly affected by the repressive nature of the New Order cultural policy, as it demanded a more distinct attribution of male and female roles.[20]

The aim of the New Order cultural policy, it appears, was to impose a proscriptive model of gender which more comfortably accorded with the national project of modernization. Paradoxically, the New Order embedded this ambition within yet another version of tradition, one which clearly transgressed Indonesia's broader and more diverse historical renderings of gender, including the social status of women and third gender *bancih* (transvestites, transgender). Indeed, there are a number of scholars who argue that Indonesia had managed to resist the extreme patriarchal systems that are evident in other Muslim-dominated nations, and the rigid role ascription that was institutionalized by the New Order was anathema to the diversity and tolerance that had characterized the archipelago for centuries. Even during the national revolution and the Sukarno presidency, there was very little direct institutional exclusion of women from public activities; women had, in fact, played an important part in the revolution and colonization process. The New Order "national development campaign," however, promoted women as the "mothers" of the nation, ascribing them to a more refined and modern domestic role. Indeed, in a strange and somewhat paradoxical mimicry of the "modern" Western mother-consumer at the time, the New Order presented a form of "tradition" which was largely artificial, formed around the notion of *kodrat wanita*—the refined woman.

This ideology and the cultural policies which supported it were inevitably promoted through the nation's education system. The ideal of feminine refinement was woven into the very potent conception of nation and its ideological framework (*Pancasila*), creating for young women a new social dignity for their destiny as wives and mothers. Inevitably, however, this containment of women not only limited their public role, it also contributed to an increasing level of stigmatization of those women who did not fulfill this destiny. In Bali, for example, studies have revealed that widows and divorced women suffered an increased level of social mistreatment during the New Order period. Whether or not these policies were successful in their own terms, they demonstrate that the New Order had developed an official public strategy which institutionalized preexisting modes of social sexism, casting alternative female identities into the social margins. To this end, the modernization that was being promoted by the New Order invoked a politically constituted notion of "tradition" which may well have existed but which was only one historical trend among many.

A number of commentators have argued that this invocation of tradition was part of the New Order's general strategy of social stabilization. Thus, the brutal and repressive regime of military coercion was fortified through an ideology which solidified the family and the household. Nation, at this level, was grounded within the restrictive, domestic order provided by women. Yet, as we have already noted, modernizing states have a habit of fixing their trajectory of progress against a particular origin; this origin becomes the foundation and vindication for the particular social destiny the state imposes over its people. History in this sense is "written" and "rewritten" according to the specific interests and political perspective of a given social group. The New Order dignified its political purpose through the application of a notion of origin and destiny: once again, women's bodies were at the center of these propagated political conceits.

YOUNG WOMEN, VIRGINITY, AND NEW BALI

In Bali, specifically, the traditional roles of women are heavily inscribed with religious and ritual meaning. While male bodies are also replete with ritual value, the actual maintenance and performance of daily libation have been more frequently ascribed to women, especially lower-caste women. Thus, the ritual life of the Balinese has been largely supported through the labor and sexual iconography of the female body. This iconography, as we noted earlier, has itself been central to the cultural and libidinal focus of international tourism. Whether through the celebratory representation of Balinese ritual or the more direct depictions of young female figures, the Balinese tourism industry has, in many ways, been constructed around the highly eroticized imagery of female bodies. And indeed, even in the context of the more recent tourism boom, many young Balinese women remain trapped in low-paid jobs, waiting for their opportunity to marry and be relieved of the tedium of eighty-hour working weeks in the service of foreign tourists. Caste, "class," and gender combine to frustrate the life ambitions and opportunities of these women. For most young women the choice is simple: a difficult and monotonous job in the tourism industry or an equally constricted life in ritual and domestic responsibility. Frequently denied the social, sexual, and economic freedoms enjoyed by their male counterparts, many Balinese women find themselves confined to a domestic role in a marriage marked by hardship and penury. It is common for married women to endure long periods of isolation from their husbands who work in tourist zones at considerable distances from the family home. While sexual fidelity is expected from women, it is widely accepted that men may have several girlfriends or a second wife. Sadly, the difficulty of this modern life has contributed to a suicide rate among young Balinese women that belies the impressions held by many foreign visitors that the Balinese are a happy and contented people.

This image of the new Bali and the transformation experiences of young women is not the full story, of course. Even through the crisis of change, many Balinese experience genuine and enduring joy in their lives, as well as profound difficulty. Laura Jane Bellows, an anthropologist who has conducted an extensive study of Balinese sexuality, has identified significant transformations within this customary female role in Bali through the progress of modernization.[21] In particular, Bellows has identified particular difficulties for young Balinese women as they confront the new behavioral and sexual freedoms associated with Western sexual permissiveness. The notional sexual revolution that has taken place in the West over the past four decades has been introduced into Bali through tourism, television, and other global media. Young women whose sexual behaviors have been constrained through the imperatives of ritual, "tradition," reproduction, and

3.3. Young Balinese women comfortable in Western clothing styles, Kuta (2007).
Courtesy of Belinda Lewis.

"nationhood" have confronted a new set of values that promotes sexual desire as both "natural" and "modern." In a peculiar clash of historical intensities, younger Balinese women are now encouraged by modern sexual codes and practices to explore new forms of sexual expressivity—including clothing styles and forms of bodily display which offend customary prohibitions.

Traditional "Balinese-ness" and the Threat of Modern Sexual Practices

To many cultural preservationists in Bali, the adoption of sexual practices associated with foreigners implies a rejection of traditional Balinese religious orthodoxy, most particularly the conception of three zones of female physiology. According to this orthodoxy, the body parts below the waist are considered most impure and thus the hips, thighs, and lower abdomen should not be visible or accentuated through modes of dress. Certain sexual positions are also considered impure—men should never place their own head below the waist of a woman, so all forms of oral pleasuring by men on women are considered obscene, a corrupt practice introduced by foreigners. The cultural politics of cunnilingus reflect a woman's social subordination, as well as the religious separation of the upper and lower parts of the body. Thus, sexual decision-making by young women is not only significant for upholding their own prospects as future wives and mothers—but also for the preservation of Balinese-ness in the context of wider cultural and social change.[22]

At the center of this clash is the female hymen, the organic indicator of a woman's moral purity, ritual value, and capacity for ensuring appropriate reproductive and kinship bonds. A young woman's virginity, and hence her maiden purity, represents the core of marriage, fertility, and thus social and communal cohesion. A woman is thus burdened by sexual self-denial in order to uphold a moral order which is the legacy and behest of deep history. In her study of virginity in the sexual and ritual life of the Balinese, Laura Bellows cites Tjok Istri Putra Astiti who presented a paper in Bali for the Association for Family Planning in Indonesia (*PKBI–Perkumpulan Keluarga Berencana Indonesia*). According to Astiti, the sexual and moral health of Balinese women like herself could only be assured if "women were careful like before"—

> The advice that we frequently hear from our elders is that a maid must be careful to protect her maidenhood, because her maidenhood [virginity] is a sign of her purity as a woman. In the past era families protected their female children from interaction with the world at large, specifically from interactions with men, by sequestering the maid. Such was the purity of maidenhood in society, to the point where a young woman, whose virginity had already been taken by a man before marriage, was said to be a "maid who was no longer pure," and often became the object of ridicule and gossip within society. What's more, if this relationship outside of marriage results in a pregnancy, for the young woman and her family this situation represents a kind of disgrace. A young woman who brings disgrace upon herself, through pregnancy out of wedlock such as this, often takes immoral or illegal action such as abortion or the abandonment of the child, who is innocent, because the young woman feels such shame. [23]

Virginity, Fertility, and Premarital Pregnancy

While Balinese tradition still insists on the privilege of virginity before marriage, there are also a range of traditional strategies for managing the cosmic dimensions of premarital pregnancy. As Bellows and Megan Jennaway demonstrate, the dishonor of premarital loss of virginity can be absolved if the union results in a pregnancy and a marriage is conducted between to the two young people. The impurity of premarital sex is "erased" and both the relationship and the unborn child are legitimized through a Hindu ceremony. Bellows describes this as the "transformation of transgressive sex" whereby premarital sex (*seks pranikah*) is reformed into a practice that maintains the traditional integration of "fertility" and "sexuality" within Balinese religious orthodoxy. In fact, for some women, premarital sex is seen as a fertility test. A pregnancy compels the male partner to offer marriage, thereby providing both children and a husband, which are markers of a woman's status and security in customary Balinese culture. Young women convert transgressive sex into marital sex and thus restore libido and desire to the traditional Balinese cosmic and social order.

While this issue of the sanctity of virginity will be discussed in greater detail below, it is clearly worth noting that Astiti is acknowledging that the sexual practices of young women are linked to Bali's spatial and cultural transformations, and that the problems associated with the body and desire are very much fixed within a social and historical setting that denies the very "naturalness" of nature. In Bali, virginity, as in the Western experience, is not merely a biological phenomenon, but a social condition which defines the political status of the body. In this context, femininity becomes formed, identified, and institutionalized as the predicate of masculinity. As men are generally relieved of responsibility for maintaining the purity of self within the sanctity of the family, their masculinity becomes a site of domination and inevitable desiring.

Of course, the subjugation of the female body has been the primary grievance of Western feminism, and it is now emerging as a central point of contention within the sexual politics of modernizing Bali. Within a contemporary setting, these battles over the meaning of bodies are reawakening the considerable complexity and diversity of practices and values that are attached to sexuality. Anxieties over the impact of modernization and Western influences are stimulating new disputes over sexual identity and the threat of permissiveness on the family and social stability. As we will also discuss later in the chapter, these anxieties are manifest in the very personal decisions regarding virginity and sexual deployment, as well as major national debates over pornography and sexual censorship. Before addressing these debates, however, we will discuss in greater detail the various forms of sexual expressivity and meaning disputes that are evolving in contemporary Bali.

THE MEANING OF TRADITION: WATER AND LOVE

The Dutch and the "chosen" Balinese elite constructed a version of preservation and tradition which clearly suited their social, political, and economic interests. However, behind this traditionalism, as we have noted, lies a diverse set of practices, values, and beliefs which, when assembled together, comprise the fullness and complexity of Balinese culture. This culture is not closed or historically fixed, as the preservationists might claim, but is open and dynamic, most especially as it begins to absorb the influences of Western culture, nationalism, and its own forms of modernization. Having recognized all of this, we would also suggest that within this assembled culture there are a number of distinctive and durable themes which identify Balinese culture within the general confluence of a globalizing world. In essence, we can distinguish local permutations and nuances within a global momentum: adapting a Japanese business term, the sociologist Roland Robertson refers to this interchange of local and global flows as *glocalization*.[24]

Indeed, the ancient absorption of the Hindu faith and Vedic culture into local and indigenous Balinese culture represents something of an historical precedent for the current global transformations. Hinduism provides the historical and cosmological base for many of the cultural practices, rituals, and religious beliefs which distinguish Balinese culture into the present. This, of course, is pertinent to our discussions on sexuality where a particular cosmological perspective is clearly drawn into the social formations of marriage, caste, kinship, and reproduction, as well as the more ineffable dimensions of desire and libido. In particular, the motif of "flow" is central to the Balinese understanding of the universe and the promulgation and volition of nature and natural forms, including the human body.

As we noted in our discussion of water and nature in chapter 2, flow is the fundamental momentum that ensures the regeneration and repurification of spiritual and natural conditions. A substantial volume of anthropological research has demonstrated that these cosmological flows are drawn around the three manifestations of "water"— semen (*kama putih*), holy water (*toya*), and other life-flow waters such as rivers, irrigation water, and amniotic fluids (*yeh*). Critically, all three of these forms of water are said to flow downwards, from *kaja* to *kelod*. While there are various translations of these two terms, they are the essential direction orientations used by the Balinese and are most usefully understood as upstream and downstream. This is not merely a literal or geographical orientation, but is a metaphor for the cosmological orientation of all nature: waters flow from high to low, center to periphery, unity to duality, order to chaos, purity to pollution, interior to exterior. As we have noted, in the social order, which should always mimic the natural order, these downward flows are to be encompassed through high caste to lower, male to female, human to animal.

While some anthropologists claim that this downward flow is associated with a single ancestral line, others view this idea as primarily theoretical. To this end, the volcanic mountain Gunung Agung is regarded as the pinnacle of the divine in Bali, and Lake Batur the derivation of all life flows. The holiest of all waters are drawn from the rocks near the volcanic opening of Agung, while Batur provides the elemental source for rivers and irrigation waters which nourishes the living bodies of the Balinese themselves. In this way, the three waters—holy, irrigation, and semen—have a common source.

Semen and sexuality, therefore, are logically contained within the natural unity and flows that characterize the universe. Within this context, the interruption of flow would necessarily bring forward the downstream conditions of *kelod*, resulting in death, impurity, or disorder. To this end, flow must not only be downstream but also continuous in order to ensure the proper orientation of bodies and nature. Historically, Balinese landforms, agriculture, and architecture have all been designed around the principles of flow, ensuring that the bodies which move within these spaces are aligned in accordance with cosmological principles. Just as different parts of the house are organized around different parts of the human body and bodily needs, the house design, openings ("doors"), and pathways must allow for the free flow of good and evil spirits and the processes of inclusion and expulsion.

Domestic sexuality is also aligned in a similar way. According to the conventions of traditional Balinese sexual knowledge, the sexual fluids of both men and women are described as "semen." For devout Balinese who subscribe to these traditions, the correct orientation of sexual intercourse must therefore allow the male semen to flow downwards to the female semen in order for impregnation to occur. To this end, the conventional sexual position has the man on top and the woman below; any interruption to this posture creates a cosmological rupture and risks the procreation of abnormalities—stillbirth, babies with disabilities, or the birth of opposite gender twins. As Covarrubias explained in his account of Balinese culture in the 1930s, the birth of twins of the opposite gender, for commoners at least, was seen as a deadly omen for the whole village. In Covarrubias's example, such births frequently resulted in the exile of the whole family for forty-two days, the incineration of the family house, and a costly series of purification rituals which could lead to the loss of land and bankruptcy of the family. Covarrubias also points out, however, that the birth of opposite gender twins was welcomed by royal families in Bali, since it represents a unity from which only a divine lineage could prosper. To this end, brothers and sisters were permitted to marry in the royal contexts since they were direct descendants of the gods and served clearly to maintain the highest level of cosmological unity.

For those areas of Bali which remain faithful to these traditions—mostly outside the tourist areas of Badung and urban Denpasar—this example remains resonant. Indeed, it clearly demonstrates how social privilege and social structure animate themselves through the control of "semen": the social order is mobilized through a belief system and ideology which ensures particular kinds of downward flow. As we have suggested throughout this discussion, however, the reason for such elaborate social and mythical systems of sexual management and prescribed practice is largely the predicate of the random and potentially ecstatic power that desire itself exerts. Moreover, the excessive repression of desire appears across all human cultures to produce the opposing effects of constraint and stimulation. In Balinese society the capacity of sex and desire to eschew or even directly challenge these frameworks of sexual management is most evident in subliminal and esoteric modes of expression and practice. While we will talk more explicitly about dance and the arts below, a potent expressivity of body and nature is to be found in the esoteric arts of magic and corporeal calligraphy.

Sex and the Divine Scripts

To this end, the high-caste Brahmana priests and other keepers of esoteric knowledge have over time helped to create and interpret a complex lexicon which maps particular meanings against the letterings of the divine, the physical terrain, and the human body. These letters (*aksara*), found in the ancient palm leaf manuscripts, connect specific deities to specific spaces such as markets, waterways, gardens, or forests. Other script are associated with the flower offerings that Balinese make daily to the gods, and there are also scripts which form the basis of potent symbols and formulae prescribed in various forms of magic and spells. Through courting rituals, these scripts and associated magic formulae are used as sexual and attraction stimulants. Attraction formulae were essential to the erotic dance genre of the *Gandrung* which entranced and deluded audiences into believing that male performers were actually women (see below). Even in Bali today, it is not uncommon for a courting or spurned lover to resort to the attraction formula in order to attract the interest of their desired lover.

In many respects, the scripts represent the underlying and constant tension between stimulation and constraint we have outlined above. A magic spell may provide a very good alibi for a lover who breaches social-sexual convention, or experiences desire that might be deemed inappropriate or excessive. Moreover, the application of esoteric knowledge inscribes the high caste with a sexual and social privilege that may not be mimicked by the lower castes. Since their status is fundamentally "archetypical," as it is divinely sanctioned, the high-caste members may engage in sexual practices that are locked exclusively within their own social group. While this esoteric sexual knowledge is contained within the script of ancient palm leaf texts, even today they may only be examined and interpreted by Brahmana priests and others linked to the high caste and regal lineage. The texts themselves celebrate a courtly and refined love which is distinguished from the more base behaviors of the commoners. The scripts, therefore, constitute a highly politicized *poetica* which guides the sexual engagements of priests, nobles, kings, and even the gods themselves. The "quality" of copulation, as indicated above, has a direct bearing on the quality of the offspring and hence the quality of rulers and the kingdom more generally. Written in the higher echelon languages of Sanskrit, Old Javanese, and Old Balinese, the texts quite consciously exclude the sexual interests and practices of commoners who are condemned, it would seem, to manage themselves through aspiration, community law, and the inevitable conditions of impurity.

Thus, according to the palm leaf scripts, sex within the high-caste context is informed by the notion of quality over quantity. This conjugal refinement is encased more generally in the language structures of high Javanese and high Balinese, both of which prescribe a specific vocabulary, syntax, and mode of address for specific social levels and communication situations. While the language of the palm leaf texts and related oral stories is recounted in high language, the sexual engagements of lower-caste commoners are represented in low Balinese. The key descriptor for sexual engagement in the lower caste is *makatuk*, a word with similar connotations as the English "fuck." The lowest form of sexual engagement—nonmarital and same-gender sex—is considered essentially bestial and is referred to as *masaki* or chicken fucking. The front-to-rear animal posture is a common caricature for sex that is not fundamentally human, but polluted by a desire for pleasure which lies outside the rituals and rites that connect human to the divine.

In practice, of course, the sexual behavior of the higher-caste members has been extraordinarily diverse. Moreover, the linguistic subjugation of the lower castes is part of a broader ideology of control, as it has been for most social elites across history. Even so, the fundamental principles of divinity and flow remain powerful for many communities in Bali, even where the political force of caste privilege and esoteric knowledge has been challenged or erased altogether. Within the broad panorama of modern Balinese sexuality, the essence of flow and purity remain resonant for many, adding complexity to a modernizing conception of sex and new modes of social interaction.

THE TRANSFORMATION OF KUTA BEACH

In chapter 1 we argued that the establishment of the Hotel Bali Beach in Sanur marked a moment of rupture in Balinese history. Bali's first five-star, multistory hotel appeared on the skyline during the genocide killings of 1965/1966, the first human-made structure that could dwarf the social icon of the tiered-temples which for centuries had dominated the island's cultural and spiritual landscape. While the civil war that had erupted around the foot of this new, grand structure represents in part an invasion by Cold War ideologies, the hotel itself represents the arrival of a new incarnation of global consumer capitalism. At the center of this modernization process was a subliminal but potent compound of hedonism, imagination, and sexual desire. These desires and the bodies that bore them were thus inscribed by a complex matrix of cultural beliefs, practices, and ideologies which were distinctly modern. The Hotel Bali Beach, therefore, was not constructed exclusively out of Bali's own human, natural, or cultural resources; it was shaped and formed out of the desiring body of the foreign tourist. In essence, the Hotel is a hybrid of flesh, concrete, and culture—the prescience of Bali's social and spatial transformation.

As we have noted, each of these desiring bodies contributed to the tourism boom and the diversity of cultural knowledge and cultural practices in Bali, including the meanings that are constituted around sex. Already loaded with preconceptions about Bali's sexuality and bearing their own baggage of values, practices, and sexual experiences, the mass tourists swarmed across the Badung district, eliciting change through the very demands of their own imagining and hedonism. Albert Falzon's film, *Morning of the Earth* (1972), depicts the interactions between the new tourists and the local Balinese in terms of a mingling uncertainty. Itself a hybrid genre of travelogue, documentary, and grassroots surf movie, *Morning of the Earth* plays on Nehru's famous description of Bali as "the morning of the world," a convocation of primitive beauty, danger, and spiritual elevation. The natural perils of the island are personified through the bodies of the surfers and their vulnerability to shadows, mysterious rituals, and an imagery of powerful but desolate surf beaches. In one very telling scene, the surfers are naked, smoking marijuana, and mingling with the local community at Uluwatu. Young Western women are seen swimming topless, a somewhat ironic allusion to Julius Jacobs's iconic photographs of the bare-breasted Balinese women.

However, unlike Jacobs's photographs, which had been taken nearly a century earlier, Falzon's Romanticism is more distinctly globalized. That is, the Western surfers appear to have adopted a cultural cognizance that was already filtered by the approbation and adoption of local custom. Falzon is at pains to present his version of Bali as a form of pure imagining or "dream." The nude scene is not merely an expression of the sexual revolution, but a genuine attempt to adopt the *sexualis natura* he believed to be an Eastern cultural derivative. Fanciful or not, Falzon's imaginary is a clear hybrid of sexual and cultural forms, drawing the images of the island and its people into the consciousness of a rising Western youth culture. For many surfers, in particular, *Morning of the Earth* was an extravagant and attractive representation, providing an image of Bali which would become the core of the new mass tourism allure.

More particularly, Falzon's film, along with many other 1970s Western texts, reconfigured the Kuta beaches as pleasure zones, sites of sexual self-presentation and cultural interplay. While surfing and beach recreation had been adopted by young Balinese men, female sex workers also began to congregate around the shoreline at night. With the setting sun, the shadowy figures would materialize, wearing tight tops, jeans, and heavy makeup in order to distinguish them from the local and traditionally clothed Balinese women. While most of the prostitutes were Javanese, a few Balinese women, especially widows and divorcees, were also appearing at night on the beaches, seeking payment for sexual favors. In this context, there were actually very few sexual exchanges between Western men and Balinese women.

Western Women and Kuta Love

The Kuta beaches were also an important site for Western female sexual expression and desiring. At its simplest, the beaches were sites for display where Western women could expose their bodies through various forms of auto-erotica and *sexualis natura*, including topless and nude bathing. More significantly, perhaps, the beaches became important places for Western women to encounter and interact with Balinese and other Indonesian men. Often too poor to frequent the nightclubs or bars, these young men would frequent the beaches, seeking the company—sexual and financial favors—of Western women. It was common for Javanese men to pretend they were of Balinese origin, adding some local mystique to their exotic, seductive strategies. While the early gigolos at Kuta were mostly Javanese, the young Balinese men quickly adopted the practice of beach wooing, striking up friendships with Western women on the basis of their knowledge of local culture and proficiency as tour guides, traveling companions, and lovers. Through this reversal or "re-gendering" of the Romantic-Orientalist ideal, Western women were able to express their sexual freedom and desires in a context which was not constrained by Western modes of patriarchal sexism. The "exotic erotic," which had been the province of male-dominated imperialism, was thus reimagined for many young Western women who felt more powerful, wealthy, and liberated in the island paradise.

In many respects, the young Western women of the 1970s and their Indonesian paramours established an historical pattern that has proved extraordinarily durable. With Balinese women largely confined to the matrimonial expectations of virginity and marriage, Western women provided a central source of sexual gratification that community values could largely accommodate. Moreover, these ongoing sexual-romantic relationships with Western women (and from the 1980s onwards, Japanese women) have often been accompanied by significant financial benefits for these young men and their families.[25] During the 1980s, the groups of men who trawled the beaches between Kuta and Seminyak looking for women, including much older women, became so distinctive, they were dubbed the "Kuta Cowboys."[26] This group developed their own subculture and social values which were generally scorned by traditionalists who saw them as threatening the fabric of community life and the *adat*.

Indeed, the practice of Balinese (and Javanese) men seeking romantic and sexual engagements with wealthy foreign women has become far more diffuse over recent years. Even from the 1970s and 1980s a number of these liaisons evolved into more substantial relationships, including long-term marriages. But for the majority of those Balinese men (and more recently women) who engage in transnational sexual affairs, their practices are not regarded as "sex work" or prostitution. Rather, the young men who exchange their local knowledge, mystique, and youthful beauty for reciprocal pleasures see themselves simply as *gaid* or "tour guides for the lonely heart." Their transactions do not always involve money, and these men see their associations with Western women as providing new and legitimate opportunities for freedom, comfort, and social mobility. While holiday romances between Western women and their Balinese lovers can lead to ongoing relationships, these men are well aware that they must strike a balance between meeting their immediate fiscal needs through fleeting associations with women and investing in the possibility of a more substantial, noncommercial relationship.[27]

Our own research and conversations with young Balinese men in general suggest that the desire for a relationship with a Western woman is fairly widespread. As the Kuta culture has become more cosmopolitan and diffuse, and the Balinese themselves have become more modernized, the advantages and pleasures associated a transnational sexual relationship have become more broadly recognized and accepted. Customary values and practices around sex have been diluted through the presence and imperatives of international tourism and global culture. Many of the more urbane Balinese men and women, in fact, have established significant relationships with foreigners; educated professionals especially have adopted a more globalist perspective of love and personal aspiration. Of course, many of the lower-skilled Balinese and Javanese men continue to trawl the beaches, bars, and shopping malls seeking the financial and sexual companionship of foreign tourists. But these are no longer an entirely predatory or identifiable gang of cowboys. Rather, the dream permeates the hearts of many of the men in the tourist zones of Bali. For these men the foreign woman's body is transcribed by another prayer: the script of her love, the prospect of marriage and release from the arduousness and daily grind of survival. They will tell her, of course, that she is the only one. And the woman will express her compassion in her smile and the warming rhythms of her body. In most cases there will be no marriage. They will lie to one another, and the romance will last as long as her visa. Sometimes indifferent, sometimes forlorn, the lovers will part and return to the discord of their respective journeys. A few letters and checks may follow, but generally the affair will resolve itself into the broader confusion of Balinese transformation and the bewildering collusion of this economy of pleasure.

CLASH OF CULTURE: TIRTA GANGGA, HOLY WATERS, AND DOG MEAT

The changes and cultural hybridizations of Kuta are somewhat more advanced than in many of the more provincial or holy areas of the island. In the holy sites, especially, the clash of meanings and culture seems considerably more acute, as locals try to mediate the impact of tourism and the new economy with indigenous values and customary practices. Tirta Gangga on the east side of the island is a site of divine pilgrimage for many Balinese. The holy gardens of Tirta Gangga are located in the mountain foothills of Karangasem, near the small city of Amlapura. Many locals believe that the springwaters that rise on the hillside and gather in natural and man-made pools have their divine source in the holy waters of the Ganges River in India. While the pools are used for bathing by tourists and people from the nearby villages, they are also an important source of holy water for priests and others engaged in divine libation.

One nearby village, Kebus (pseudonym), is also famous for its sale and consumption of dog meat, considered perhaps the "hottest" of all meats,

3.4.   Bathing pools at Tirta Gangga (2007).
Courtesy of Belinda Lewis.

which are the hottest of all foods.[28] The variable "hot" and "cold" qualities of a particular food refer both to its spicy qualities and also its effects. While vegetables and fruits are relatively cool foods and conducive to rational practice, the meats are "hot" and generate energy and bodily activity. Dog meat is often being prescribed for various forms of sexual dysfunction and also as an aphrodisiac. It is a food that should be consumed sparingly as it is inclined to produce irrational behaviors which are of themselves "polluting"—especially for people of high caste who are the purest of beings. The men of Kebus are known for their high consumption of dog meat and are thus regarded generally as base and inclined toward impure thoughts and actions.

These characteristics, according to other villagers in the area, are manifest in the sexual engagement between Kebus men and the Western women who visit Tirta Gangga. Rather than seek legitimate employment, the Kebus men notoriously proffer their services as "guides" for visiting women. If a woman is receptive, the Kebus men engage with them sexually, often in the lush gardens at night since the Kebus are generally excluded from staying with women in local hotels. The Kebus, in this sense, are regarded as contaminated and base, though they remain "human." Those whom they "consume" in the downward flow of social and natural categories, are more base and therefore regarded as being equivalent status to the dogs: that is, they are regarded as "animal." When the men of other villages speak of these sexual activities, the copulation is nearly always caricatured as animalistic and conducted in a front to rear posture. Thus, while these Western women may believe they are expressing their social and political right to sexual choice—a key tenet of Western liberal feminism—their practices have very different meanings for the local Balinese. As part of a broader Balinese imaginary, Western women in particular are often regarded as promiscuous and base, since they are prepared to have sex without respect for social context, customary law, or the sensibilities of the Balinese themselves. At Tirta Gangga, where this sex takes place outside of history and social structures, it is deemed to be "animal" and thus beyond the realm of the divine. This is particularly offensive for local villagers, as it takes place within and around the holy waters.

While the Kebus story is only one of many around the glocalization of sex in Bali, it is significant for its focus on the meanings of women's sexuality. As we have noted above, within traditional Balinese culture, women carry the considerable burden of social and cultural maintenance including the daily management of ritual, family, and fertility. Even in the lowest castes, it is the women who are the final barrier to impurity and dissolution. If "the feminine" ruptures and is lost, then the essence of Balinese culture is also lost. Indeed, in the hybrid, cosmopolitan tourist areas, this is precisely the challenge facing many younger Balinese women and girls. Modernization and the pleasure economy are inevitably creating new opportunities, but also new threats to the valence of virginity and the domestic and fertility roles traditionally prescribed for Balinese women. As we noted above, the preservation of virginity is still regarded as a primary responsibility of young women and their families. The Balinese practice of strict segregation of males and females has been largely constituted around the objective of controlling sexual arousal and the seductive power of male desire. Even in the villages, strict prohibitions on male-female physical contact are enforced. Thus while physical affection between members of the same sex (such as hugging and holding hands) is permitted and common, the same privilege is denied intergender contact. Families are extremely careful to ensure that girls are protected from the sexual interest and wooing of males, who are considered notoriously incapable of controlling their own libidinal natures.

Within this customary and provincial context, therefore, Western women have been located at the lower end of the animal-human sexual scale. The sexual engagement of female tourists with Kebus men is seen as degrading the purity of the Tirta Gangga waters; while these women themselves may understand their actions in terms of legitimate sexual expression as sanctioned within their home cultures. While this dispute over meaning can be isolated and polemicized in a relatively small, provincial community like Tirta Gangga, there is a far greater diversity of perspectives in the more cosmopolitan tourist zones such as Kuta and other tourist centers. The Kebus example helps to illustrate how these "zones of change" have become central and sensitive sites of cultural exchange and transformation for the Balinese.

NEW BALI: NEW WOMEN

Quite clearly, international tourism has dramatically altered the spatial conditions in which women and men interact in Bali, substantially disrupting the community practices of segregation and protection. The young Balinese women who work in hotels, restaurants, shops, on the beach, and in the streets are continually exposed to the physical contiguity and sexual interests of men, including Westerners. The remarkable resistance demonstrated by young Balinese women to constant sexual entreaty and harassment by foreign and local men is perhaps an indication of the durable force of older sexual norms and mores. It is certainly clear that community law (*adat*) and the supporting ideology of patriarchy not only constitute a system of control, but also of social and personal protection. Women's sexuality, bodies, and community roles were often sustained in a repressive and self-interested social order; but this order also protected them from temptation, harassment, and sexual exploitation by men who, in an often-repeated patriarchal myth, are "unable to control themselves and their sexual desires." And while the traditional organization of space complemented these protective practices, the new economy has dismantled many physical barriers to male-female contact, facilitating relatively unsupervised and more intense interactions between genders. For young Balinese women and girls, exposure to new consumer styles and practices provides excitement, pleasure, and a bodily arousal that had not been forewarned by village life.

Thus, this reorganization of economic and cultural spaces has provided pathways for new forms of sexual expression and pleasure for young Balinese women. In tourist service industries—especially massage, escort services, and sex work—customary taboos on touching have been clearly discarded. However, change is also evident in courtship and relationship formation where younger Balinese men and women continually struggle with transitional sexual norms and morality. The new pleasure economy has certainly impelled young men to replace dowers of pigs and cows with symbols of modern identity and advancement—motorbikes, personal jewelry, brand-name sunglasses, guitars. Young Balinese men are convinced, with very good reason, that their capacity to attract a girlfriend or wife is largely contingent on their material success. Like many young people in the West, the Balinese who live around the tourist zones have become entranced by a narcissistic blend of brand-image advertising and sexual display.

Young Balinese are thus caught within a cultural dialectic which celebrates tradition on the one hand and the modern cosmopolitanism on the other. These celebrations are further complicated by the presence of Westerners who seem attracted by an imaginary of traditionalism, but who constantly mediate it through their own hypermodernism. Many of the younger Balinese have, thus, adopted a hybrid sexuality which conflates residual elements of an imagined tradition with a frequently bewildering volume of modern sexual modes and images—including those delivered through magazines, DVDs, CDs, television, the Internet, and the presence of international tourists themselves. In this way, younger Balinese are forming new subject identities that are very much embedded in the global "mediasphere" and its broader cultural spaces. As in Western cultures, the imagery and narratives of popular culture, including pornography, are used by young people to exchange knowledge about sex. Discussions among young Balinese and letters to youth magazines show an increasing interest in sexual expression, especially within the Westernized categories of "boyfriend" and "girlfriend" (*pacar*). Central to these discussions is a desire for sexual engagement that doesn't pose a threat to the hymen—and hence virginity, fertility, and marriage. Letters to the *Bali Post* from young women typically catalog their sexual experiences in relation to these concerns, closing with enquiries such as, "Am I still a virgin?"[29]

Our reading of Covarrubias might suggest that the "problem" of virginity has always been central to Balinese sexual practice. According to Covarrubias's observations in the 1930s, Balinese commoner women were rarely virgins when they married. Often couples cohabitated prior to marriage and often the woman was pregnant. If this is the case, then it appears that the preservationist ideal somewhat miscalculated the role of virginity in Balinese community life. The same, of course, may be true today, where the ideal of virginity is largely a fantasy designed to maximize "responsibility" over "desire." Research by the Indonesia National Family Planning Coordinating Board claims that around seven out of ten Balinese women are already pregnant when they marry.[30] Young Balinese women, echoing Western adolescents, claim that contraception is very difficult to negotiate "in the heat of the moment," especially prior to intercourse.

New Sexual Practices: Contraception, HIV/AIDS, and Suicide

Thus, while premarital sex is becoming more common among Balinese young people, condoms are not widely used to protect against pregnancy out of wedlock. The use of condoms has complex and contradictory social and cultural meanings for young people in Bali. According to our interview respondents, condom use implies that the sex is "recreational" (*main seks*). It is often young women, rather than men, who refuse to use condoms, and this is primarily because they want men to take responsibility for sex by demonstrating their preparedness to marry in the event of a pregnancy.[31] By rejecting condoms, Balinese women see themselves maintaining the traditional integration between fertility and sexuality. That is, they are adopting aspects of modern sexualities whilst, at least to some extent, protecting Balinese values and traditions.

While resistance to condom use can be interpreted as a resistance to the disintegrating influences of modern sexual practices, it is also posing new public health challenges. According to Professor Muninjaya at Udayana University,[32] suicide rates in Bali have rapidly escalated in recent years—with rates being higher among young women and particularly those with unwanted pregnancies. Furthermore, the prevalence of HIV/AIDS is also increasing. While promotion of condom use would seem a pragmatic solution to prevent these tragic deaths, sexual health workers in Bali face a difficult challenge of finding ways to help young sexually active people to reconcile the competing meanings associated with sexuality and fertility within the context of modern sexual practices.

As we noted earlier, customary law imposes considerable sanction on a young man who does not fulfill his responsibilities. While many Balinese fear that this sense of responsibility is being degraded by Western and modern influences, deeper anxieties about the moral integrity of Indonesia have mobilized a more strident response in the national parliament (DPR). A range of legislative proposals have been presented to the parliament by an alliance of purist Islamic parties (see chapter 5), seeking to impose a more stringent moral order over the Indonesian archipelago. While the most recent legislation is focused on censorship and pornography, the general intent is to restrict sexual expression and sexuality. In a barely disguised invocation of customary Islamic *shari'ah* law, early iterations of the bills sought to impose heavy sanctions, including a jail sentence, for a man who impregnates a woman whom he then refuses to marry. Similar sanctions were proposed for adulterers where men and women have clearly breached the marriage code and they refuse to accept their social and marital responsibilities. Proponents also saw the legislation as an opportunity to criminalize marginal sexualities, such as homosexuality and transgenderism, deemed aberrant and demonstrably outside the practices sanctioned by the Qu'ran and *shari'ah*. In this sense, the new law aimed to fortify the institutional status of marriage against the degrading effects of modernization and the West, which are generally seen by the conservative religious parties in Indonesia to be morally decadent. According to conservative Islamic spokesmen, this decadence is due, at least in part, to the "false emancipation" and obsessive sexualization of women in the West.

Divorce rates are relatively low in Bali, and in Indonesia more broadly, and polygamy has a greater legitimacy than in Western societies. Only those Balinese men who have largely rejected customary and communal life in Bali seem prepared to risk divorcing a wife. It is more common in Bali for men to take a second wife, though unlike polygamous cultures in the Middle East, Balinese multiple marriages usually involve an entirely separate household and dwelling. The cost, complexity, and duress of such arrangements have more recently inclined Balinese men toward a new tenet: "*Satu isteri, banyak pacar*" (One wife, many girlfriends). In the tourist zones, Western, and Japanese women, as we have noted, have become the favored focus of these extramarital arrangements, bringing with them the possibility of financial assistance as well as sexual gratification. Yet these arrangements also become complicated when a Balinese man wants to establish a more substantial relationship with the "other woman." Through the course of our own interviews, we have encountered numerous examples of cultural dissonance where different values and perspectives have created considerable difficulties in the forming and unforming of transcultural relationships. In one case, a Balinese man who had become very wealthy and modern wanted to marry his Japanese girlfriend. While the Balinese wife was prepared to accept a second wife, the Japanese woman would not embrace polygamy or her Balinese status as a "co-wife." In this instance the Balinese man proceeded with a divorce on the grounds that his Balinese wife was "mentally ill."

GAY SEX, TRANSVESTISM, AND THE *GANDRUNG*

Same-gender sexual relationships and cross-dressing (*bebancihan*) have long been part of the sexual diversity of Javanese and Balinese culture. It is reasonable to speculate that the strict prohibitions placed on opposite gender touching by customary law in Bali may have contributed to communal tolerance of same sex consorting—at least until the establishment of colonial rule in the early twentieth century. Thus, same sex consorting and transgenderism may have been part of the silent and undisciplined spaces which sex often inhabits within a culture, spaces which are largely overlooked by ritual or prohibitive surveillance as they pose no great threat to the sanctity of law, kinship, or reproduction. Those commentators who argue that it was the Western aesthetes, like Walter Spies, who transformed Bali into a "homosexual paradise" seem somehow to disregard a range of practices which were well-established by the time of European colonization and the invasion of Western cultural influences. Perhaps the most spectacular of these practices was constituted around the *Gandrung*, an erotic dance form in which the female characters were performed by young men. While the dance had been performed inside the courts during the eighteenth century, it had achieved widespread popularity in the villages during most of the nineteenth century and into the early part of the twentieth century. By the time of Spies's arrival, it had largely disappeared, perhaps transmuted into a newer form of erotic dance, the *Joged*, in which women dance flirtatiously with male audience members and the gender roles were "normalized."[33]

A few of the last dancers to perform the *Gandrung* are still living, and anthropologists have been able to map the character of the dance, along with the social and sexual mores it encompassed. *Gandrung*, which can be translated as "desire," facilitated specific kinds of sexual touching in the performance between the gandrung (principal *Gandrung* dancer) and a man selected from the audience. The performance always began with the principal performing a duo with another member of the dance troupe (the *pengeleb*). This preamble dance was designed to tease and arouse the audience, as well as provide a model which the chosen audience participant could follow. At the conclusion of this dance, the gandrung principal would select a specific audience member from those sitting at the rim of the dance stage and who expressed their "desires" through eye movements, gestures, and voice. The choice of partner was generally predicated on the dancer's own personal interests or "debts," as well as the relative status of the audience members. Once selected, the audience member would dance in close proximity to the gandrung; uninvited sexual touching or kissing from the audience member, however, would be met with a forceful blow from the gandrung's fan. A gandrung may, however, invite intimacy through various dance movements and gestures, including the gentle rubbing of noses and lips. At the conclusion of the dance, the audience member would pay a fee and in return often receive a shroud of flowers. The gandrung could dance with as many as twenty-five partners in an evening.

The same-gender erotica upon which the *Gandrung* was predicated occupied a particular cultural space for the Balinese. While not considered "natural," the erotic play between males, in particular, was not entirely "unnatural"; rather, it was a transitional condition which could be produced by distinctly human interventions in the natural and divine order. For Balinese culture this was entirely permissible, provided it was not effected through the workings of the *leyak* or evil witches. According to the *Gandrung* dancers, male-to-male attraction was considered against the general laws of nature. Thus, in order to achieve the aesthetic effect of same-gender erotica, magic formulae (*pengeger*) were interposed, enabling the gandrung principal to be conceived as female. This combination of script, holy water, and various other magical elements was cast across the gandrung, propitiating the *jiwa perempuan* or "soul of a woman" which would enable the male audience to believe that he was truly female. Under the spell, the gandrung himself would believe in his own femininity, adopting a sexual demeanor which attracted him to men rather than women.

The stories of the *Gandrung* dancers and others who had been audience participants indicate clearly that sexual attraction between the men was a facility of this particular mode of magic. While some suggest that the spell was relatively ephemeral, others claimed that the spell would last years, only being broken by the intervention of the *dukun* (ritual magicians). It was not uncommon for *Gandrung* dancers to be the focus of obsessive adorations, sometimes becoming the lovers of powerful audience participants. One of the former dancers reported an effect of "madness" in which ardent admirers—including high-caste Brahmana—had been known to sell their properties and cattle in order to lavish the favored gandrung with expensive gifts and have them as permanent concubine. And indeed, the gandrung would sometimes surrender to these loving entreaties, participating in long-term relationships (*makasihan)* with their consort. Even so, the potent attraction magic was commonly identified as the source of these obsessions which continually deluded and maintained the sexual interest of the same-gender partners. However, as the following testimony of a retired dancer indicates, this madness could strike at any man in any social condition and thus produce damaging consequences:

> Once we stopped [dancing for the evening] the ritual specialist (*dukun*) came again. Then my body would be touched and anointed. Because the partners would follow the gandrung and want to sleep here. But this was prohibited by the head of the village. They loved us too much. They were not allowed to sleep here. They were not allowed to bother people sleeping. They were sent home.

But the next day we would dance again, every day it was like that. . . . We danced all the time, but only for six months. Because the partners were stealing. Those who did not have money stole chickens, bananas. [The performances] were stopped because the village had fallen into chaos. Then I moved to Klungkung. . . . At that time Dewa Agung fell in love with me. . . . The king was in love with me. First he came here to watch. Then he came the next day, and the day after that. Then he wanted to dance with me. He was already in love. He was a beautiful dancer. He kissed me, then he forgot himself and kept coming back. . . . He was the one who loved me the most. In Klungkung I always slept with [the king] I was not allowed to sleep with anyone else. Because he loved me so much, I was taken in bed.[34]

Same-gender relationships of this kind were an implicit, if not clearly visible, part of the Balinese sexual and cultural landscape up until the 1920s. Even the 1910 edict, by which the Dutch colonists sought increasingly to impose their political, economic, and moral will over Balinese sexual diversity, seems not to have inhibited same-gender relationships until some time into the 1930s. Older Balinese recall the *Gandrung* dance and the *Makasihan* relationships, although Covarrubias, writing in the late 1930s seems unaware of their existence. Thus, while Covarrubias refers specifically to "unnatural" sexuality being forged around European tourism and prostitution, the older Balinese speak of the makasihan (literally "to love") as a relational form that was common to both men and women during their early lives. Even today, villagers speak of these long-term love relationships between same-gender couples "who have never married or had family."

Women, Cross-Gender, and the *Arja* Dance Form

While it was common in Balinese dance-drama for males to perform in cross-dressed roles as women, it was less common for women to assume the roles of men. However, the classical *Arja* dance drama provided an important space for a more liberal gender agenda. The *Arja* is a classical dance form, emerging through grassroots and community practice during the early part of the nineteenth century. According to most accounts, *Arja* is linked to the Old Javanese word *reja* ("beautiful") and was probably first performed in 1825 at the cremation ceremony of I Dewa Agung Gede Kusamba. While it was originally performed in the courts by all male performers, the particular characteristics of the dance drama attracted increasing numbers of female performers. Specifically, the principal performer is required to sing the entire part and there has been a durable belief in Balinese theater that female voices are more suited to singing the *tembang* (songs) of which there are many in the *Arja* dance-drama. In either case, the romantic and comic style of the *Arja* proved extremely popular with Balinese audiences, and by the early 1920s, female troupes had begun to dominate the dance with women cross-dressing as men and adopting both the male and female roles.

The popularity of the *Arja* derives, as least partly, from its canny blend of classical myth and contemporary social comedy and commentary. There is no script in the dance so the principal must create the narrative and songs from ancient legends such as the *Panji* romance or *Malat* Javanese stories, reshaping them into a contemporary context. Recent events, community disputes, and local characters are woven into the story, and thus the success of the troupe is largely contingent upon the creative skills, joke-telling, and grace of the principal dance performers. This convocation of ancient and contemporary artifice creates a rich and ethereal atmosphere in which the romance is both arousing and seductive, transporting audiences beyond the minutiae of everyday life into the more ethereal realm of transcendent pleasure.[35] This combination of secular and spiritual aesthetics seems to have been intensified by the grace of the female form and quality of the female voice. While principally an entertainment, the *Arja* was and still is occasionally performed at temple ceremonies, weddings, and cremations.

Unlike the *Gandrung*, there is little anthropological evidence that the *Arja* promoted female-to-female sexual engagements. However, the emergence of female dominated troupes with females playing the part of male lovers has clearly contributed to the diversity of social and artistic sexual expressivities in Bali. The erotic and sensual grace of the women created a distinct motif of same-sex dalliance and female transvestism. Moreover, the social prominence of the female *Arja* troupes presented an image of female public agency which was clearly at odds with women's prescribed roles of wife and mother. Indeed, the *Arja* constitutes an important alternative to the New Order regime's repressive and deterministic approach to gender which invoked a very particular notion of tradition and traditional sexuality. As we have noted, the New Order sought to standardize and institutionalize gender difference through the promulgation of a rational and patriarchal state power. Suharto sanctioned only particular forms of traditional art which conformed to the objectives of nationalism, state power, and the preeminence of male-centered systems of control. As DeBoer notes—

> Many of the important traditional "classic" theatrical forms . . . even the once wildly popular *Arja* . . . have fallen into relative neglect while . . . two new genres created during the 1960s which are closely associated with Indonesia's New Order . . . received strong encouragement and support from the central Indonesian government in Jakarta.[36]

Little doubt, the privileging of male dominated public culture and the rise of national arts institutions in Indonesia contributed to the revitalization of the all-male male *Arja* (*Arja Muani*) in the early 1990s under the New Order. Some commentators argue that the revitalized *Arja Muani* may have contributed to a decline in popularity of the female *Arja*, as audiences sought the sanctioned spaces of masculine aesthetics and social authority. On the other hand, the transgression that was coded within male transvestism may have intensified both its erotic effects and its potential for political subversion. That is, the subversion of New Order authority and its rigid gender prescriptions may have been more powerful when expressed in male rather than female transvestism.[37]

Walter Spies and European Prohibition

Bali's more recent reputation as a paradise for gay men probably owes more to the fame of artists like Walter Spies and Donald Friend than it does to the *Gandrung*. Even so, in 1938 when Spies was arrested for having sex with minors of the same gender, the artist was himself a great patron of the *Gandrung*. The arrest and trial marked a critical moment for sexual diversity within Balinese communities, a moment when the Dutch made clear that they were transforming the meaning of same gender sexuality into a matter of colonial law and management of the population. That is, Spies's trial marked the moment when "homosexuality" was translated into the Balinese lexicon as "criminal" and aberrant, rather than transitional or uncertain. As

3.5. Traditional Balinese *Arja*, "Sukreni Gadis Bali" (Sukreni Balinese Maid), adapted from a novel of the same title by Panji Tisna, published in the 1930s. Performed on 22 December 2007 by Geok Group, directed by Wayan Dibia.
Courtesy of Alit Widusaka.

with the prohibitions around intercaste marriage which, for the Balinese, had been a matter of social debate rather than legal sanction, the relabeling of same-gender erotica as criminal attached new meanings to a cultural practice that for centuries had been encompassed within a general frame of cultural diversity. Thus, it was less likely that Spies contributed to the creation of Bali as a homosexual paradise, but rather that the Spies trial drew the mythical and mystical status of same gender erotica from the historical shadows and into the harsh light of global gay politics.

It is within this context that Spies was martyred to a modernist colonial rationalism which oppressed sexual practices and sexual aesthetics that deviated from its standards of normality. As we have indicated, modern states became obsessed with the legislative management of their populations, including the control of labor, reproduction, and hence sexuality. The Spies's trial and conviction, in effect, introduced to Bali a modern political dichotomy which distinguished legal from illegal modes of sexual behavior. In this context, too, the *Gandrung* and *makasihan* clearly possessed a ritual and sexual aesthetic which challenged the framework of modern functionalism and rational order. To the European mind, the magic formula and its bewitching spell are comprehensible only in terms of superstition or a mysticism which permitted men to engage in same sex dalliances without community stigma or the dismantling of their socially inscribed masculinity. Thus, the atrophy of the *Gandrung* during the colonial period might be explained in terms of its transferal into the legalistic and prohibitive language of the Dutch rulers. But its survival and resurgence into the tourism boom might equally be understood as a transferal into the language of antiquarian entertainment with its own culturally peculiar homoerotica. For the Balinese, however, the *Gandrung* was always an entertainment, a sexual aesthetic which enabled a dangerous but delightful erotic expressivity.

Of course, this form of free expressivity was precisely what the Dutch feared, since it posed a direct threat to the masculine rationality of the state and state power. As we have noted, masculinity is the contingent opposite of femininity, and any challenge to these categories was seen in terms of a more percussive threat to the state and imperial order. The Dutch certainly believed that they would need to protect themselves from the more "natural" but "uncivilized" sexual practices of the Balinese. As with the edict demanding that Balinese women wear blouses, the prohibition on homosexuality in Bali was clearly designed as a cultural shield for the protection of Dutch moral sensibilities and masculine virility. The colonialists feared the seductive beauty of the Balinese, not only because it rendered them more difficult to control (and exploit), but because it threatened perpetually to distract and disable their own people. Spies, who had been a friend of the Residency and who had access to high levels of the colonial administration, was suddenly recognized as one of the Fallen. The sexuality he represented and ultimately encouraged may have weakened the instrumental (and masculine) force of the Residency, as well as contaminated the reputation of the Dutch administrators and their colony. Certainly, the notion of Balinese licentiousness that had been propagated by writers like Julius Jacobs was clearly fortified by Spies and others in his community who had openly paraded their sexuality to the wider world.

Nonetheless, homosexuality in Bali was not erased. As was typically the case in Western societies, same gender attractions merely went underground and became resignified in terms of illicit sexual practice. This relabeling contributed to the formation of new sexual subcultures, which also became appended to the new practices and influences of the tourism economy. In this way, same gender practices in Bali were absorbed into the global culture and the range of disputes and agonisms associated with the processes of developing world Westernization. Thus, while heterosexual Western imaginings were representing Bali in terms of a hedonistic *sexualis natura*, the gay community, especially in America and Australia, were constructing their own same-gender sexual idyll which was not constrained by a chronicle of repression and instrumental order. For these communities, the long history of same gender and transvestite sexuality in Bali and Java provided inspiration for their own romantic ideal of release and free expression.

Of course, gay prostitution and patronage continued in various underground forms in Bali, but a more "legitimate" gay tourism industry also began to blossom during the development boom. Integrated resorts catering specifically for the gay and lesbian market have been established in various parts of the island. These resorts offer integrated recreation and lifestyle services similar to those in mainstream resorts, and they are associated with identical environmental and cultural problems (see chapter 2). In particular, the sexual interaction between wealthy visitors and far less wealthy Balinese continues to raise issues about sexual and cultural imperialism. The intimacy of sexual exchange, that is, becomes implicated in much broader questions of ideology and the global economy: is genuine consent possible within a context of such significant differentials of power, status, and wealth? As we noted in the previous chapter, such a question is itself linked to issues of territory, cultural control, and appropriation; a Balinese might readily exchange his or her dignity and bodily self-determination for financial security and material gratification.

While this issue is significant for all visitors, questions of exploitation and sexual engagement have a further, potentially more devastating dimension, especially in relation to HIV/AIDS. While the vast majority of the increase in infections is associated with intravenous drug use, nearly 10 percent of new infections are related to sexual activity, including gay male sexual activity. Again, power differentials complicate sexual negotiations, including the use of condoms and other protective practices. Balinese men and women who are HIV positive have been subjected to considerable stigmatization by the broader community, with even local health workers refusing to treat infected patients.[38] This sort of discrimination is amplified in national political debates where conservative Islamic parties are proposing to outlaw homosexuality and transvestism. As noted above, these political parties and their supporters claim that homosexuality is principally a manifestation of Western moral and sexual decadence. HIV, in this sense, is seen as god's punishment for unnatural sexual acts, a view that has also been expressed in Western conservative Christianity.

The Indonesian Waria and Transgenderism

The conservative groups supporting a ban on homosexuality and transvestism have typically invoked Indonesian history and traditional values to support their claim that these new sexual forms are an impurity derived from the West. In this sense, the conservatives employ a vocabulary of sexuality which is also derived from the West—*gay, homoseks, lesbi*. Opponents of the prohibition, however, argue that this version of tradition is itself embedded in a very modern iteration of anti-Western ideology and the social and political interests of the radical Islamicists themselves. Indeed, the conservatives' version of tradition critically ignores Indonesia's long history of sexual tolerance and diversity, as well as the culture's own sexual vocabulary. Thus, current battles over sexuality are being waged as much over language and labeling, as they are over sexual practice and identity.

Significant transvestite communities were reported in the trading areas of Indonesia as early as the 1800s and are still evident in Jakarta and East Java today.[39] Indeed, by 1830 it appears that the transvestite communities (*waria*) around Jakarta constituted a significant presence in local popular culture. The Bantji Batavia (Batavian transvestites) were distinguished by their cross-dressing and particular dance forms which had become evident in the street culture of the city. However, it appears that transgenderism seems not limited to any particular ethnic group or locality. Over time, these communities have adopted their own nonpejorative descriptor *wadam*, which appears to have been first sanctioned by Ali Sadikin, mayor of Jakarta from 1966 to 1977. As an appointee of Sukarno, Sadikin's progressive and enlightened policies allowed these communities to take a more dignified place in Indonesia's social landscape. However, the term *wadam*, a compound of WAnita (woman) and aDAM, caused offense to some of the purist Muslim communities. In particular, the male name "Adam" refers both to the Biblical first man and a significant prophet in the Islamic faith. By the 1970s the battle over meanings and labels became intense, and the minister for religion, Alamsyah, sanctioned the new term *waria*.[40] This New Order descriptor situates the transvestite as a social and human perversity, sitting outside the norms of human gender. Like the other favored term, *banci* (often also "effeminate male"), the term *waria* has been adapted by the community as a genuine rubric for their status as "third gender," a label which the *waria* themselves appear to have embraced.

Seemingly unperturbed by social stigma or pejorative labeling, many *waria* continue to live on the social margins, establishing extremely powerful communities and social support networks. These networks are characterized by social welfare and a socialistic microeconomy constituted around sharing, mutual care, craftwork, and sex work. Many commentators, however, challenge familiar stereotypes of Indonesia transvestites, arguing that the *waria* are an extremely diverse social group. Thus, while some *waria* identify as "third gender" (neither entirely male nor female), others see themselves as more predominantly male or predominantly female. A number of *waria* work as prostitutes, but others have professional careers and only cross-dress in the evenings. Some *waria* have wives and families; they may be "out" or principally clandestine, engaging in *waria* activities in secret. To this end, many *waria* only have sex with men; others with both genders; and still others exclusively with women (*waria lesbi*).[41]

The challenges posed by conservative political and religious groups in Indonesia have prompted a new form of political activism among many *waria* who have sought to promote their civil rights through a range of protests and public stunts. This sort of political activism has expressed itself through the celebrity status of several *waria* who host talk shows and perform on television. Miss Waria Indonesia, Merlyn Sopjan, has written several best sellers, including *Perempuan Tanpa V* (Woman without a Vagina), which she uses to celebrate the community, culture, and sexuality of the *waria*. In Bali the evolution of *waria* is evident in the bars and nightclubs of Seminyak, where transvestites mingle with tourists, adding a further richness to the sexual euphoria that pervades the island's pleasure culture. While particularly attractive and feminine *waria* perform drag shows in the gay bars, other transvestites float like sequined ghosts in the giddy air of the nightclubs, inverting the sexual norms of gender just like their forbears in the *Gandrung* dance.

COMMERCIAL SEX AND THE TOURISM INDUSTRY

As we have noted, modernization is continuing to reorganize cultural and physical space in Bali, including the space that segregates males and females. It is perhaps this transformation of space, along with the consequent dilution of prohibitions on male-female touching, which has enabled the revival of heterosexual erotic entertainment. The disappearance of the *Gandrung* is contemporaneous with the reemergence of the traditional *Joged*, in which the female principal dancer performs with a chosen male audience member. The *Joged* has also become popular in the resort areas

3.6. Waria "Ani," Seminyak (2007).
Courtesy of Belinda Lewis.

where Western men (generally middle-aged) engage in various forms of stylized flirting with young Balinese female dancers. In some districts of Bali, dancers have become notoriously explicit in their performances, exchanging theatrical touching, kissing, and more intimate dancing after the show in return for financial payments.

3.7. Traditional *Joged* performance.
Courtesy of Nyoman Wija.

According to I Nyoman Darma Putra, the *Joged* became increasingly "wild" and sexually explicit after the *Reformasi* period. Distribution of a pornographic *Joged*, filmed on amateur video in 2002, sparked considerable public controversy about whether the *Joged* had gone too far. Within Bali, concerns were expressed about the offense to moral values and, in 2004, the *Joged* was removed from major cultural events such as the *Bali Arts Festival* which is televised throughout Indonesia. Although it was widely accepted that this was to cater to the tastes of the growing number of Muslim Javanese tourists and television audiences, critics argued that the move represented a capitulation to the growing influence of conservative Islam. The *Joged* reappeared in 2005 in a modified and more restrained form which emphasized the aesthetic qualities of the dance. While *Joged* dancers in general were encouraged to play down the sexual aspects of audience participation, hip-shaking and kiss-stealing have definitely not disappeared.

While Bali has not embraced the level of explicit sexual performance evident in Thailand, the Philippines, or Western countries, the *Joged*, nevertheless is part of a continuum of tourism-based libidinal body-trading. As we have noted, tourism in Bali is fundamentally organized around "sense," sensuality, and bodily pleasures—alcohol, dancing, languor, swimming pools, sunsets, lush foods, indulgence, and tropical greenery. Further along this continuum, the visitor's body may be lavished through more direct sexual touching—massage, massage *complit* (erotic massage), escort services, prostitution, casual sex, and sexual romance.

While the notion of "sex tourism" often suggests a more organized form of holiday prostitution, the term is not clearly defined or applied in studies of developing world tourism and sexuality. We noted above, for example, that sexual relations between tourists and Balinese are often complicated by significant differentials in power and wealth, even when the exchange does not involve direct payment for services. Thus, the concepts of "prostitution" and "sex tourism" might need to accommodate a more subtle form of sex tourism in which visitors engage sexually with locals in return for gifts, meals, and various other forms of financial support or "patronage." In many respects, this form of sexual patronage has been practiced within all hierarchical and patriarchal societies; however, it has become a distinctive feature of developing world tourism whereby younger women seek relationships and marriage with first world men as a means of social mobility. For middle-aged men, younger consorts are attractive, not only because of their relative beauty and vigor, but because they often supplicate themselves to masculine and patriarchal authority. The imperatives of poverty persuade the consort to exchange her youth and beauty for care, comfort, and security. In what we might call the "sugar-daddy syndrome" such arrangements lead on occasions to marriage and family.

As we have noted above, these sexual practices are also evident among female tourists in Bali. An increasing number of middle-aged Western and Japanese women are using their Bali holiday as an opportunity for sexual engagement with younger Balinese men. Many of these women reject a fee-for-service arrangement, preferring a more subtle transaction of youth and remuneration. Once again, the younger Balinese and Indonesian men readily exchange the aesthetic and symbolic value of their bodies for the patronage and care of an older, and sometimes less attractive, female tourist (*mama manis* or sugar mamas). For the men of Kuta, older women are often regarded as more generous and accommodating than younger women; there is a sense in which the partners in these ephemeral relationships are sharing their respective personal qualities or resources in a more or less equivalent exchange of sexual pleasure—youth and beauty on the one side, wealth and maturity on the other. For this reason, a number of social commentators have excluded these relationships from a more general criticism of the sexual exploitation of people in developing countries.[42] Even so, it is clearly the case that bodies and culture of a developing-world people are being mobilized, if not expropriated, for the pleasure of a social group whose power is consolidated around economic superiority. Moreover, in some cases, Western women express their right to have sex with young Balinese men in terms of a Western feminist value system. This right frequently articulates itself as a form of political emancipation—freedom from the exploitative and patriarchal sexual regime of the home culture.

This same alibi is not available to Western men, of course, even where their practices and motivations may be similar to those of Western women. Indeed, many men prefer the patronage system to a direct fee-for-service style of sexual transaction with Balinese and other Indonesian women. Many of the sex workers in Bali themselves prefer patronage to fee-for-service, even though a relationship may only last as long as a tourist visa. This is not surprising, perhaps, as young female prostitutes are among the poorest and most vulnerable people living in Bali. As many prostitutes in the tourist-zones are from Java and elsewhere in the archipelago, they are subject to transmigration taxes and the constant surveillance and harassment of community gangs and the police. Known by the romantic title of *kupu kupu malam* (night butterflies), the girls often come to Kuta from Jakarta and rural districts, the children of indigent subsistence farmers. As females, the girls are generally less valued for farm work than their brothers, and with a low level of education they represent a poor financial prospect for the family. The girls' vulnerability to violence and extortion impels them into an underground system of gang protection and exploitation by managers and pimps. While these networks may offer some level of security and community support, especially in the prostitution *kampungs* (neighborhoods) of Denpasar, many workers remain exposed to violence and exploitation by clients and their pimps. For the girls who work outside the clandestine system and police-based protection rackets, these dangers are even more acute, and so the prospect of tourist patronage is very appealing. Not only do boyfriend tourists provide food, shelter, entertainment, and gifts such as clothing, they also afford security and respite from the austerity and dangers of sex work and life on the streets.

While a number of prostitutes haunt the shadows and alleyways around Kuta, many also work as "café girls" at nightclubs and other entertainment venues. Police crackdowns and heightened security measures since the Islamist militant attacks on Kuta have severely impinged on the prostitutes' work spaces, so it is now far more common for pimps and taxi drivers to approach international visitors and invite their interest in a "young girl." These "young girls" also inhabit the massage rooms and other bodily service spaces such as tattoo parlors. Indeed, while there are labor demarcations between massage and prostitution, the Kuta area has evolved a strong subterranean youth network, including subcultures of the *cuek* (literally "careless"; sl. "cool") set, drug users, and other marginalized groups. Indeed, many of the younger prostitutes in Bali have been attracted into sex work through their association with the drug subculture, moving from an amateur sexual activity to professionalism through the support and encouragement of boyfriends. The surrender of virginity and the adoption of new sexual-cultural practices, including drug and alcohol consumption, have opened the pathway for a number of girls to these alternative lifestyles, including massage and sex work.

The "upmarket" prostitution system which operates through the major hotels and resorts tends to conscript better educated and more attractive women. In these instances, prostitution is arranged by the syndicate and hotel management for the service of wealthy Indonesian and international visitors. Service prices range from US$300 to around US$2,000 for a full escort service. Outside the resorts and tourist zones of Kuta, girls work the streets and *kampungs* around Carik in Denpasar.[43] Carik is a shabby and dirty *kampung*, consisting of around 15 service houses and around 150 cubicles. The cubicles are very small and unhygienic with little more than a cane mat bed and occasionally a paper towel. The girls are paraded in the houses and the client chooses the woman, service, and price that suits. Prices vary according to the customer's ability to pay: beginning at around US$2 for the most basic service, the price can be as much as US$15 for international clients, full sex, or more demanding or unusual services.

The young women themselves receive only a small portion of these fees. In most cases, they live in Carik and must pay rent, commission, and protection money to their pimps. As Ari, a Balinese prostitute working in Carik, told us: "We live and work here because it is convenient. There are about five girls in each house, and we have a door at the back in case of raid." Such raids are usually initiated by municipal authorities and police. Failure to pay police protection money or an order from higher authorities can lead to the arrest of twenty or so women and a stint in Krobokan Prison. During their incarceration, the women are generally supported by the pimp and other girls in the community. At visiting hour at Krobokan, emissaries from Carik will be seen bearing food and other personal essentials, occasionally "paying off" the wardens for protection and support. While rehabilitation programs aim to teach the women needlecraft and a range of skills to facilitate alternative work options on their release, the majority return to sex work, and the cycle of remand and release is continued.

It has also been suggested that as many as 15 percent of the Javanese prostitute community in Bali were child brides, most of them married between the age of eleven and sixteen.[44] While an early age of marriage does not lead inevitably to prostitution, it is linked to extreme poverty which appears ultimately to predispose these young brides to sex work. This form of child exploitation is equally notable in the male same-gender community where various forms of male child prostitution continue to be reported. International policing is increasing the detection and conviction of Western pedophiles in Bali, including the recent case of a teacher who had been convicted in Australia but nevertheless was employed in a school in Bali and paying children in his classes for sex. In an equally well-publicized case, the rape and sexual abuse of Western children has been reported in five-star hotels, crimes purportedly perpetrated by Balinese men.

Child trafficking, in fact, is a substantial issue for human rights organizations in Bali. The majority of international visitors remain unaware that trafficking of children, primarily young women, commonly occurs under the guise of dance or cultural missions. Local NGOs, such as *Yayasan Manikaya Kauci*, have conducted awareness-raising programs for dance group members, families, and community leaders in an effort to prevent young women from being lured into trafficking. The sexual exploitation of prepubescent children in Bali remains a persistent and increasingly subterranean dimension of the island's sexuality. Nonetheless, while tourism may contribute to the demand for child trafficking, it also creates new possibilities for advocacy and support of Balinese efforts to take control over the ways its people engage with tourism and the globalizing pleasure economy.

NEW PLEASURE: NEW PROHIBITION

Several times in this chapter we have mentioned debates in the Indonesian parliament over new laws governing sexuality and sexual practices (*RUU APP Anti-pornografi dan pornoaksi*). While the laws went through numerous iterations, the bill was constructed around the prohibition of "pornography." In a deft political move, the conservative Islamic parties inscribed their restrictive religious codes into a populist bill which criminalizes any public activities, performances, or images which could "incite sexual desire." While this includes sexual depictions in publications and the electronic media, it also extends to any "man-made sexual materials in the form of drawings, sketches, illustrations, photographs, text, voice, sound, moving pictures, animation, cartoons, poetry, conversations and gestures." Opponents of the antipornography bill claim that it represents Islamic *shari'ah* law by stealth. Furthermore, they argue that the provisions of the bill that allow for "civil society" to help prevent pornographic acts will only empower vigilante groups like the Islamic Defenders' Front and provide justification for their often violent actions.

Many community groups and gangs that have emerged in Indonesia since the fall of Suharto (see chapter 4) have been particularly active in their support of the bill. While these groups are little more than opportunistic or extortion gangs, they have nevertheless been successful in convincing local communities across the archipelago to adopt bylaws which parallel the *shari'ah* intent. In this context, the Defenders of Islam Front (FPI) has been especially successful in its application of extortion and stand-over tactics in community politics. Despite the august title of the group, they are less focused on realizing the *shari'ah* ideal and more interested in creating a climate of fear within communities and thus generating a need for security. According to Ian Wilson, the purist Islamic credentials of the FPI are merely strategic: FPI creates a sense of threat and insecurity and then for a substantial fee offers their services and "ideals" to restore order.[45] Islam, in this sense, becomes a political and commercial weapon in disputes over sexuality and desire: "The FPI worldview sees the Islamic community in Indonesia as under serious attack from western decadence and immorality. The spread of free-market capitalism has manifested in the uncontrolled spread of businesses peddling in vice such as discos, bars, entertainment centers etc."[46]

Playboy and the Antipornography Laws

The antipornography bill has been the subject of furious debate within the parliament and across Indonesian society more broadly. In March 2006, the launch of the first edition of *Playboy Indonesia* sparked immediate protests in Jakarta, despite the fact that the magazine contained no nudity or bare breasts and less flesh was visible than in most Western women's magazines. Two months later, the Jakarta office was left in ruins after violent attacks by radical members of FPI. Consequently, *Playboy Indonesia* moved its operations to Bali where conservative Islam was considered to have less influence. Nonetheless, in Jakarta, the power of conservative Islamic lobbyists led to the arrest of the magazine's editor, Erwin Arnada, in December 2006 on charges of violating decency and civility. The charges attracted a potential jail term of up to thirty-two months.

According to Bali representative of *Playboy*, I Gusti Ngurah Harta (plate 3.8), "The content of Playboy is not dangerous. This is ordinary entertainment. There is a culture section. There is no nudity. The *Kamasutra* is more vulgar than this. . . . Infotainment is more dangerous to our culture. TV programs showing celebrities divorce, pregnant before marriage. This has a more strong influence."[47]

Sex and Freedom in Bali—Tolak RUU APP Bali!

Bali has been at the forefront of vigorous opposition to the antipornography laws. In 2006, the head of Bali TV, Satria Naradha, publicly claimed that Muslim Java considered Bali's pluralism and permissive culture as an obstacle to the spread of conservative Islam: "The credibility of Bali in the eyes of Muslim Java is no good. . . . The reason for the Bali bomb is because Bali is the infidel island." Gede Nurjaya, head of the Bali Tourism Authority, claimed that the antipornography laws would oppress the cultural and creative expression that has characterized the island for centuries. He argued they would ultimately "devastate Bali's reputation and tourism industry."[48]

3.8.   Ngurah Harta at his house in Bali, used as a temporary office of *Playboy Indonesia* following the attacks (2006).
Courtesy of Belinda Lewis.

During that same year, Bali Governor Dewa Made Beratha, officially rejected the APP bill and its deliberation, arguing that it would place people viewing Balinese cultural heritage and sacred religious objects in danger of criminal prosecution. In response, the *Majelis Mujahadin Indonesia* (MMI) threatened that if the state did not "discipline the rogue province, the MMI and other Islamic groups were prepared to finish the matter themselves." Threats of violence followed, and one MMI official publicly suggested that Bali should be named an autonomous region especially for pornography. In a more strident political gesture, the MMI issued a legal summons against Governor Beratha, accusing him of separatism and plans to secede from Indonesia.[49] While the summons was withdrawn, Bali was once again positioned as the transgressor. However, these events also exposed the deeper political dimensions of the bill and associated debates over culture, sexuality, and desire.

At the grassroots level, many Balinese expressed deep concern about the growing political influence of Jakarta-led, conservative Islam on Balinese culture and social life. In Denpasar on 12 March 2006, a delegation of the national parliament was greeted by a mass demonstration. Thousands of protestors chanted "Don't send us another bomb!" as they lamented the potentially devastating effects of the laws on tourism and local culture in Bali. Huge crowds gathered to watch performances by rock, reggae, and punk bands, drag queens, fashion models, and political activists. Ironically, and in a playful display of Balinese cultural defiance, the demonstration included a performance of the traditional *Joged* by a troupe of older women who publicly bared their breasts to dance in front of the crowd.

Public and parliamentary debates about the proposed bill continued for another two years. Despite strong support from Islamic groups such as Prosperous Justice Party (PKS), vigorous opposition repeatedly forced the postponement of the bill's ratification. Governors of three other provinces (West Papua, Yogyakarta, and North Sulawesi) supported Bali in formally

3.9. *Joged* dancers protest against antipornography laws in Denpasar. Front cover of *Radar Bali* newspaper, 4 March 2006.
Courtesy of I Made Rai Warsa from *Radar Bali*.

denouncing the bill on the grounds that it would discriminate against minority cultural groups and threaten traditional cultural practices, dress, and dance forms. In Jakarta, traditional women's groups as well as feminists from both Java and Bali held public protests claiming the bill was sexist and discriminatory and that it would criminalize women. In the national parliament in September 2008, two of the ten factions of the House, the Indonesian Democratic Party of Struggle (PDI-P) and the Prosperous Peace Party (PDS), withdrew from official deliberations over the bill. Thousands of Balinese took to the streets once again to voice their concerns about threats to tourism, civil liberties, cultural integrity, privacy, and artistic freedom. Bali's newly elected Governor Pastika publicly spoke out against the bill's lack of respect for pluralism and cultural diversity. On behalf of the Bali provincial government, he sent an official submission to Jakarta protesting against the bill's deliberation.

On 30 October 2008, after numerous iterations and much publicity, the bill was passed. Outside the Jakarta courtroom 1,500 police were on hand as pandemonium erupted between cheering supporters and angry opponents of the legislation. Human rights groups denounced the harsh penalties for violation of the laws. They argued that the bill would criminalize women who "incite desire" simply through bodily gestures or in choosing not to follow restrictive Islamic clothing codes such as being seen in public without a head scarf or fabric covering shoulders, arms, and lower legs.

Even before the bill had been signed off by the president, several erotic dancers were arrested, fined, and jailed in Jakarta. Under the provisions of the bill, any person creating, possessing, distributing, or downloading any form of pornography would face hefty fines and up to four years in prison. Consistent with conservative Islam, penalties were doubly harsh for women. Any person, performer, or model (primarily women) caught "displaying nudity" in public could spend up to ten years in prison and be fined up to $50,000.

In the week after the new legislation was passed, Bali's Governor Pastika publicly declared that the province would not be able to enact the bill saying, "We cannot carry it out because it is not in line with Balinese philosophical and sociological values."[50] This is the first time a province has rejected a parliamentary bill. A West Papuan delegation of church leaders threatened that that if the law was enforced, their province would secede from Indonesia. Governors of the dissenting provinces joined Bali's Governor Pastika in formally calling for a judicial review of the controversial bill at the Constitutional Court.

Over the coming months, commentators expressed grave concerns about the potential impact of the bill. Opponents claimed the new legislation was designed to curb civil rights, violate personal freedoms, and regulate private behavior based primarily on the moral standards and religious beliefs of a conservative Muslim majority. The bill was criticized as part of a growing monopoly on cultural values which could destroy Indonesia's unity, threaten cultural harmony, and shatter the right of citizens to exercise their traditional culture and values under the nation's founding principle of *Bhineka Tunggal Ika* (Unity in Diversity). Concerns were also expressed about the bill's potential to give rise to conflict and political violence by bolstering the country's already unswerving fundamentalists.

In Bali, there were vigorous grassroots responses to the bill. Working under the Commercial Arts Workers (PSK) banner, youth artists held a protest art exhibition called "Barak Sengamma" (Sex Barracks) depicting sexual activities among animals ranging from rabbits, frogs, grasshoppers, and fish. The exhibition was opened and endorsed by the sister of former president Megawati Soekarnoputri. Artisans in Gianyar, Bali, continued their work carving small statues, many of beautiful women with breasts exposed. Ironically, the buyers are mainly domestic tourists from Muslim Java. According to local artistan, Kandi, "When your mind is dirty, you will see any object as pornographic or as something that arouses your lust." Gianyar regent, Cok Oka Artha Sukawati, publicly announced that his administration would protect local artists' and artisans' freedom of expression despite the new laws.[51]

Gay and queer activists in Bali lamented the implications of the bill for people of marginal sexualities. Over recent years, there has been substantial progress toward greater tolerance of sexual diversity and support for sexual health programs to address the growing issue of HIV/AIDS. Under the new bill, activities such as the innovative Q Film Festival, would be deemed illegal. However, organizers remained undaunted, claiming that the festival would continue in Bali and elsewhere in Indonesia—even if it meant screening the films in foreign embassies where audiences would be untouchable under the new Indonesian legislation. Public health authorities also expressed concern about the bill's impact on freedom to speak about sexual health and prevention of sexually transmitted infections as part of education programs for young people. HIV/AIDS continues to rise in Bali, and recent figures from the Bali National Family Planning Coordinating Body (BKKBN) state that only 0.1 percent of Balinese boys and men use contraception.[52]

By late 2008, there was considerable concern in Bali that the new legislation could lead to insecurity arising from conflict between the island's administrators and the police. While Governor Pastika had declared he would not enact the bill, the Bali Police chief inspector, Teuku Ashikin Husein, was of a differing view and he pledged to uphold the law. Husein publicly described the legislation as "positive" and made it clear that he would enforce it.[53] Pastika, as former chief of Bali Police, was confronted with the challenge of averting a serious crisis of governance founded primarily on religious and cultural difference.

At the national level, the refusal of four provinces to enact the bill presented a constitutional crisis that exposed the limitations of the democratization and decentralization process. The bill's passing had been timed to coincide with the lead-up to the presidential election in April 2009 with President Yudhoyono hoping to demonstrate support for conservative Muslim values and secure votes from the Islamic community. However, the bill was signed amid fears that the controversial legislation could become a more serious cultural and religious battleground. Many commentators saw the bill as a dangerous political move to appease conservative Islam, fortify moves toward a *shari'ah* agenda, and empower vigilante groups to use the bill as justification for their violent actions. The bill was passed in the same week as the Bali bombers were executed and hence canonized as martyrs by their followers. For the Balinese, of course, the confluence of these events was particularly resonant. In many respects, the new laws represented a victory for the bombers, whose overarching objective was the establishment of an Islamic state across Indonesia—the centerpiece of which is *shari'ah* law.

In Bali's vortex of modernization and social change, therefore, libido has become subject to intense and often violent contests of meaning. The persistent harassment and violent attacks on the office of *Playboy Indonesia* ultimately forced its relocation from Jakarta to Bali—a migration that parallels much deeper resonances of history and culture. In the world imaginary, Bali is sex; a spectacular misreading in some ways, but also a symptom of a deep historical yearning. It would seem, therefore, that the antipornography bill, like the terrorist attacks of 2002 and 2005, seeks to destroy the island's cosmopolitan hedonism and sexual decadence. But the prohibitions, like all that have preceded them, are themselves deluded by the steamy delights they imbue on the island's sexual character. The *Playboy* brand and the libidinal flush of the Kuta nightclubs are merely the propagated ensigns to Bali's profoundly rich and complex sexual aesthetic.

NOTES

1. Michel Foucault, *The History of Sexuality*, vol. 1 (New York: Penguin, 1981).
2. Adrian Vickers, *Bali: A Paradise Created* (Ringwood, Australia: Penguin, 1989).
3. The Dutch continued to rigidify the caste system until the mid-1920s when educated commoners, tired of the arrogance of the upper castes, began to challenge its structures and power relations.
4. Thomas Reuter, introduction in *Inequality, Crisis and Social Change in Indonesia: The Muted Worlds of Bali*, ed. Thomas Reuter (London: Routledge-Curzon, 2003).
5. Margaret, J. Weiner, *Visible and Invisible Realms: Power, Magic and Colonial Conquest in Bali* (Chicago: University of Chicago Press, 1993).
6. Geoffrey Robinson, *The Dark Side of Paradise: Political Violence in Bali* (New York: Cornell University Press, 1995).

7. Weiner, *Visible and Invisible Realms*.

8. See Edward W. Said, *Culture and Imperialism* (London: Chatto and Windus, 1993); Suvendrini Perera, *Asian and Pacific Inscriptions: Identities, Ethnicities, Nationalities* (Melbourne: Meridian, 1995); Alison Broinowski, *The Yellow Lady: Australian Impressions of Asia* (Melbourne: Oxford University Press, 1992).

9. Jean Baudrillard, *Simulations*, trans. Paul Foss (New York: Semiotext(e), 1984); Pierre Bourdieu, *Distinction: A Social Critique of the Judgement of Taste* (London: Routledge, 1984); Pierre Bourdieu, *Language and Symbolic Power* (Cambridge: Polity, 1990).

10. Michael Hitchcock, *Bali the Imaginary Museum: The Photographs of Walter Spies and Beryl de Zoete* (Oxford: Oxford University Press, 1996). Also Walter Spies and Beryl de Zoete, *Dance and Drama in Bali* (London: Faber and Faber, 1938).

11. Geoffrey Gorer, *Bali and Angkor: A 1930s Pleasure Trip Looking at Life and Death* (Singapore: Oxford University Press, 1986).

12. Miguel Covarrubias, *The Island of Bali* (New York: Alfred A. Knopf, 1937), 140.

13. Covarrubias, *The Island of Bali*, 141.

14. Tessel Pollman, "Margaret Mead's Balinese: Fitting Symbols of the American Dream," *Indonesia* 49 (April 1990): 1–35.

15. Covarrubias, *The Island of Bali*, 145.

16. Megan Jennaway, *Sisters and Lovers: Women and Desire in Bali* (Lanham, Md.: Rowman & Littlefield, 2002).

17. Jennaway, *Sisters and Lovers*, 91.

18. Jennaway, *Sisters and Lovers*, 143.

19. Mark Hobart, "Engendering Disquiet on Kinship and Gender in Bali," in *Male and Female in Developing South East Asia*, ed. Wazar Jahan Karim (Oxford: Berg, 1995), 121–44.

20. James L. Peacock, *Rites of Modernization: Symbolic and Social Aspects of Indonesian Proletarian Drama* (Chicago: University of Chicago Press, 1968).

21. Laura Jane Bellows, "Traditional Sex/Modern Meaning: Desire and Foreign Influence in Bali," PhD thesis (Baltimore: University of Virginia, 2003).

22. Laura Jane Bellows, "Like the West: New Sexual Practices and Modern Threats to Balinese-ness," *Review of Indonesian and Malaysian Affairs* 37, no. 1 (2003): 71–105.

23. Tjok Istri Putra Astiti, cited in Bellows, "Like the West," 81.

24. Roland Robertson, "Glocalization: Time-Space and Homogeneity-Heterogeneity," in *Global Modernities*, ed. Mike Featherstone (London: Sage, 1995), 25–44.

25. See Jennaway, *Sisters and Lovers*.

26. Their counterparts in North Bali were known as the Lovina Lone Rangers.

27. See Jennaway, *Sisters and Lovers*.

28. See Bellows, "Traditional Sex/Modern Meaning." The following discussion is based on Bellows's work. "Kebus" is a pseudonym used by Bellows to protect the identity of the village.

29. Helen Creese, "Reading the *Bali Post*—Women and Representation in Post-Suharto Bali," *Intersections: Gender, History and Culture in the Asian Context* 10 (August 2004). See also Bellows, "Traditional Sex/Modern Meaning."

30. See Evi Arifin, "Factors Affecting the Discontinuance of Contraception in Bali, Indonesia," *Asian Meta-Center Research Paper Series* (Singapore: Asian Meta-Center, 2003).

31. Bellows, "Like the West," 71–105.

32. Interview with Professor Muninjaya, Udayana University, 2006.

33. There is some disagreement among anthropologists about the genealogy of the dance. Laura Jane Bellows and others argue that the *Joged* is the antecedent of the older form, the *Gandrung*. However, Natalie Kellar claims that the *Gandrung* evolved from the *Joged*. See also Bellows, "Traditional Sex/Modern Meaning"; I Wayan Dibia and Rucia Ballinger, *Balinese Dance, Drama and Music* (Singapore: Periplus, 2004).

34. Natalie Kellar, "Beyond New Order Gender Politics: Case Studies of Female Performers of the Classical Balinese Dance-Drama *Arja*," *Intersections: Gender, History and Culture in the Asia Pacific* 10 (April 2004): 418.

35. See Colin McPhee's discussion of Balinese music in *Music in Bali: A Study in Form and Instrumental Organization* (New Haven, Conn.: Yale University Press, 1966).

36. Fredrik DeBoer, "Two Modern Balinese Dance Genres: *Sendratari* and *Drama Gong*," in *Being Modern in Bali: Image and Change*, ed. Adrian Vickers (New Haven, Conn.: Yale Southeast Asia Studies, 1996).

37. Kellar, *Beyond New Order Gender Politics*.

38. T. Merati, Supriyadi, and F. Yuliana, "The Disjunction between Policy and Practice: HIV Discrimination in Health Care and Employment in Indonesia," *AIDS Care* 17 (Supplement 2) (July 2005).

39. Identifiable groups of "effeminate" males were recorded in local histories and traveler reports as early as the fourteenth century. However, increasing trade and the spread of Dutch occupation led to increased reporting of these *waria* communities. See Tom Boellstorff, "Playing Back the Nation: *Waria* Indonesian Transvestites," *Cultural Anthropology* 19, no. 2 (2004).

40. Tom Boellstorff, "The Emergence of Political Homophobia in Indonesia: Masculinity and National Belonging," *Ethnos* 69, no. 4 (2004).

41. Irian Kortschak, "Defining Waria," *Inside Indonesia* 90 (October 2007).

42. Sheila Jeffreys, for example, rejects the idea that women can be sex tourists, arguing that the differences between sex that is freely given and sex that is transacted represent entirely different categories of behavior. See Sheila Jeffreys "Sex Tourism: Do Women Do It Too?" *Leisure Studies*, no. 22 (July 2003).

43. See Sugi Lanus, "The Triangle of Denial, Indifference and Silent Hope: Drug Abuse and Prostitution," in *Bali: Living in Two Worlds*, eds. Urs Ramseyer et al. (Switzerland: L Scwabe Basel, 2001).

44. Lanus, "The Triangle of Denial."

45. Ian Wilson, "The Changing Contours of Organised Violence in Post New Order Indonesia," Working Paper 118 (Asia Research Center, Perth, Australia, April 2005).

46. Interview with Alam quoting the Defenders of Islam Front. Cited in Wilson, "The Changing Contours of Organised Violence," 18.

47. Interview with Ngurah Harta, Denpasar, December 2006.

48. Interviews with Satria Naradha, Bali TV, and Gede Nurjaya, Bali Tourism Authority, 2006.

49. See Laura J. Bellows "Indonesia's Politics of Porn," *American Sexuality Magazine*, 23 August 2008. Retrieved from nsrc.sfsu.edu/MagArticle.cfm?Article=655&PageID=0.

50. Ni Komang Erviani, "Police Chief Pledges to Uphold Porn Law," *The Jakarta Post*, 11 November 2008. Retrieved from www.thejakartapost.com/news/2008/11/11/police-chief-pleadges-to-uphold-porn-law.html (accessed 16 November 2008).

51. Ni Komang Erviani, "Bali's Artisans to Keep Working Despite the Passage of Porn Bill," *The Jakarta Post*, 10 November 2008.

52. Luh De Suriyani, "Contraception Use among Males Dismal 0.1 Percent: Official," *The Jakarta Post*, 14 November 2008. Retrieved from www.thejakartapost.com/news/2008/11/14/contraception-use-among-males-dismal-01-percent-official.html (accessed 16 November 2008).

53. Erviani, "Police Chief Pledges to Uphold Porn Law," *Jakarta Post*.

4

In the State of Transition

Civil Society, Corruption, and the New Risk Culture

Civil society? This is a police state. Bali once had a civil society. Now it is a corrupt state.

—Palguna, 2005

There is a crime epidemic in Bali. You can buy your way out of any misdemeanor, including murder or drugs crime. If you want someone killed, you only have to pay around 2 million rupiah. To have a foreigner killed, around 10 million.

—www.fugly-bali.org[1]

In Indonesia they give terrorist killers like Abu Bakar Ba'asyir six months but they lock up Australians for twenty years for a bit of dope. Murder two hundred innocent people and you're a hero. Smoke a little happy weed and you're the devil. They're warped. No Australian or American should go to Bali: ever! It's just a sick, corrupt system.

—"Jonty," protesting over the sentencing of Schapelle Corby, 2005

TRANSITION AND THE NEW DEMOCRATIC ORDER

Putu was born in Tianyar, a small village in the northeast corner of Bali. Tianyar is very poor. Its soils are shallow and hold little moisture. Located on the leeward side of Mount Agung, the village does not receive enough rainfall for rice farming and barely enough for drinking or cooking. In some villages, children are sent to walk five kilometers to reach the only well in the area, a small spring lying at the bottom of a dry, volcanic valley. For many Balinese, Tianyar and its people are cursed, contaminated somehow by genealogical forces which deprive the people and nature of fertility and the redemptive flow of water. In either case, the crops are sparse, and farmers are barely able to feed themselves and their families, let alone generate enough surplus for cash. When rain does come, it usually sheets across the surface, drawing out the shallow nutrients and washing them into the valley and out to sea. Putu and his family have watched such rains. They have crouched beneath the unwalled canopy of their house, sometimes touching the raindrops or playing in the eddying pools of rubbish and mud. But even as the rain is falling, they know that tomorrow the water will be gone and things will be exactly as before. The soil will be dry, the family will be hungry. Tomorrow the children will take turns again to draw water from the well. They will miss school and they will play in the dirt.

For Putu, though, there was a moment of ecstasy in his childhood. When he was twelve years old, his grandfather won a cow in a *tajen*, a cockfight. It was a surprise, as Grandfather's cocks never seemed as strong and healthy as the birds down on the coast and he nearly always returned from the gambling pits with his proud rooster, a limp and shameful carcass. But one rooster won him an honorable victory. Despite his relatively diminutive size this bird was a demon fighter. Grandfather's history of losses and the size of this particular cock had enticed gamblers to bet heavily against Grandfather. But the small rooster destroyed his adversaries with swift and surgical efficiency. Putu had witnessed many of his grandfather's humiliations, and, despite his parents' disavowals, had continued to believe in the old man's skill. And this day, his belief was vindicated. As surely as a dream, the small cock nimbly evaded the talons and blade of his opponents, cutting deep into their throats as they flagged or lost concentration, spilling blood onto the dust to the incredulity and howling of the onlookers.

"You are my good luck," Grandfather said to Putu, as they led the prize heifer home that day. "I am too old to tend this beast, but I will share her with you, if you look after her." And it was arranged that the boy would receive half the profit when the heifer was sold. There was no school for Putu and each day he would walk the animal down to the spring and to the grassy verges along the road to the coast. For nearly two years the cow had to be penned, fed, watered, and kept free of pests. When the time came, it was sold in the market and returned a very good profit. Sadly, during that time Putu's grandfather passed away and his share, plus a little of Putu's, was set aside to pay for the funeral. However, here was enough left over to send Putu down to Kuta Beach where he walked its length buying and selling cheap copies of brand-name sunglasses. Like many Indonesians who had followed the tourist gold rush in Bali, Putu's story might have been a happy one. For four years he worked around the beaches, and every few months he was able to send money back to his family in Tianyar. But when Islamic militants attacked two nightclubs on 12 October 2002, Bali's precarious economy collapsed. While many of the workers and vendors returned home to their villages in Java or provincial Bali, Putu tried to find alternative work around Kuta, hoping and believing perhaps that if he could survive long enough, the tourists and his good luck would return.

This was not to be. New government security measures made his task more difficult. Putu's status as an internal migrant (someone originally from another district) meant he was required to pay for an identity card (*KIPP*) which provided a permit to live and work in the tourist zones and also ensured a form of surveillance of outsiders. Even at 10,000 rupiah (US$1) for three months, this fee was a challenge for Putu. While these new restrictions were focused more specifically on the *orang Java* (non-Balinese), Putu and other "outsiders" were also viewed with suspicion. Without an income and with new taxes to bear, Putu was forced to leave his rented room and live on the streets. The terror incited by the militant attacks intensified the already fragmented character of the Kuta cosmopolis, deepening the fractures and borders which separated its various communities. Thus, property owners and businessmen tended to congregate around their own threatened sources of wealth. Members of the established neighborhoods and communities that had underpinned the new cosmopolis were now asserting themselves and their interests through an invigoration of tradition, ritual, and customary law. In particular, this invocation of the older grounding of Balinese society was expressed through the revival of the *pecalang*, the traditional ritual guards who had become increasingly active in the post-Suharto period as a community police and security force. While the *pecalang* had historically protected religious rites and festivals, they had become increasingly involved in broader community affairs, vigorously supporting the revival and preservation of the *adat* customary law and traditions. After the 2002 bombings, the *pecalang* had become increasingly visible and vigorous in the execution of their community policing roles. Outsiders, including those from impoverished outlying districts like Putu, became increasingly targeted as the community sought to flush out individuals and groups who might threaten the image of harmony upon which the whole economy depended.

Along with many other outsiders, Putu began to live his life in the shadows, avoiding police, the *pecalang*, and other community and public officials who might apprehend or attack him. Increasingly, Putu would keep the company of people living on the margins of society around Kuta. Among them were prostitutes, petty criminals, and bottom-tier drug traffickers. Mostly young people, they used much of their limited income to adopt Western practices and styles as a means of distinguishing themselves from the older generation and the Indonesian mainstream who had spurned them. New modes of drug consumption, alternative clothing styles, tattoos, and sexual practices were all drawn from images of the West and Western media texts. Putu's integration with this lifestyle clearly contributed to his engagement with Balinese drug culture and minor-level trafficking activities. Early one morning, the police burst in on Putu and several companions while they were still sleeping in a rough shelter behind the *pasar* (market). His arrest and subsequent conviction led to a fifteen-year sentence in Krobokan Prison.[2]

THE SUHARTO LEGACY:
FOUNDATIONS OF A NEW CIVIL SOCIETY

Putu's story has become increasingly familiar in Bali. According to Bali's former police chief, Governor I Made Mangku Pastika, there were virtually no Balinese serving custodial sentences in Krobokan Prison five years before the first Kuta bombings. During the 1990s, however, the Balinese had become increasingly involved in crime, nearly all of which were associated with petty theft and the narcotics trade. In 2003, Pastika estimated that almost 50 percent of the people in jail were from Bali. While most narcotics traffickers were previously from outside Bali, recent figures estimate that almost 30 percent are now Balinese. According to Pastika, who was elected as governor of Bali in July 2008, the influence of Western tourists and media has stimulated a new form of greed and materialism which has contributed significantly to the fracturing of customary law (*adat*) and the traditional Bali-Hindu belief system. Without the solid base of ritual and faith, Pastika claims, young people have turned toward the worst excesses of Western culture including the use of illicit drugs:

> This idea of Indonesian "cool" is something that has been invented by bad minds, faithless minds. It replace the things in life that really matter. Bali was once very, very peaceful. It was a highly integrated society. There was harmony. Now the cultural values of the Balinese are declining. . . . Now our children are turning to crime. Why? It's because of the change of values . . . by tourism, by the TV, by the consumer . . . they are no longer satisfied. They don't understand karma any more.[3]

This ideal of harmony, as we have discussed throughout this book, is largely a cultural construction fabricated over time by numerous interest groups within and outside Bali. In this context, Putu's story contains many of the elements of disharmony that have continually challenged the veracity of this fabrication, resonating with the violence of a social order—a New Order—which underscored development, social transition, and the tourism boom in Bali. That is, Putu's story, like many others, is not the happy ideal of Bali harmony or Bali paradise, but a calamity of uneven parts that have been generated throughout the New Order and the incendiary of its inception in the genocide of 1965/1966. In this light, the tourism boom, which has fostered and depended upon the "Bali harmony" discourse, was itself constructed over the violence, terror, and deaths of the Balinese people themselves. Thus, the potential benefits of modernization have been constantly compromised through a tyranny of social and political oppression.

Not surprisingly, the inchoate civil practices and political institutions which Sukarno had attempted to shape around the official state ideology (*Pancasila*) were largely erased by Suharto, whose overriding concerns were with civil obedience, the maintenance of autocratic power, and the wealth of his military plutocracy. To this end, parliamentary democracy was a farcical promulgation of self-interest; all forms of public debate or dissent were crushed by an uncompromising military dictatorship. Governance, including judicial process, was largely structured through the military hierarchy, as privilege and the perpetual threat of brutality and coercion were inscribed into all levels of social life. Indonesia's modernization was recast through older forms of plutocratic avarice which manacled economic development to the interests and corrupt practices of the military and political elite.

This culture of explicit and clandestine financial "remission," became a social, legal, and commercial imperative that infected the entire society. The New Order created an institutional framework for complicated double-coding, kickbacks, graft, and corruption. As we noted in our discussion of development in Bali (see chapter 2), this system of unofficial remissions also undermined public policy and planning, and contributed to the formation of a complex network of invisible relationships, bonds, and indebtedness. Contracts and other commercial processes were perpetually frustrated by "favors" and a flaccid legal system which was essentially an arm of the military. Development and the financial sector were laden by a system of patronage that continually distracted international investment away from productive activity and toward only those projects which would further enhance the Suharto plutocracy's already grotesque wealth. According to the 2003 Asian Development Bank report on corruption, Indonesia's ongoing development problems were largely rooted in these weaknesses in governance which the Suharto regime has left as a principal legacy.[4] While managing to grow strongly during the 1980s, Indonesia could not overcome this fundamental weakness in public sector infrastructure and private international investment. As the ADB report argued, governmental corruption not only presents a profoundly fallible moral paradigm to its people, it leaves the national economy with a two-fold challenge—

1. Corruption, under evolving economic institutions, discourages private investment and, thus, long-term growth prospects.
2. Corruption limits public sector resource mobilization and lowers the return to society from public sector spending and investment.

It was most certainly these factors, along with the underlying ineptitude of the Indonesian bureaucracy, which contributed to the depth and extent of the 1997 Asian monetary crisis in Indonesia. As many commentators have noted, the intensity of the crisis in Indonesia, which ultimately led to the collapse of the Suharto presidency in 1998, was the unavoidable outcome of several decades of exploitation, corruption, and mismanagement.[5]

Even so, it was the evolution and growth of a distinct middle class which determined the timing and character of the regime change in Indonesia. While President Suharto had managed to strangle the development of a labor movement and proletariat political parties in Indonesia, the middle classes emerged during the 1980s and 1990s as a significant and potentially powerful political force. Not surprisingly, many of these better-educated and more affluent professionals were interested in the processes of economic liberalism, reform, modernization, and democratization. While a considerable proportion of these people preferred the separation of state and religion, others (including the first post-Suharto elected president, Abdurrahman Wahid) sought to vulcanize the new democracy to a Javanese tradition and Muslim morality. An even smaller group sought a more chauvinistic and visible role for the faith, believing that Islam should be the center of government and social law. These Islamic leaders, many of them educated in Saudi Arabia, were able to marshal their educated and less well-educated followers into various forms of political congregation and expression.

Of course, the more radical wing of Islamicism had been active during the period of Dutch occupation and many were key fighters in the national revolution (1945–1949). Sukarno had to work strategically to ensure that the national constitution and the state ideology (*Pancasila*) were not appropriated by religious interests seeking to have Islam nominated as the national faith and *Shari'ah* Islamic law installed as the basis for the nation's entire judicial system. Ultimately, *Pancasila* evolved as a secular and pluralist framework which protected the rights and dignity of Indonesia's minority religious and ethnic groups, including the Hindu Balinese. Even so, the more radical political Islamicists felt somewhat betrayed by Sukarno and the secularist national model. While representing only a minority of Indonesian Muslims, the political Islamicists nevertheless constituted an important and influential social group. Both the Old (Sukarno) and New (Suharto) Order regimes had to manage them very carefully.

Acceding to the presidency in the mid-1960s, Suharto pursued a strategy which was simple enough. He merely subjected the Islamicists to the same vicious will he had imposed over the whole country—and in general the Islamicists preferred Suharto's secular order to the class warfare, communism, and chaos that Sukarno's rule ultimately threatened. But Islam, in its most pure or extreme forms at least, rejects all authority that is not centered on Allah and His Law. In this context, therefore, Islamicism constituted a significant and ongoing threat to the New Order regime, most especially as the middle class began to grow in size and social influence, and began increasingly to be interested in questions of democracy, devotion, and law. Thus, while the moderate and liberal-minded Islamicists threatened the autocracy through their interest in a devout democracy, the more radical Islamicists challenged the Suharto government on the basis of its secular and materialist nature. As we will discuss in greater detail in the following chapter, this latter group was influenced by the scholarship and education framework of Saudi Arabia which advocated a purer form of Islamic governance, one which privileged *shari'ah* law over secular autocracy or secular democracy.

Thus, while the radical Islamicists remained relatively inconsequential in numerical terms, their views were mediated through a middle class who were becoming increasingly dissatisfied with the austere and uncompromising authority of Suharto's government. From the 1980s many in the Indonesian middle class began to adopt a more devout and observant religious demeanor, invoking their faith, perhaps, as an antidote to the corrupt, authoritarian, and illicit practices of the Suharto military plutocracy. What is clear, however, is that in the last decade of the twentieth century increasing numbers of the population were expressing their faith in a more public way. And as if to placate the rising tide of Islam and its political expression, Suharto in the latter years of his presidency began to wear the *songkok* (black Muslim cap) and offer a range of social legislative concessions that acknowledged the relevance of a resurgent religious morality. Thus, while the monetary crisis catalyzed the collapse of the New Order, it was the economic power of the middle class and the violent protests of radical Islamic students which ultimately isolated Suharto from his support base and grip on power.

The U.S. government, which for decades had supported Suharto as a bulwark to Asian communism, now saw the ageing tyrant and his corrupt government as a significant threat to financial and political stability in the region. With the collapse of the Soviet Union and international communism more generally in the early 1990s, America and its principal regional ally, Australia, ultimately switched their support from Suharto toward a more democratic state framework in which secularism and a liberal economy could prevail over religious fundamentalism. The establishment of political institutions would lionize democracy, democratic values, free trade, and the prosperity of the middle classes. The violent attacks on the Chinese community by Islamic radicals during the 1998 crisis reminded external governments and the local plutocracy of the considerable dangers posed by Indonesian Islamicism. Eventually, even many of his closest allies abandoned Suharto, and he was forced to resign on 21 May 1998.

After a brief transition, the new elected president, Abdurrahman Wahid, embarked on the extraordinary challenge of rebuilding Indonesia's civil society and political institutions. A devout, but pluralist Muslim, Wahid was an unexpected victor, outmaneuvering his much younger and more publicly popular rival, Megawati Soekarnoputri, the daughter of Sukarno, Indonesia's first president. While Wahid soon lost control of the government and was replaced by Megawati, he nevertheless embarked on a program of reform (*Reformasi*) which remains the centerpiece of Indonesia's political project—a transition from a military and highly centralized governance structure to a genuinely civil society. The change to a directly elected presidential system (as opposed to an appointment by the parliament) for the 2004 presidential ballot has not altered significantly the direction of these transitions, even though President Susilo Bambang Yudhoyono has devoted himself to a new anticorruption purge and a more strident approach to effective national governance. As we will discuss in detail below, the great challenge for these presidents, especially within a context of increasing Islamic militancy and global insecurity, has been the entrenched nature of Indonesian corruption and weaknesses in civil process. The three primary tenets of the *Reformasi*—democratic and participatory governance, decentralization, and demilitarization—are encountering considerable challenges and resistance from those whose interests are most directly threatened by the reforms.

Indeed, while some commentators have suggested that the *Reformasi* ended with Wahid's presidency, others claim that Suharto's death early in 2008 marks an historical and symbolic closure for the reforms and their political impetus. Our own view is that the trajectory of civil transition is continuing albeit with a more uneven and complicated volition. Thus, the essential conditions of a genuinely civil society remain largely incomplete in Indonesia. Democratic governance, rule of law, judicial transparency, and the political-social engagement of nongovernmental institutions are disturbingly immature, if not fractious. Indonesia's complex religious, military, and social histories continue to frustrate the consolidation of the *Reformasi* and the more resonant reforms that are the conduit of this new phase of modernization.[6]

TRANSITION AND ITS EFFECTS IN BALI

The difficulties of executing the *Reformasi* are particularly evident in Bali. The cultural and environmental trauma generated by genocide, political exclusion, and uncontrolled development have provided a distressingly unstable platform for the island's modernization. Islamic militancy and the broader context of global insecurity further accentuate these problems, exposing the distended economic belly of the island to deepening uncertainty. As the propagated image of harmony begins to fracture, underlying

tensions and frustrations are revealing themselves through a range of political, cultural, and ethnic agonisms. The transition policies and the *Reformasi*, in fact, have been greeted with suspicion by the Balinese who have for
years been victim to a powerful Javanese political and military elite. And indeed, within this new regime of civil order, decentralization, and increased
provincial autonomy, the Balinese are struggling to overcome the historical
conditions which have deprived them of dignity, civil expression, and an effective political infrastructure.

Thus, while Bali had developed highly sophisticated protocols and institutions for community governance and self-management in the premodern
period (before Dutch occupation), these institutions, the *banjars* and *ben-
desa adat*, were substantially dismantled during the New Order. Rather than
replace these community management systems with a modern civil infrastructure or blended infrastructure as Sukarno had planned, the New Order
installed a corrupt, authoritarian, and largely inept system of centralized,
military-based control. While decentralization and autonomy should have
led to a better governance and stronger civil society, the reform processes
have largely been top-down, with little room for participatory decision-
making. Those benefiting most from the reforms have been local elites, bu-
reaucrats, new businessmen, and aristocrats. With little recent experience of
democratic and participatory civil management, the Balinese are clearly
struggling with the autonomy associated with reform, and in many cases,
they are recasting the old hierarchies and governance "traditions" that had
once served the community as part of the old system of kingdoms.[7]

The Balinese are trying to mediate the imposed cultural and spatial transformations brought by development with the new political potential of the
Reformasi. More particularly, they are seeking ways to mediate the complex
elements of change that have taken place within their own consciousness
and sense of self: they must join the dots between past and present, benefit
and loss, autonomy and predetermination.

To this end, the transition policies have reawakened tensions between the
state (*negara*) and the people (*rakyat*), tensions which might seem a normal
symptom of a modernization process. At the dawn of the New Order in
1965/1966, these tensions were being played out in various ways through
civil and institutional channels, though they became radicalized through
Suharto's counter insurgency and political purges. In the current context,
the revivification of these debates is occurring around policy reform focused on demilitarization, a policy designed to remove the military from judicial, policing, and civil governance processes. While on the surface this
may seem a relatively straightforward matter of institutional realignment, it
is complicated by the pervasive and often subterranean engagement of a
people, culture, and "system" within virtually every aspect of private and
public life in Indonesia. This is particularly manifest in the judiciary and

police force which has now been separated from the military and is designed to emulate the community policing practices of other modern states.
Nonetheless, while the police force in Bali now operates as an independent
arm of government, the inherited practices of nepotism, kickbacks, and corrupt practices remain heavily entrenched. With an average officer income of
around US$60 per week and a personnel comprised largely of former mili-
tary servicemen, the new police force continues to supplement its meager
income with a range of self-funding activities, including unofficial fees and
fines, protection rackets, drug trafficking, and stand-over. As the former police chief, Governor Pastika informed us, the police are largely drawn from
the higher castes in Bali and they have not adjusted to the idea of civil service; rather, they see themselves as exercising a privilege and authority that
is sanctioned by tradition, as well as the state:

> It is not easy to change that way of thinking. But we must change because of
> the new paradigm, from ruler to servant, The servant of the people. . . . In the
> caste system in Bali, the Brahmana are for the priests, the Satria for the rulers,
> the soldiers, the police . . . and the lowest caste is the Sudra. I come from Su-
> dra. I come from Sudra and now I am chief of police in Bali. But I must keep
> thinking that I am the servant. I must talk to my men and say "Even though
> you are now in the caste of Satria, you are still a servant of society. The people
> is our boss, not you." That is not easy. I must talk very much to these people
> because it is the culture. It is in the mind. It is very hard.[8]

Not surprisingly, these attitudes have also led to considerable tension and
even competition with the military, who are feeling increasingly alienated
by the civil transition policies.

Of equal significance, however, are the actual mechanics of policing itself.
As the inept forensic work in the 2002 bombings indicates, the police still
lack adequate training and resources. While the number of police per head
of population in Bali is high compared to the rest of Indonesia (approximately 1:300 compared with 1:1,000), police officers are largely ineffectual
and incapable of managing serious crime. To the Balinese themselves, the
police are still generally perceived as a malevolent and entirely untrustwor-
thy social unit which is to be silently endured, avoided, despised, and
ridiculed. Even in 2005, the police were unable to quell the violent demon-
strations outside Krobokan jail calling for the immediate death of convicted
Bali bomber, Amrozi. Eventually, local *pecalang* leaders were called in to
pacify the angry mob of several thousand people.

> People come here because they have strong feeling. Amrozi cause Bali to lose
> millions of dollars. There was no organizer, we just know by mobile phone.
> The mob tried to enter the prison yard. They damaged the wall. The police tried
> to stop them . . . People called me to the demonstration to avoid further clash

between the mob and police. To stop the violence. I want to stop the clash because it will give bad image for Bali to tourists.[9]

To this end, the real conditions of social order within communities relies on traditional civil institutions, including the *banjar* (neighborhood and village council) and the community "police" or *pecalang*. As we noted above, the role of the *pecalang* has evolved from the protection of ritual to become a more general form of community policing body.

In the context of demilitarization and state police ineptitude and corruption, the *pecalang* is one example of a social and civil organization which has emerged since the fall of Suharto to fill the security void created by demilitarization. In the previous chapter, we made mention of one such group that has assumed the role of vigilante in Indonesian community life, the Defenders of Islam Front (*Front Pembela Islam*). As we noted, the FPI uses violence to create an environment of insecurity and threat, and then uses extortion methods to elicit payment for the restoration of order. Like many other social vigilante groups, the FPI invokes the force of Islamic tradition and morality to fortify its status and extortion strategy, convincing communities across Java that its claim is legitimate and that *shari'ah* bylaws should be adopted.[10]

While invoking Bali's distinct Hindu traditions and the *adat*, the *pecalang* are assuming a similar role in social management in Bali. Reinvigorated after the fall of Suharto, the *pecalang* have become actively engaged in local and national politics, and have adopted a distinctly chauvinistic posture in community security, particularly since the Islamic militant attacks of 2002. This role of community policing has become somewhat confused, particularly in the tourist zones where the intersection of state and people is complicated by the globalization of culture and the amorphous nature of "community" itself. As the *pecalang* seek to generate and contain a sense of order within a customary social framework, they frequently appear atavistic and clumsy, more like a self-appointed vigilante than a well-formed agent of communal protection.

This ambiguity is situated in the historical reemergence of the new *pecalang*.[11] For example, during the 1998 presidential elections, the Denpasar and Kuta-Legian *pecalang* were particularly active mustering support and providing security for their preferred presidential candidate, Megawati Soekarnoputri. In the post-Suharto era, the *pecalang* have been able to assume a far more assertive political demeanor than had previously been permitted, and were active during the preelection campaign in denouncing the former dictator while valorizing Megawati whose mother had been Balinese. And while this is not universally the case, there are certainly a number of *pecalang* members who have harbored a strong sense of Balinese nationalism, advocating the expulsion of all non-Balinese from the island and the promotion of a form of Balinese secession similar to that offered to the Acehnese in northern Sumatra.[12]

Perhaps the most notable demonstration of this new mode of community aggression was evident in the 1999 attacks on the beach vendors at Kuta-Legian where local *pecalang* mustered and expelled the non-Balinese beach-sellers, incinerating their food stalls (*kaki-lima*) and denying them access to the beachfront. News reports of this aggression, however, seriously compromised the propagated mantra of Bali harmony, resulting in a direct reduction in tourist numbers for that year. The *pecalang* were thereby rebuked and have since adopted a less visible approach to their community policing. Following the 2002 bombings, the *pecalang* actively supported the police and their security management. According to the former police chief, Governor Pastika, this support was very welcome, and while there was always the danger of vigilante policing, the *pecalang* clearly contributed to a new regime of social management in the midst of community crisis. This was especially the case as police and government officials sought to impose a new regime of surveillance designed to check the identity of non-Balinese Indonesians who may constitute a threat to civil order. Responsibility for checking the status of the non-Balinese transmigrants was largely assumed by the *pecalang*. Unfortunately, while the vast majority of non-Balinese came to the island for legitimate purposes, mostly to work or sell products, the licensing system (*kippem*) was often crudely administered and there have been reports of bullying and violence by *pecalang*, especially against Muslims from Java.[13] To some extent, this excess can be explained by the political disposition of the group and their actual composition. While *pecalang* members are often community leaders, there are also many who are unemployed or underemployed men with no experience or training in civil management and little social profile except for their participation in the *pecalang* and their robust fidelity to Balinese tradition.

More recently, the transition to community policing has also involved the recruitment of honorary police. Members of this unpaid civilian police force are selected from a range of ethnic and religious backgrounds in a strategy designed to overcome the ethnic tensions arising from the excesses of *pecalang*-based security and to improve community integration and cohesion. However, problems such as inadequate training and lack of cohesion still provide challenges for effective implementation.

The Challenges of Community Policing

Police force reforms and the transition to community policing are key strategies for strengthening security and civil order in Bali. While the engagement of traditional community organizations such as the *pecalang* has been replete with problems, the transition is further complicated by the presence of another unofficial security group known as the *preman*. These gangs of thugs provide "public support" in exchange for political protection and relative immunity from police intervention in their criminal activities. Some are aligned with the major political parties (Golkar or PDI-P), and the major *preman* organization, *Forum Peduli Denpasar* (FPD), claims to have an agenda of "bottom up" social reform around issues such as development, protection of regional culture, and the fight against drugs. With substantial criminal connections in the gambling and entertainment areas, the *preman* are notorious for conducting violent attacks on citizens and property as well as execution-style murders of public figures. Engaged to protect business interests, intercede in village feuds and wider civil disputes, the *preman* rarely receive criminal convictions for their brutality and violence. In 2003, *preman* Manik Parasara murdered his own brother as part of a local political dispute and, after appearing in court with hundreds of followers, was handed only a six-month sentence.[14]

In 2008 we observed the *preman* at work. Tall young men, equipped with mobile phones and truncheons, were brutally beating a man they had deemed an undesirable presence in the tourist strip. Doubled-over and screaming for assistance from local shopkeepers, this man knew he had to attract the attention of onlookers in order to embarrass his assailants with public scrutiny. But most people just looked away. An American surfer interrogated the men, asking them why they were acting like "fucking Gestapo." The allusion, however, was lost on the black-shirts who simply continued their assault until the youth lay in a bloodied heap on the sidewalk. Obviously poor and living on the margins, the youth was clear evidence that the new security system and its propagated image of community harmony was barely succeeding to mask a much deeper condition of disorder.

In another incident in 2006 a journalist, who had published an article criticizing a development in West Bali, was arrested by local civilian police. The arrest and detention of the journalist had been directed by the Head of the District, a prominent *bupati* and university professor. The district head was outraged by the article and sought to reassure potential developers that such criticisms would not be tolerated. The case raised the ire of other journalists and received substantial publicity in the *Bali Post*. The subsequent investigation by Bali Police saw the journalist released from detention and despite rumors that the *bupati* would be charged with misconduct, no legal action was taken.[15] Clearly, the transition to community policing remains a substantial challenge for Balinese communities, their political representatives, and the official police force.

In practice, the transition to civil policing and management in Bali is still falling well short of the ideal. This is also the case for the policy of decentralization which has given regional autonomy to each of the Indonesian provinces, including Bali, and the specific districts within them. The extensive decentralization process, shifting power from the Indonesian central government toward local provincial autonomy, has created new debates about the ways in which the people of Bali might take greater control over the island's governance, development, and economic prosperity. As we have noted, however, the levels of non-Balinese, especially foreign, property ownership and capital investment have relegated most Balinese to the status of wage-earner or petty shopkeeper. In a sense, and as community leader Viebeke Lengkong has declared, the Balinese have become marginalized in their own territory:

> That's the reality, I'm sorry. . . . Other people are in control. All the tourists, the expatriots, the migrants living here. Even though they are Indonesian, they are in control. The Balinese are losing the generation. The Balinese are being pushed out . . . marginalized. When you come to the hotels, the developments, who's your general manager? He's not Balinese. Who's your manager? He's not Balinese. Who is Balinese? The Balinese is the sweepers. . . . That's all we are. The sweepers of Bali.[16]

With these powerful economic forces at stake, provincial and district decision-making is perpetually constrained by the demands of wealthy business owners and international corporations. In a province which relies almost entirely on tourism as a source of economic welfare and cash employment, it's not surprising that development is the primary mantra of the provincial government.

Balinese Ritual and Apoliticism

A number of commentators argue that the Balinese are fundamentally apolitical: that is, they have no great interest in civil process, political institutions, and public debate.[17] For many, the Balinese fidelity to their Hindu rituals and faith and the *adat* predisposes them against modern political expression, debate, or activism. Along with their low economic and social status on the island, the Balinese religious and traditional affiliations disincline them toward representative politics at either national or provincial levels. Tourism expert at Udayana University, Professor Ardika, argues that the religious libations of the Balinese actually leave them with little time for political engagement and the intellectual energy required for critique and social challenge.[18] Other commentators suggest, in fact, that these libations so distract the Balinese that they have become essentially unreliable workers who could never aspire to a management position as they could, at any time, have to leave their workplace and attend some "important village ritual." Hindu faith and the *adat* provide all the necessary answers, Viebeke bemoans, "leaving the Balinese to wallow in their beautiful but powerless spiritual condition."

Other commentators have supported these arguments, claiming further that the propagated notions of "Bali harmony" and "Bali paradise" have helped to convince even the Balinese themselves that political action is fundamentally dangerous since it might upset the sacred cow of international tourism. And it is certainly true that the precarious condition of the tourism industry has proved very sensitive to disturbances. Following the 1999 beach burnings, international tourist numbers declined by almost 15 percent, while the 2002 bombings had the immediate effect of reducing international visits by around 80 percent, a figure that has been repeated following the 2005 bombings in Kuta and Jimbaran Bay. In all these instances, the Indonesian national government, the Bali Tourism Authority, and the Balinese themselves have exerted considerable effort to promote the ideal of Bali harmony through both official and informal channels. Following the 2005 bombings, however, the ideal seems to have been less convincingly restored. According to Gede Nurjaya, head of the Bali Tourism Authority, at the close of the 2006 season tourist numbers remained critically short of recovery levels with an average hotel occupancy of only 10 percent.[19] When finally the tourism numbers recovered over 2007 and 2008, the mix and character of the international visitors had changed markedly (see table 5.3, chapter 5).

AJEG BALI AND THE POLITICS OF BALINESE IDENTITY

The trauma of the bombings and the ensuing economic downturn has been accompanied by a different form of political discourse, one which blends religion, identity, culture, and political agitation. The rise of the *Ajeg Bali* movement has convinced a number of observers that Bali is experiencing a new kind of religious, cultural, and political revivalism. This revivalism, a little like the evangelical nationalism in America, is formed around a sense of civics and civic duty that is distinctly and assertively Balinese.

Ajeg Bali is a cultural revival movement which reflects a desire for self-empowerment among Hindu Balinese. It seeks to reinvigorate Hindu Balinese cultural identity and address growing concerns among many Balinese regarding the rapid pace of change, growing social inequalities and their marginalization from decision-making about the future of their island. *Ajeg Bali* literally means "Stand strong for Bali!" Its originator and most prominent advocate is Satria Naradha, Bali's major media entrepreneur and director of the Bali Post Media Group (BPMG) which includes BaliTV and *Bali Post* newspaper. *Ajeg Bali* directs people in Bali to consider all of the cultural, social, economic, and environmental issues associated with development. According to Satria, the movement is about agenda-setting, public debate, and self-determination so that Bali can "advance slowly, step by step, together."

Ajeg Bali first received substantial public exposure in May 2002 (just prior to the bombings) at the launch of the new television station, BaliTV. Timed to coincide with the lead-up to the presidential elections in Indonesia, Satria Naradha strategically obtained political support for both the new TV station and the *Ajeg Bali* movement. Bali Governor Beratha and all major political candidates, including Megawati Soekarnoputri and the now president Yudhoyono, provided signatures of support which were later carved in stone (*prasati*) and mounted into the imposing façade of the new BaliTV premises as enduring evidence of support from Jakarta.

Ajeg Bali: Social Equity and Community Capacity Building

Satria Naradha (pictured below) studied journalism in Surabaya and took over the directorship of *Bali Post* in 2001 following the death of his father who had founded the newspaper in1948 (as *Suara Indonesia*). In addition to his media interests in Bali, Satria also owns seven TV stations and numerous radio stations across wider Indonesia. After the 2004 tsunami disaster in Aceh, he established the first nonprofit, community TV station to assist with the community recovery.

4.1. BaliTV production studio (2007).
Courtesy of Belinda Lewis.

BaliTV is a major supporter of *Ajeg Bali* through its media programming which aims to facilitate Hindu-Balinese cultural revival and raise awareness about important environmental, social, and economic issues affecting Bali. Early in 2005, Satria Naradha announced the formation of *Koperasi Krama Bali (KKB)* a cooperative aiming to support less affluent, informal rural and more traditional sectors. KKB funds a range of community programs. One example, "Balinese can do it," aims to develop the skills and employability of Balinese who are without jobs or formal training. The *Koperasi* has collected considerable sums of money from *Ajeg Bali* supporters, government, and political candidates (particularly during the 2005 local elections) and redistributes funds to small businesses and community groups to provide educational opportunities for the "informal sector." Training courses are provided at no cost to participants in areas such as business management, bread-making, hairdressing. Support for the revival of Balinese foods has seen a proliferation of small businesses selling traditional *bakso balls* and *sate kambing* from the *kaki lima* carts in tourist areas and local villages. *Ajeg Bali* is also working to reduce the negative effects of globalization of the food supply, now flooded with cheap, energy-dense Western foods, confectionery, and soft drinks. BaliTV provides vigorous counteradvertising to balance the paid advertising and pervasive influence of multinational food chains such as KFC and McDonald's.

The TV program *Dharma Wacana* (literally "religious preach") is one of the highest rating programs on BaliTV. Still on air three times daily in 2008, this talkback program also provides sermons from leading priests regarding *Ajeg Bali*. Filming occurs at the studio and on location across Bali in rural villages.

According to Satria Naradha, the BaliTV studio is "low tech" and low budget and employees are largely drawn from local youth who are trained on the job: "I have a small studio, but a big mission. Little steps, but slowly, all together, we will get big result."[20]

Since 2002, *Ajeg Bali* has been vigorously promoted through BMPG, and the movement has been proliferating through various popular, political, religious, and media discourses. According to Balinese academic and journalist, I Nyoman Darma Putra:

Ajeg Bali was already in existence and it would probably just have remained a cultural cliché, but the 2002 bombings and the associated economic and spiritual crisis created the conditions for it to become a substantial cultural and political/moral social movement.[21]

Through *Ajeg Bali*, the apoliticism inscribed in religious affiliation and ritual is being transformed by a form of "fundamentalism"—the convocation of cosmological sanction, cultural tradition, and identity politics.

4.2. Corby dope: Bali police and onlookers examine the four-kilogram bag of marijuana found by customs officers in Schapelle Corby's surfboard bag (Prosecutors Office, Denpasar).
Courtesy of I Nyoman Darma Putra.

While the proponents of *Ajeg Bali* reject the general tag of "fundamentalism," it is clear that Bali's emergence from the tyranny of New Order is releasing a cultural politics which for many Balinese draws together traditionalism and a resurgent desire for autonomy and territorial control. To this extent, the concept of *Ajeg Bali* (literally "Bali stands strong") articulates a territorialism which seeks to redeem the island from the cultural and environmental degradation inflicted by rapid and uncontrolled tourism development.

As we noted in chapter 2, the foundation of this reemergent territorialism was evident in various environmental protests during the 1990s. However, Balinese secessionism and "nationalism" have been present throughout the whole period of the Republic—and earlier. At the time of its completed annexation into the Dutch East Indies colony (1908), Bali was a largely independent territory with eight regencies, each dominated by its own royal family, and a diverse but distinctive Hindu faith. The cultural and cognitive standardizations imposed by colonial rule, somewhat paradoxically, contributed to the ferment of a national consciousness which ultimately rejected external control. This new consciousness drew many Indonesians, including many Hindu Balinese, into a national revolution which was essentially dominated by Muslim Java. Indonesian nationalism, however, was not universally embraced by all Balinese, and there remained a small but significant core of Balinese separatists who sought the restoration of independent sovereignty. This brand of Balinese nationalism had both secular and religious dimensions, and adherents were motivated by a range of interests and political dispositions. As we have noted, Balinese secessionism was largely silenced during the Suharto years, emerging more recently within the constellation of political and cultural grievances we have outlined above and in previous chapters.

Ajeg Bali, in a sense, continues this tradition, although it has a more contemporary edge to it. In many respects, *Ajeg Bali* extends the notion of Balinese-ness (*kebalian*) that has always been at the edge of Balinese territorialism, and which, as we noted above, is linked to anxieties about Javanese hegemony, development degradation, and the presence of large numbers of Muslim migrants in the Bali tourist areas. In this context, *Ajeg Bali* aims to strengthen self-esteem and a sense of Balinese identity as well as helping Balinese people to participate in local decision-making. Satria Naradha claims that *Ajeg Bali* is instrumental to the transition to a more participatory democracy because it is not directly political but rather exerts a subtle influence on government through its agenda-setting role. He acknowledges the challenges of working with governments which are still emerging from the authoritarian legacy of New Order, but he is adamant that the transition to more democratic forms of public participation should occur slowly.[22]

Critics of *Ajeg Bali* claim it is an elite, "top-down" movement with little representation or influence on the ground in local communities. Naradha, through his control of the media, is considered to be a self-appointed "second governor" whose leadership and authority over Balinese identity politics is more reminiscent of old forms of aristocratic domination than of new modes of democratic political participation.[23] Concerns are also expressed that the *Ajeg Bali* discourse may be used to stifle debate about challenging the traditional hierarchies associated with class, caste, gender, and ethnicity. However, Naradha argues that the movement is gradually transforming the previously limited political arena into a more public and participatory space. The aim of *Ajeg Bali* is to mobilize a greater range of civil society groups in pressuring governments for democratic reform:

It is difficult to change government . . . they need time to change . . . so that people in government cannot just do what they like any more. Now, with *Ajeg Bali*, the community is telling the government that they must consult. If they are concerned about *Ajeg Bali*, they will adjust their plans and policies depending on what people are thinking. . . . This is a good thing.[24]

Critics of *Ajeg Bali* also claim the movement offers the Balinese a forum for the expression of increasingly radical regionalist sentiments, whereby local culture is presented as exclusively Hindu and in tacit opposition to Islam. *Ajeg Bali*, it is argued, has been instrumental in promoting an exclusive ethnic profile of Balinese culture and religion, and is thus potentially a constraining and divisive social influence.[25] However, according to Satria Naradha, *Ajeg Bali* seeks merely to revive the spirit, morale, and confidence of the Balinese whilst maintaining a strong relationship with wider Indonesia. He is acutely aware of the risks associated with divisive politics of identity and is careful to emphasize that *Ajeg Bali* is not "anti-Muslim or anti-Javanese":

> Ajeg Bali is very Hindu. But I don't like to say about the Hindu, because Hindu is a minority in Indonesia. Hindu Bali is little and Indonesia is big . . . but Indonesia can't exist without the minority of Bali: the big cannot exist without the small.

More recently, the discourse of *Ajeg Bali* has included the notion that a stronger, pluralist Bali can contribute to Indonesian unity and security:

> Just now the motto from BaliTV is "The sun rise from Bali." The message is . . . we care for other regions. If Bali maintains good economic growth, good social goal, no conflict, no bombs, this is very good for other regions in the country. I need Bali to be example for our brothers in Java—as a model. But only time will test our actions.[26]

Taking the *Tajen* out of the Temple

Part of the difficulties with the Hindu-Balinese cultural revival movement is that it draws together a diverse range of cultural and political interests, transposing significant social differences into a disarmingly simple ideal of redemption. One of the most potent of these divisions is expressed by the former police chief, Governor Pastika, a significant advocate of the integrity and purity of Bali's Hindu revivalism. As chief of Bali Police, Pastika had embarked on a radical program of social reform which sought to prohibit Balinese cockfighting (*tajen*) and associated gambling activities. According to Pastika, the cockfights had so mesmerized the Balinese people that they were ruining their livelihoods through gambling. Pastika claimed that people were of the mistaken belief that the *tajen* were holy sanctioned cultural activities and, by conducting cockfights around temples and other religious sites, they had been frequently transgressing sacred territory and ritual. However, Pastika's attempts to close down the cockfights were themselves considered a betrayal of cultural integrity and tradition by the populace, particularly in outlying villages, where the *tajen* had been a long established and entirely sanctified communal activity. Paradoxically, this kind of grass-roots resistance posed a challenge to Pastika's "cultural revival" platform during his recent campaign for election as governor of Bali. In order to re-orient community opposition and strengthen support for his approach to the revitalization of Hindu-Balinese traditions, Pastika conducted an extensive program of consultations and forums in villages across Bali. He was elected governor in July 2008.

As we have noted numerous times, the invocation of tradition is used by opposing political groups in order to ground their respective political claims. Thus, far from being apolitical, the Balinese are expressing their politics and claims to power through various dimensions of community and civic life. This life, however, and the sense of "being Balinese" is neither uniform nor monolithic; rather, the assertion of Balinese cultural territorialism is being formed around an increasingly pluralized constituency of interests, experiences, and perspectives. *Ajeg Bali*, gambling, the cockfights, and the intense modification of ritual and religion—are all part of a cultural transformation through, and reactions against, the crisis of modernization and its new political order.

CIVICS AND THE ELECTORAL PROCESS: CHALLENGING OLD HIERARCHIES

The democratization process is providing a new context for civil society in Bali and it is reshaping politics at the provincial, district, and village level. While there is much excitement about *Ajeg Bali* and its political potential (and dangers), recent election results also suggest that the Balinese are becoming increasingly engaged in a range of political reforms, including the breakdown of traditional hierarchies and power structures based on caste. Thus, electoral democracy is giving rise to more vigorous critical public debate and new political leaders are emerging from increasingly diverse social backgrounds. While the nine district heads have traditionally been drawn from members of the Balinese nobility, recent elections have resulted in these positions now being dominated by commoners. In the 2005 local elections (*Pilkada*), heads of districts were, for the first time, elected by popular vote rather than appointed by senior government officials. The 2005 *Pilkada* saw the election of six commoners with only three of nobility background. District heads now included entrepreneurs, politicians, a dentist, and others of mixed education and occupational backgrounds.

To some extent, this change parallels the battles being waged over culture, religion, and caste within the official Hindu organization, Parisada Hindu Dharma Indonesia. Since the *Reformasi*, caste conflict has intensified within PHDI and two factions have emerged—the conservative Parisada Campuan, which is loyal to the *adat* traditions and the preservation of old hierarchies; and secondly, the modernist Parisada Besakih, which rejects caste differences based on birth, supports more egalitarian relationships (including commoner representation in district administration), and advocates more modest rituals to facilitate broader participation in civic, religious, and economic life. While recent local elections could have provided the context for the powerful traditional elite to reenter the political arena, it is clear that a new kind of politics emerged in which political candidates and their affiliations were no longer aligned along lines of class and caste.[27]

In 2008, the complex dynamics of democratization became evident as Bali participated in the first direct election of the island's governor. Among various groups of Balinese, there were different views about the opportunities provided by electoral democracy. Since Bali's independence, the office of governor has always been assigned to a member of the nobility from either the Brahmin or Ksatriya clan. This is the result of old conflicts arising when the influential and respected *Pasek* leaders were replaced by the new power structures of the imposed caste system. Governor candidate Mangku Pastika is from the commoner *Pasek* clan, one of the largest clan-based organizations in Bali. For the *Pasek*, the election was seen as a crucial opportunity to challenge the hegemonic grip of the nobility on Bali's political and social institutions. For other groups, the election was about challenging power imbalances associated with regional identity. While the office of governor has always been held by politicians from South Bali, Mangku Pastika was the first governorship candidate from the northern coastal region. For the people of Bulelong district in the north, the election of Pastika was an opportunity to challenge the unbalanced distribution of resources which had seen the poor areas of North Bali long neglected at the expense of development and resources for the South.[28] Furthermore, the election of a governor from a commoner background added new legitimacy to critical debates about the ways in which traditional Hindu Balinese culture and religious practices may be contributing to Bali's social crisis. In 2008, Pastika argued that lavish Hindu Balinese rituals and extravagant festivals should be constrained so that spending could be redirected toward improving welfare and addressing serious inequalities in health, education, and employment opportunities for many Balinese:

> We should change our mindset. It doesn't mean we should abandon our tradition or religious heritage, but we should put it into the present context and find the proportionate balance. By doing so, the religious aspect of our society would play a significant, concrete role in the development of Bali into an advanced society.[29]

According to Darma Putra, *Ajeg Bali* also played an important role in the 2008 election. Pastika's strong campaign on Hindu Balinese revivalism resonated with the *Ajeg Bali* discourse, while his clan and caste affiliations offered new opportunities for commoners to see their interests represented in local politics. To some extent, the potential of *Ajeg Bali* to reframe traditional social hierarchies is personified in the movement's progenitor, Satria Naradha, who is himself a commoner. While *Ajeg Bali* is regarded by its critics as fundamentally elitist and conservative, Naradha's media companies have been pivotal in the promotion of public debate, which is essential for the functioning of a modern democracy and the access of all citizens to public office. Indeed, the 2005 and 2008 elections have been distinguished by new forms of political campaigning in which the mass media have been mobilized to an unprecedented extent. Naradha's BPMG (especially through BaliTV and *Bali Post* newspaper) emerged as the dominant source of public information and opinion about politics in the province. By presiding over a balanced coverage of all candidates as well as strategically mobilizing revivalist debates around Hindu Balinese culture, Satria Naradha has positioned himself has a powerful force in the political and cultural life of Bali.[30]

For many commentators, the dynamics of these recent elections demonstrate that several transitions are taking place in Balinese civil life:

1. Hierarchical relationships of caste and clan are being challenged, particularly within civil society organizations.
2. Authority is becoming more available to the lower commoner caste.
3. Religion is no longer exclusively framed in caste hierarchy.

However, while an emergent electoral democracy may be challenging old power relations and facilitating new forms of political expression and participation, new political debates continue to evolve. In particular, the reform process is yet to address the relative status and political participation of women and of people from diverse religious and ethnic backgrounds. Community activists such as Viebeke Lengkong express much frustration about the slow pace of change:

> Where are the women? Women are excluded from all significant decision making on this island. Women do not sit in the *banjar*, and this is where the important decisions are made. The *adat* and the religious laws are really only part of this complex web of governance. Balinese are surely the most governed people on the planet.[31]

While significant shifts in power and representation across the island's civic communities are releasing new forms of political interest and impetus, Bali is still struggling to acknowledge its own internal diversity and the political-cultural claims of those who participate at the margins. Paralleling the challenges faced by other modern democracies, Bali must account for the emergence of new kinds of social control and domination, including the power and influence of a media which may become increasingly centralist as it replaces one power elite with another. Thus, the caste-based nobility which justified itself through a cosmological ideology may simply be replaced by a different form of self-validating nobility, a Hindu-based meritocracy that oppresses the diversity it claims to represent.

DRUGS, YOUTH, AND RESISTANCE

The complex dialog between tradition and modern discourses underpins everyday life and everyday practices for the Balinese. Contemporary Balinese culture, therefore, is a cacophony of meanings, claims, and contentions. Expressed at various times and through various spaces, these meanings are sometimes consonant and overlapping, and sometimes disjunctive or entirely discordant. The interchange of past and present, ritual and change, pleasure and outrage are all scoped within a broad and transitional cultural canvas. Tradition, in this context, may be deployed for the redemption of cultural and environmental degradation, or as a form of pure spirit, something that is parenthesized from the secular conditions of material life. In this latter context, religion and tradition survive in Bali, as in many Western contexts, as a modern aesthetic which resists the intrusion of rationalist order. Faith, thereby, is not in contention with modernity, but is merely another component of culture which, like European romanticism and the arts more generally, extends the human experience beyond instrumentality and Enlightenment-derived reason.

Other Balinese take a more pragmatic view of tradition, ritual, and religion, deploying them as commodities within the tourist economy. Thus, the aesthetics of Balinese culture—dance, religious iconography, art, gamelan music, and even cremation ceremonies—are modified for an international audience and sold as cultural artifacts. Many of these more commercially oriented and pragmatic Balinese quite consciously create hybrid expressive forms designed specifically for cosmopolitan and international consumers. Dancers in the *Joged*, for example, are reshaping the traditional dance form into a more directly erotic and creative play space, a hybrid of older modes and Western-style tabletop erotica. While deploying traditional dance dress and styles, the female principal dancer arouses the sexual interest of her audience, engaging in suggestive gestures, body movements, kissing, and intimate touching which would be prohibited in customary law. While this transition may be explained in terms of economic imperatives, the dancers themselves are far less sanguine, claiming that their performances are both "fun" and "respectful," representing "a new way of dancing in a new Bali." In this sense, the *Joged* dancers are doing what cultural agents have always done with tradition: they are modifying the art in order to adapt to new circumstances, economic conditions, and expressive forms.

As we argued in the previous chapter, these new modes of sexual and aesthetic expression constitute a new cultural space in Bali, one that has been shaped around the modernizing consciousness of the Balinese themselves. As we also argued, women's bodies and the meanings inscribed on femininity are essential elements of these transformative or alternative spaces. While women continue to be excluded from participation in customary village governance such as the village council (*banjar*) and the *pecalang*, modernization has opened up some alternative opportunities for women's social, economic, and public participation. Of course, historically, high-caste women had greater resources for such participation; however, the tourism boom has provided young, commoner women with greater opportunities for education, social mobility, personal prosperity, and occupational independence. This is especially the case for the daughters of Bali's small but significant class of entrepreneurs, as well as those born into mixed marriages where education and social mobility are highly valued.

More generally, the politics of civil transition have directly affected young Balinese who have become increasingly engaged in Indonesian youth culture. Clearly influenced by internal modernization processes and Western media and culture, many Indonesian youths are challenging the moral and ideological authority imposed by older generations. Some commentators refer to a particular dimension of this youth culture as Indonesian "cool" or *cuek*.[32] In particular, the slang *cuek* usually refers to a "take it easy" attitude and probably derives from the Malay word *cuai* (negligent). Popularized in the 1980s by Ruth Sahanaya's song *Astaga!* the notion of *cuek* has become identified with a Western style of "cool" which is tolerant, open-minded, and sexually liberal. *Cuek* is thus a style which rejects the authority of an older generation which has been predicated on power, exploitation, and brutality. The social status of the political elite, in particular, is morally questionable as it preaches civic duty while plundering the nation through corrupt and violent practices. For many of the *cuek*, this hypocrisy is evidenced in the highly Draconian and prohibitive drug laws introduced in 1997 in the twilight of the Suharto dictatorship. The laws were largely a concession to pressure from conservative Islamic forces inside Indonesia and conservative leaders in the region more broadly. With his grip on power slipping, Suharto and others in the military elite saw an opportunity to attract greater support from conservative Indonesians through a range of social reforms. The 1997 Law on Psychotropic Drugs and Law on Narcotics expanded the 1976 Narcotics Law, broadening the range of illegal substances and crimes which could attract the death penalty. In a gesture of anti-Westernism, the Suharto legislature demonstrated to the Indonesian public that they were still tough and capable of denying the contaminant effects of Western cultural practices.

For many younger Indonesians, however, these laws were sponsored by a class of people who had themselves committed a range of atrocities and who had long since surrendered any claim to moral authority—most particularly as the generals had been notorious for their participation in the Indonesian drugs economy. Thus, *cuek*, in its various cultural permutations, is seen by many Indonesian youth as an antidote to this hypocrisy. Though not advocating the use of drugs, *cuek* is broadly understood as an anti-establishment attitude or style which rejects false or overbearing authority and its prohibition on pleasure, including the pleasure of drug use. Whether described as *cuek* or not, this new youth subculture in Indonesia is in clear contention with the rising conservatism of religious devotion which many in the new Indonesian middle class valorize as a moral shield to modern decadence. While in Java this conservatism is rallying around Islamic devotion and practice, in Bali the conservative Hinduism represented by figures like Governor Pastika and Satria Naradha is frequently invoked as the island people's salvation from the moral dissolution associated with Western drug culture. To the conservatives, this decadence is embodied in the practices of young, modern Balinese women, in particular those who wear tight jeans and engage in premarital sex. Many older and more conservative community members regard the cultural values and practices of sexually active younger Balinese women with deep suspicion.

As our story of Putu indicates, drug use has become a significant problem for Indonesia, especially in places like Bali where Western cultural practices have exerted considerable influence over young people. As numerous studies have shown, the rates of narcotics use and addiction have been increasing exponentially in Indonesia over the past decade.[33] While various kinds of drug use have been practiced for centuries in Indonesia, the emergence of a youth drug culture is clearly associated with social restructure and modernization. In particular, the reorganization and rationalization of agriculture in Indonesia has driven many young people away from the family farm and into the major cities and tourism zones to seek employment. With little education, training, skills, resources, or support, many of these young people huddle in social ghettos, seeking out a living through marginal activities such as prostitution and petty crime. Over time, these populations have formed their own communities and subcultures, evolving particular rites, vocabulary, social hierarchies, economy, rules, and practices. Many of these street kids or *tikyan* are heavily involved in narcotics consumption and low-level trafficking. The boys and young men, in particular, have a hardened and dissolute demeanor which rejects mainstream social norms and values. Like many street kids across the world, *tikyan* reinforce their sense of social alienation through a profoundly nihilistic vision of themselves and their future. In this sense, their vision is strangely apocalyptic, combining comments like "there is no tomorrow" with an idea that they "are with god" in the midst of their pleasures and despair.[34] To this end, the *tikyan* seem almost entirely unconcerned about illness, including sexually transmitted diseases, drug-related infections such as HIV/AIDS, overdose, or vulnerability to abuse. When they do have money, it is usually spent on clothes, drugs, commercial sex, or other instant gratifications.

This drug problem, however, is not simply an outcome of structural modernization and the contaminating influence of Western media, tourism, and cultural values. Indeed, while religious and political conservatives in South East Asia would like to blame the West for their drug problems, it is clearly the case that the use of narcosis-inducing substances has a deep history in the region. Marijuana, mushroom, and beetlenut, for example, have been widely used for personal pleasure and various forms of religious and community rites in Indonesia. Magic formulae, trance performance, music, dance, and other ceremonies have often involved the use of mesmeric or mind-altering substances. The Chinese traders who settled in Indonesia brought opium to the archipelago, and it became one of the East Indies Company's most profitable traded commodities during the period of Dutch colonial occupation. Indonesians also adopted the practice of distillation, creating a potent liquor, *arak*, from local coconut milk. Even today, in the villages and *kampongs* men and youths gather in the evenings, ingesting a volatile mix of *arak*, pills, mushrooms, and root vegetables. These gatherings have evolved their own ritual value, providing relief from the daily routines of hardship and poverty and strengthening social cohesion between men.

It is clear that traditional substances and social rituals have been supplemented, and in some cases replaced, by more powerful narcotic compounds. The ritual and consumption practices surrounding these new drugs are located within a global economy and trade system in which the notion of "nation" and "national health" have become clearly implicated. Thus, the introduction of injectable drugs like heroin, along with new forms of psychotropic drugs like ecstasy and crystal meth, is seen by prohibitionists in Indonesia as entirely alien, a symptom of Western culture and global economic integration. According to prohibitionists, these new drugs and associated cultural values threaten the psychological and physical health of Indonesia. The rapid escalation in heroin use, along with its associated risk of HIV/AIDS and addiction, has been seen by many in the conservative elite as a significant danger to the nation's youth, moral fabric, and future.

The reasons for this escalation are somewhat more complex than many of the prohibitionists seem to appreciate. While it is certainly true that narcotics and arms are the most heavily traded of all illicit global goods, it is also clear that senior public and military officials are among the key players in drug trafficking throughout the region. As Indonesia modernized and the economic elite in Jakarta came to recognize the financial potential of illegal drug trading, the archipelago evolved as a primary transit zone for modern narcotics, especially injectable heroin. With a well-developed crime network and many people prepared to risk their life and liberty in order to escape extreme poverty, a strong drug-trafficking network was quickly established. While not a major producer of narcotics in 1997 when the new laws were instituted, Indonesia had inadequate border controls and a corrupt customs service which enabled the easy flow of narcotics to Australia and the United States.[35]

Since 1997, rates of addiction have radically escalated as Indonesia graduated from being a mere transit zone to become a principal producer and consumer of narcotics. While these figures need to be treated with caution, the official drug addition rates announced by the Indonesian government increased from around 130,000 people in 1995 to 1.3 million in 2004. The Indonesian government claims around 25 percent of addicts will die within five years of becoming "hooked." While these practices are largely located in the poorer sectors of Indonesia, the adoption of injectable heroin has been noted across all levels of the community. This seems particularly the case in Bali where a recent report on Intravenous Drug Users (IDU) found that all users surveyed had attended high school and several in the sample had attended university.[36] Consistent with Indonesian government data on addiction rates, the significant majority of users were aged under twenty years, with first use frequently beginning in the early and mid teens. While there is an equal mix of Balinese and non-Balinese Indonesians using drugs around the Kuta area, the majority of IDUs in Denpasar fall into two distinct categories, each residing in particular parts of the city. Several hundred users are located in the downtown area of the city with several hundred more located around the military barracks. This latter group is principally the Balinese-born children of military personnel who are originally from Java or other parts of the archipelago. Much of the petty crime around these areas is attributed to the "Barracks" group, many of whom engage in petty theft in order to support their habit. This group is also notable for a low level of conviction, a situation generally attributed to the protection afforded by connection to the military and high-level officials.[37]

As we have already intimated, this regime of criminal protection is more broadly associated with the involvement of the police and the military in the drug industry. Urine tests on rank and file police and military personnel have identified a high level of substance use, including low-grade heroin, amphetamines, and ecstasy. Court officials and police notoriously "on-sell" confiscated drugs, and senior members of the military are frequently seen smoking *potauw* (sabu-sabu) with well-known dealers. Suharto's own grandson, Ari, is frequently cited in Jakarta as a major drug trader; his arrest and conviction for possession was regarded as a major accomplishment for antidrug campaigners—although their rejoicing was somewhat compromised by the astonishingly light sentence delivered by the courts. Such light sentences are the norm for major dealers in Jakarta, as the network of senior military and judicial officials continues to protect an inner sanctum of elite drug traders.[38]

This network remains a major obstacle for the anticorruption commissions established by the Yudhoyono government. Not surprisingly, antidrug campaigners have over recent years formed their own vigilante groups, identifying, summarily beating and apprehending people suspected of drug dealing, and bringing them to the attention of the authorities. While many of the vigilantes are motivated by a form of Islamic morality, some are seeking vengeance for the death of a loved one who had become involved in serious drug abuse.[39] In either case, however, the vigilantes see drugs as part of the contamination of Western influence. Invoking a powerful sense of Islamic purity as a mechanism for social and political resistance to modernization, these groups have on occasions beaten their suspects to death. While clearly a transgression of the higher principles of civil society and rule of law, these vigilantes have to some extent been sanctioned by senior public officials who seem to overlook the excesses of summary justice. In Bali, specifically, members of the *pecalang* and other community vigilantes have summarily executed outsiders on the pretext of crimes such as theft and drug trading.[40]

More broadly, the national government Minister for Youth and Sport publicly announced that drug users should be dealt with by "street justice." In the early 2000s, chief of Bali Police at the time, Inspector General Pastika, also declared war on drug dealers, claiming that narcotics posed the greatest threat to the integrity and moral condition of Balinese youth. Urban neighborhoods across the archipelago have stated their support for the vigilantes, hanging banners around the streets of Jakarta and Jogjakarta with slogans such as "Drug-Free Community," "Death to All Drugs Dealers and Users," and "Destroy Drugs Dealers and Users." One prominent antidrug campaigner even offered a prize to anyone who detected a drug user and informed the police. The prize was around US$80, a significant sum paid out to around fifty Jakartan whistle-blowers.

The truly unfortunate aspect of these retributive attacks is that they generally target the lowest link of the drug trade chain—impecunious users and small-time couriers. As we have suggested, this group includes people like Putu, who are among the most vulnerable of Indonesian citizens. Many of the lower-chain recruits are themselves *jungkies*—impoverished and desperate. As the 1999 Report on Injecting Drug Use in Bali notes, the great majority of injecting drug users are using shared needles which renders them vulnerable to HIV/AIDS and Hepatitis C. Health statistics indicate very clearly that infection rates for both of these diseases have escalated dramatically over the past decade. The report also notes that new forms of drug use are appearing in Bali, most particularly associated with the rising "party scene" in which Westerners and wealthy Indonesians are ingesting or inhaling substances such as ecstasy, ice, speed, and *sabu-sabu*. These party drugs, which have become increasingly popular among Western youth, particularly for those involved in rave and dance culture, have been more broadly distributed in Bali through the nightclub scene. More recent research conducted at Udayana University in Denpasar reports that these trends have intensified, even in the period since the Bali bombings. Concomitantly, a broad public conversation has emerged surrounding the illicit drug industry and entrenched corruption. Indeed, several Balinese blogs have hosted online discussions in which a number of private sources allege that a local amphetamine-manufacturing industry has been established under the aegis of senior police and military officials.[41]

TWO SIDES OF THE LAW

In Bali, as in Indonesia more generally, state and civil processes have not yet entirely liberated themselves from several decades of systemic nepotism and corruption under the Suharto regime. Despite recent clean up efforts, police corruption in Bali is both endemic and tacitly tolerated. Police officers and other government officials continue to supplement their meager wages through an unofficial system of fines, fees, and taxes extorted from local people as well foreign visitors who are directly targeted as a source of additional income. Mangku Pastika, in his role as chief of Bali Police, sought to address corruption by changing the mind-set of his police force:

> Police officers must understand they are civil servants. They must perform the will of the people and, of course, of the government. The government that the people have chosen.[42]

This high ideal, however, seems entirely at odds with the daily practices of a police force which not only creates its own jurisdiction of unofficial income generation, but is also reportedly engaged in a range of criminal activities. This is a problem common to paramilitary law enforcement agencies across the globe where notions of criminality are shaped in various ways by the culture of a very powerful social agency such as the military. The really distinct feature of the Indonesian police, and the Balinese police force in particular, is the breadth and pervasiveness of its corruption. Across all social levels, in fact, the Balinese seem inured to this unofficial economy which, through its haphazard implementation, intensifies social inequalities and suppresses genuine opportunities to address the causes of poverty and crime. Foreign visitors also participate in this economy without recognizing their role in sustaining it. Most tourists, for example, quickly learn that they can bypass the official judicial process when they commit a minor traffic offense or seek to have some minor trading dispute resolved. A police officer, just like a shopkeeper, will invite a direct payment for services or payment of a traffic fine, rather than go through the court system; the officer usually assesses the "client's" capacity to pay and requests a fee accordingly. The officer will remind the offender of the severity of the Indonesian legal process and of the various higher officials who will, no doubt, seek additional payments over and above any formal fine or punishment. In a characteristically Balinese process of negotiation, the offender will often haggle over the fee, and it is common for the officer to apply the same rhetorical tactics as the shopkeeper. In this sense, officers will frequently claim—"I am a poor man. . . . Education for my children is expensive in Bali. . . . This is for my mother's cremation. . . . I help you, you help me, etc." While foreign tourists may be amused or irritated by this process, their willingness to pay the unofficial fine merely legitimates and sustains a system that is intrinsically corrupt and socially damaging.

Fees are also applied to tour guides, drivers, and others engaged in the tourism industry. Police have their own geographic jurisdictions, and any driver from outside the jurisdiction seen with tourists on board is likely to be stopped, registration papers checked, and an on-the-spot fee demanded. In a trip of less than 50 km to the northeast from Kuta, a driver can be stopped at least three or four times, unless he has prearranged his payments to the controlling officers. Tourists can also expect to pay fees in all public processes, including immigration and customs. Prior to the 2002 Kuta bombings, visa extensions were controlled unofficially by one senior *Immigrasi* officer who would bargain with tourists for the official visa extension stamp. This officer's name was well known among the Kuta backpackers, who generally prefer the unofficial payments to the more complicated and expensive formal processes. The same is true in customs. With many Westerners establishing import-export businesses in Bali, an unofficial network of exchange has been established at Ngurah Rai airport and the dock areas at Benoa Harbor. Through the direct payment of unofficial fees, traders are able to move their goods in and out of Bali without the imposition of taxes, limits, and burdensome administrative processes—which are excessively applied if the trader refuses to pay the informal fees.

While these illegal practices are observable in most major ports across the globe, they are periodically, if not commonly, constrained by public agencies with the authority to counter corruption. The great problem in Bali and Indonesia more generally is that low salaries and an embedded history of graft have entirely neutered whistle-blowing and prevented the establishment of effective anticorruption agencies. There appears to be very few people in these public organizations—military, police, customs, the judiciary—who are genuinely clean or courageous enough to expose the clandestine networks. Moreover, the temptation to act corruptly is exacerbated by the magnitude of the economic disjuncture between the official and the foreign visitor. In a relatively crude way, officials explain their graft in terms of international equity and wealth redistribution: civil servants see themselves as imposing a justice tax on those often vulgar and imperious tourists who are representatives of past and present colonial crimes.

Officials also explain and justify graft in terms of community and familial networks. Fees are considered essential for the economic survival of lower-ranking officials and their families. However, this system of graft and clandestine payment severely undermines the taxation system, investment, and the principles of rule of law—all of which contribute to security, wealth development, and distribution. As the Indonesian experience clearly demonstrates, those groups with greater access to, and control of, coercive power draw a disproportionately high level of reward from the system. Payments within the system tend always to move upwards, or at best laterally; the lower ranks pay for their rights to exercise graft by sending a percentage of their fees to higher ranks. The system seldom works in reverse.

Indeed, according to Transparency International's Corruption Perception Index of 2005, Indonesia is the sixth most corrupt nation of 159 nations surveyed—on a par with war-ravaged Iraq. While for many tourists in Bali, this may simply represent the forfeit of some loose change, corruption at higher levels continues to frustrate business relationships, effective social management, and economic development. By condemning Indonesia to an impoverished and politically volatile future, corruption contributes to loss of life and the destruction of livelihoods for people in Bali. Even the new anticorruption measures recently introduced by President Susilo Bambang Yudhoyono are proving largely ineffectual. Amid the massive graft and corruption that dominates Indonesian civil life, only one significant conviction has been recorded to date: the governor of Aceh, Abdullah Puteh, was sentenced to ten years in jail for embezzling nearly a third of the US$12.6 million paid for the purchase of a Russian helicopter.[43] Of course, there are a number of other well-known figures awaiting trial, including Suharto's half-brother, the business tycoon Probosutedjo. However, in a system which is replete with corrupt practices, it is difficult to see how these high-profile arrests will impede such an entrenched and pervasive graft culture.

Anticorruption Measures

To this end, there is considerable public disillusion with the Corruption Eradication Commission (*Komisi Pemberantasan Korupsi, KPK*) which was established in 2004. The KPK is an interdepartmental commission which has been designed to identify and prosecute public officials suspected of embezzling more than a billion rupiah (around US$100,000) from government funds. Despite success in the Puteh case, the KPK is struggling to assert its authority. In one instance, investigations into the possible corrupt practices in the Indonesian Supreme Court were met with outright defiance by Chief Justice Bagir Manan who refused to obey a KPK summons. Even though Bagir agreed to be questioned in his own offices after the intervention of the president, the case highlights critical weaknesses in the commission's civil power, as well as the aggressive and entrenched power of corrupt agents themselves. In this light, a whistle-blower in the KPK's investigation into irregularities in the 2004 presidential elections has himself been accused of corruption in a separate KPK investigation. Khainansyah Salman, a former analyst with the Supreme Audit Agency, identified irregularities in his audit of the elections. However, Khainansyah has himself been accused of embezzling 10 billion rupiah from *Haj* pilgrimage funds that are managed through the Ministry of Religious Affairs, placing in doubt the auditor's recent anticorruption award presented by Transparency International. While the situation remains unclear, members of Indonesia's own Transparency Society argue vigorously that these accusations are simply a payback for the auditor's whistle-blowing in the electoral commission case.[44]

In 2005, the Office of the Attorney General, with over 6,000 prosecutors in 350 offices across the nation, received information on nearly 450 graft cases, but acted on none. According to the central attorney general's office, the cases are not worthy of interest as they are generally about petty complaints in provincial areas. However, when we more closely examine these complaints, they bear the same insidious qualities as the larger cases being investigated in Jakarta. One such case in Bali involves the police protection racket which ensures security for local businesses against various competitive and criminal threats. In one case, a German expatriate and his Balinese wife established an Internet access business, largely for use by tourists and Balinese businesses. Invoking the aegis of international law and a Western notion of civil rights, the German business operator Frederick[45] refused to pay protection money. Frederick believes that a local competitor, who had established a financial relationship with the police, insisted that the authorities act against him. Without issuing a summons or presenting charges, the police confiscated the couple's equipment and asked once more for a payment of fees on the grounds that the equipment was a "health hazard." Frederick reported the incident to the KPK, but in the meantime his wife, Iluh, was arrested for noncompliance with the police summons. The KPK agreed that the arresting police and prosecutor should be investigated, but the incident had now escalated and Frederick himself was to be charged with operating unauthorized equipment. The peculiarity of the story deepened further when the officials accused of corruption mounted a libel case against Frederick for reporting them to the KPK. Frederick fled from Indonesia with the couple's daughter, while Iluh was convicted on the charge of operating unauthorized equipment—the first case of its kind in Indonesia, even though the same machinery is used everywhere across the nation.

THE BALINESE JUDICIARY: A TALE OF TWO CASES

Schapelle Corby

Many local observers argue that case of Iluh was a complete fabrication, an example of collusion between corrupt police, the prosecution office, and the judiciary. In order to survive in this context, even local lawyers must cooperate with the clandestine network. Frederick's own legal advisors encouraged him to settle the dispute through direct, unofficial payments rather than become involved in a confrontation which he was destined to lose. This was the same advice given by the same lawyers to Australian woman Schapelle Corby during her well-publicized drug importation case in 2004/2005. Schapelle, aged twenty-seven years at the time, was arrested when entering Bali with 4.2 kilograms of cannabis in her body-board bag. Constantly proclaiming her innocence, Schapelle was ultimately convicted and sentenced to twenty years imprisonment. The case caused extraordinary perturbation to Australians who comprise the majority of international visitors to Bali and who believed they had established a special and enduring relationship with the island people. In the view of many Australians, this relationship was fortified by the shared tragedy of the 2002 Kuta bombings in which eighty-eight Australians were killed.

Debates about the Corby case have centered on three critical issues. First, and somewhat inevitably, observers of the case, including Australian and international media audiences, wanted to know whether Schapelle was innocent or guilty of the crime. Secondly, very significant questions were raised about the forensic investigation, the level of proof, the police and customs services, and most importantly, the judicial process. Thirdly, observers asked whether Schapelle had received anything that might vaguely resemble justice as it is understood in the West: that is, given the intrinsic corruptness and cultural conditions of the Indonesian system, was it even possible for a trial and appeal process to be fair and reasonably prosecuted. The great difficulty for international observers was, of course, Indonesia's appalling record of state and civil management, and the legislative framework which imposes sentences that are far more severe than in modern Western societies. To this extent, many of the observers of the case in the West believed that the Indonesian judiciary was actually incapable of prosecuting the case and determining Corby's innocence or guilt. Despite the gains of the *Reformasi*, the Indonesian legal system remained shadowed by ineptitude, corruption, and inconsistency: it appeared to many in the West that the young woman had simply been delivered into a pernicious and chaotic state apparatus that was essentially indifferent to the historical integrity of rule of law and natural justice.[46]

Within the context of increasing global terror and the ossifying divide between East and West, the amplification of the case through the international media intensified popular Western hostility toward the Indonesian state and the indecency of its legal processes. More specifically, Australians felt deeply betrayed by Bali, whose people they had befriended and learned to trust through the mantra of "harmony" and decades of tourist interaction and occupation. This special relationship had failed to protect one of their own from the perfidy of the Indonesian state to which, in this moment of crisis, the Balinese seemed simply to supplicate themselves. Propitiated by the popular media, the Australian imaginary saw another side of their Balinese friends, a political pragmatism which was largely indistinguishable from the Javanese overlords. In Australia, there were calls for a boycott of Bali following the Corby conviction and although these actions were repudiated by the serious media, academics, and political *cognoscenti*, it was clear that public sentiment of this nature was articulating a deep sense of betrayal and a belief that the Balinese had allowed themselves to become the servants of a pernicious and corrupt Indonesian state. These views were further fortified by the reinvigorated and rather cavalier antiterrorism policies of America, the United Kingdom, and Australia, which had been largely propagated to enlist public support for the war in Iraq but which had overflowed into a broader suspicion of the East and "Oriental outsiders" more generally. It was precisely this outrage and suspicion which informed the calls for tourists to abandon Bali and for the Indonesian government to return the millions of dollars donated by Australia for the 2004 tsunami disaster in Aceh, Indonesia.

Our own research has shown that, in general, most Balinese were only moderately interested in the Corby case and were somewhat bemused by Australia's intense interest. While expressing a level of sympathy for Schapelle Corby, most Balinese interview respondents could see very little difference between this case and numerous others involving foreigners and drug trafficking. After thirty years of Suharto and their own political holocaust, the Balinese find it difficult to be outraged by the fate of a single Western woman; most interview respondents expressed surprise that Corby had not simply paid her way out of trouble, which was the normal practice when dealing with the legal process. In many ways, the Balinese have become inured to the corrupt practices of the system and so it wasn't surprising that they saw foreign calls for a boycott as being somewhat disproportionate.

Moreover, the Balinese in the tourism areas of Badung have also become inured to many of the cultural practices of Western visitors, including consumption of illicit drugs. What is clear, however, is that the Balinese had very
little trust in the country's police or customs service, and even less faith that
a Jakarta-controlled court system could deliver justice.

Model Prisoner: Michelle Leslie

This appears to be the more pragmatic position adopted in another recent drug case involving a young Australian woman, Michelle Leslie (Lee).
Arrested in 2005 in possession of two ecstasy tablets, Leslie clearly accepted
the advice of local defense lawyers. Unlike Corby's original legal team
which promoted her innocence through the Australian and international
media, a strategy designed presumably to embarrass the local judiciary into
an acquittal, Leslie's team sought to manage the case through the clandestine networks. Leslie gave no interviews to the Australian media and at one
point even adopted a new mode of dress, wearing traditional Muslim *burqa*
as testament to her penitence. It is well known that a fee was paid to the
wardens at Krobokan Prison (around US$8,000) in order to secure a cell
with electricity and only two other inmates; this contrasts significantly with
Schapelle Corby who refused to pay bribes and has had to occupy a tiny,
cramped cell with no electricity and fourteen other inmates. Leslie's plea of
guilty was negotiated through the chief prosecutor's office, resulting in a
three-month sentence, the period which she had already spent in detention

**4.3. Prominent local cartoonist Putu Ebo depicts Balinese concerns about corruption
in the Leslie drug case (December 2005).**
Courtesy of Putu Ebo.

awaiting trial. Her plea also included a claim that she was addicted to drugs, a confession which brings an automatic reduction in sentence (though there is no evidence that ecstasy is addictive). And while a number of apologists for the Indonesian judiciary viewed the sentence as "within the norm," it contrasts significantly with the ten-year sentence delivered to a local woman for an identical crime. Since her release, Michelle has claimed that she was actually innocent of the crime and that her family has had to mortgage their house in order to pay the huge bribe required to secure her release.

In fact, apologists for the Indonesian legal system, including academic Tim Lindsay and Australian Federal Court Justice Ronald Sackwell, have claimed that the Leslie sentence was "within the norm."[47] They also claim that the Leslie case and the Corby case have been prosecuted flawlessly and within the particular framework of the Indonesian legal system. There was, in the minds of these august gentlemen, no sign of corruption or contaminated process. In the midst of popular outrage over the Corby case, Tim Lindsay in particular became the front row defender of the Indonesian judiciary, reassuring a cynical Australian public that the Corby case was being prosecuted effectively and that the verdict and sentences were reasonable. In order to make such a claim, of course, Lindsay had to overlook the poor forensic work conducted at airport customs and the plausibility of Corby's own explanation for the drug's appearance in her baggage. More importantly, however, Lindsay and Sackwell overlooked the judiciary's standard of practice, which is clearly infested with corruption, systemic dishonesty, and inconsistency.

The prosecutor's offices, in particular, have demonstrated an extraordinary willingness to recommend mitigation, as in the Leslie case, or to entirely redefine particular crimes committed by Westerners. For example, just prior to the Corby case, charges against Australian man Chris Curral were completely reformulated. Curral was found with around 50,000 ephedrine tablets hidden in various parts of a cargo warehouse near Kuta. Rather than face a possible death sentence for manufacturing narcotics, Chief Prosecutor Made Herawati recommended to the Bali District Court that Curral be convicted of the lesser crime of unauthorized manufacture of pharmaceuticals. The conviction brought a ten-month sentence (the period served in detention) plus 5 million rupiah fine. In her submission to the district court, the chief prosecutor claimed that there was insufficient evidence to convict Curral of the more severe crime of narcotics manufacture, claiming that the unauthorized production of pharmaceuticals presented a danger to public health. Ephedrine is a key component of methamphetamine tablets and a range of designer-based recreational drugs. It is difficult for the Balinese to reconcile the prosecutor's recommendation against the numerous drug convictions that have been delivered through the Bali courts to local Balinese.

In essence, this returns us to the original question: did Schapelle Corby receive justice? The answer, quite simply, is that a fundamentally corrupt system is not capable of delivering justice in any case. Corby denied herself the opportunity to work through the clandestine network once her defense team adopted a strategy of public advocacy. To some extent, the Corby family's compliance with this approach was affected by their own inexperience in dealing with people like Ron Bakir, the Australian entrepreneur who appears to have enlisted the Corby case to support his own public and commercial profile. While representing the case in the media as an exercise of Indonesian infamy and the pursuit of justice, Bakir seemed to carry more private motives, which may have had to do with the financial difficulties he was experiencing in his own mobile phone business. In either case, once the Corby trial was so dramatically amplified through the international media, the opportunity for working the unofficial system was completely surrendered. With such critical scrutiny from international media and their audiences, the Indonesian judiciary had to do its utmost to appear both reasonable and just. Clearly, a number of Australian academics and lawyers have been entirely duped by the charade.

Sadly, while the judicial processes in the Leslie case will be investigated by the Indonesian Corruption Eradication Commission, Schapelle Corby appears destined for a disproportionately long custodial sentence for a crime she may well not have committed. The Corby case indicates, again, how the Balinese and Indonesian political environment remains fixed in highly rigid and iniquitous social structures. The police and judiciary function almost entirely out of a process of privilege and discrimination. Some observers mistakenly believe that Schapelle Corby is a victim of injustices that are formed around anti-Western sentiment. This is only partly true. More broadly, the injustices being suffered by Schapelle Corby are fashioned through the deep roots of Indonesian violence and a hierarchical system that mobilizes privilege against those it dislikes or who lack the capacity to pay. Thus, Corby's sentence is not so much a manifestation of anti-Westernism, but anti-Others—those who sit outside the clandestine network or who refuse to (or cannot) pay it sufficient homage. While it may be improving to some extent, the Indonesian judicial system is fundamentally flawed—its outward charade merely distracts from its own intrinsic corruption, human rights abuses, and civil crimes.

More generally, the drug trade in Indonesia reflects a social tragedy that is part of the negative index of globalization. Prisons across the trading world have become increasingly populated by young people who have become ensnared in the pernicious world of illicit drugs, either as consumers or traffickers. This is not a problem that is unique to Indonesia or the modernizing non-OECD world, but is rather a major social issue for the global community. The rapid escalation in Indonesian addiction rates, HIV infections, and drug convictions are related to a broader problem which cannot be solved by simple-minded policies of prohibition. As in the West, these policies merely catch the weakest and most vulnerable people in a community, and rarely apprehend the elite manufacturers and traders who control the industry and make by far the greatest share of profits. Rather than treat narcotics as a public health and social issue, criminalization and zero-tolerance policies in all countries are failing to save our young people from serious danger. Criminalization, in fact, appears to confirm the outsider status of drug-using communities, effectively blaming the victims, occluding the potential for harm minimization and recovery, and maintaining the pernicious power of the drug overlords.

WHAT IS BALINESE SOCIETY?

In this chapter we have sought to illuminate state and civil processes in Bali within the broader context of political modernization and the post-Suharto period. We have examined the ways in which demilitarization, decentralization, and the enhancement of civil processes are generating change across Balinese society. We have suggested that, specifically, the reform agenda and modernization are stumbling over a range of entrenched social groupings and institutional practices which are essentially anathema to the invigoration of a democratic, civil society. Through this context, the anti-pornography laws passed by the Indonesian parliament in late 2008 have created even deeper fissures in the ideal of *Pancasila*—national unity through cultural and religious diversity. As a form of Islamic or *shari'ah* law, the new bills impose a civil and social order which clearly transgresses many of the cultural practices associated with Balinese tradition, as well as its modernizing economy. By 2009, Indonesia's most critical constitutional crisis was looming, as Bali's governor, Made Mangku Pastika, threatened to reject and not implement the laws.

This problem of diversity is also evident within Balinese society. As the reform agenda and new forms of political autonomy struggle to establish themselves, a significant number of young people appear unconvinced, preferring in many cases to seek alternative expressive spaces. Alienated by the corrupt, violent, and oppressive practices that appear endemic within the project of "nation" and "national society," many young people are turning toward a transnational state of being—at one extreme are young people engaging in radical, purist Islamicism, and at another are those engaging in global populism and Western-style cultural practices. Against the continual assertion of corrupt and unjust power, a number of these young people are also turning toward narcotics or street life, which somehow or other salves the discord of oppression, change, and alienation. And at the bottom of it all is Bali's Krobokan Prison, a hideous social blight which marks the failure of policy, governance, and the maintenance of effective community life.

Thankfully, there is a range of nongovernmental organizations (NGOs) which have recognized the crisis and are attempting to overcome it. While the Suharto regime was very anxious about the activities of NGOs, creating a broad raft of legislative and bureaucratic impediments to their work, there have been a significant number of legitimate and well-credentialed development, welfare, and recovery agencies emerging in Indonesia, particularly since the Bali bombings and a series of recent natural disasters. The *Reformasi*, in this light, has facilitated the establishment of many local nonstate organizations which are largely constituted around emergency relief, crisis recovery, and broader development aims. While we have already identified a number of these groups which have more chauvinistic political and religious objectives, there are also many groups that are motivated by altruistic and positive social ambitions. In Bali, specifically, many of these organizations have been funded through aid organizations such as AusAID (Australia) and USAID. Notably, AusAID has funded a number of projects coordinated through the *Bali Rehabilitation Fund*. This fund has been delivered through the Australian Community Development and Civil Society Strengthening Scheme (ACCESS) designed to alleviate poverty in Indonesia through civil society strengthening and community empowerment and self-management.[48]

In many respects, the ACCESS programs, which focus on poor communities in Indonesia, are guided by a finely targeted ideology which seeks to support the political stability of the region through a ground-up model of economic development and the enhancement of civil and democratic participation. The significance of this approach became particularly evident in the aftermath of the 2002 Bali bombings following the collapse of the Balinese tourist economy. The radical downturn in visitor numbers prompted the United Nations Development Fund to call for the diversification of the Balinese economy and for a more equitable and better-managed approach to tourism and tourist development.[49] Of course, many Balinese themselves had been advocating such reforms since the late 1970s, but the dramatic collapse of tourism demonstrated the vulnerability and precarious nature of the Balinese economy—both then and now. While tourist numbers had recovered by the end of 2004 with the strongest tourist season on record, the second round of bombings dramatically reversed this recovery.

The 2006 Final Report of the Bali Rehabilitation Fund argues that ongoing international aid is needed to reduce the dependence of the Balinese on a monolithic tourism economy and their vulnerability to "further crisis." The Bali Rehabilitation Fund claimed to have helped around 4,000 Balinese develop new knowledge and skills which would provide the basis for greater economic independence. A key outcome of these projects has been the strengthening of the capacity of women to achieve greater economic autonomy and capacity for self-determination. Working in partnership with local NGOs, the BRF coordinators supported projects ranging from handicrafts, vocational and business training, through to environmental protection groups, enhancement of agricultural technology and alternative modes of production, such as seaweed cultivation, organic strawberry farming, and recycling waste as cattle feed.

While the economic benefits of these schemes are undeniable, the ACCESS program also illuminates the fundamental tensions within the development and civil society model. In general, these community development programs are constituted around a framework of global, liberal economics and an ideology that is largely determined by external interests. Indeed, the politics of international aid has increasingly received critical scrutiny over its tendency to inscribe the political and diplomatic interests of donors onto the social landscape of the recipients rather than genuinely working toward self-determination.[50] Aid, that is, remains tagged to the interests of those powerful organizations who wish to see a standardized global field in which democracy, civil society, and liberal economics are the prescribed outcome. Within this context, the Balinese must labor to create a society that provides security and civil order, but which nevertheless articulates their profoundly distinctive cultural attributes. If all is not to be surrendered to the homogenizing and absorptive amoeba of Western-based globalization, then the Balinese must seize the reins of their own history and determine for themselves the sort of society they want to be. Thus, the extraordinary qualities that distinguish Balinese culture need not be sacrificed to the momentum of modernization; rather, the culture itself, in all its complex manifestations, is instrumental in determining how the reforms should be implemented in order to create new opportunities for self-determination and security.

The bomb is the chance to learn and to plan. . . . After the bomb, the mapping of Bali needs to happen carefully, step by step. All of the people need to think again. The government, the tourism people, developers, need to think about Bali . . . what can you do for Balinese people, step by step, slowly? Not separate from Indonesia but for Balinese culture and religion to still exist. We need to minimize the difference between high economic and low so there is more equity and balance in the Balinese community. . . . How many immigrants? How many tourists? How many Balinese people? . . . And also—how should the economy grow in Bali? At this time it's too fast, other times too slow. We need stable growth for the long-term. Bali development has gone too fast and many people in Bali are not prepared for that.

Ajeg Bali is not against development but it needs the Balinese to be in control. Not development forward and Balinese move back. Just now, Balinese is in the back, I don't know who is in the front but it's not Balinese. Our community must try to solve problems—with ourselves, without government, without another from Jakarta. Yah, step by step the community can solve our problems with the economy from the inside. So we can all move forward together. But it needs a long time. . . . It needs many informal leaders. . . . I am optimistic that *Ajeg Bali* can, step-by-step, uplift Bali.[51]

The challenges for Bali are quite clear. Effective governance remains problematic and there are many questions being raised about the capacity of national and district governance structures to deliver productive health, environmental, and social programs. While national interventions have caused many of the problems associated with rapid development, the solutions require a more mixed and diffuse governance model. And while *Ajeg Bali* may seem plausible, at least in principle, the tendency to agglomerate and unify Balinese society creates its own set of social conditions which may pervert the diversity and transitional nature of the island culture. To this end, Bali might be better conceived as a set of distinctive communities and communal groups that converge through particular cultural continuities.

This is largely the view of public health professor Muninjaya from Udayana University, who argues that the central Indonesian government is not distributing an adequate share of its income to Bali and that resources are simply not reaching those communities in Bali where they are most needed. Furthermore, while autonomy and decentralization have given greater power to each of the nine district governments in the province of Bali, lack of coordination between them has become a key obstacle to effectively solving public health problems at a province-wide level. According to Muninjaya, resources are also desperately needed for capacity-building and skill development within local communities. Decentralization and autonomy are giving rise to new public health, environment, and social problems that vary between districts and thus, communities need the capacity to identify their own problems and generate solutions at a local level. He argues that empowerment of women to participate in decision-making should be at the forefront of these efforts. Clearly, this requires substantial challenges to traditional gender and village power relations.[52]

Bali's social infrastructure remains largely constituted around village and neighborhood life: there is a vast gulf between the cosmopolitan and modernizing conditions of the tourism-based Badung district, and the ways in which most Balinese live. To this extent, a political system that is constructed around district and national governance must accommodate the ways in which community life is shaped. If there is such a thing as a "Balinese society," as Satria Naradha claims, then it needs to acknowledge its constituent elements, particularly its multiple communities and lifestyles. Being Balinese, therefore, is not one thing, but is a fluid and open condition that converges through broad historical and contemporary cultural practices, expressivities, and values. Thus, while social elites might like to imagine that they are presiding over an integrated whole, the life-experience for most Balinese is focused around a far more particulated and less precise sense of community. When it is translated into a much broader "civil society," this sense of community will then rejoice in its diversity and the dialogs that exist between different layers of being—family, village, district, province, nation, and beyond.

NOTES

1. Fugly-bali.org is an anonymous website dedicated to exposing the negative aspects of life in Bali including crime, corruption, and illegal activities. Online postings are emerging as a new form of unofficial public discussion about security and civil life in Bali. See www.fugly-bali.org (20 May 2008).

2. This story is adapted from interviews conducted between 2003 and 2006. At the time of the interview, "Putu" was an inmate at Krobokan Prison in Denpasar.

3. Interview with General I Made Mangku Pastika, Denpasar, July 2004. See also Jeff Lewis and Belinda Lewis, "Taming the *Rwa Bhineda*: Challenges and Opportunities for Recovery after the Bali Bombings," in *Rethinking Insecurity, War and Violence: Beyond Savage Globalization*, ed. Paul James, Tom Nairn, and Damian Grenfell (Melbourne: Routledge, 2008).

4. See *Annual Report on the Major Activities of the Anti-Corruption Unit* (Tokyo: Asian Development Bank, 2003).

5. See J. S. Jomo, ed., *Southeast Asian Paper Tigers: From Miracle to Debacle and Beyond* (London: Routledge Curzon, 2003).

6. See Rahadian Permadi, "The Passing of a Dictator," *Inside Indonesia* 91 (January–March 2008). Also Henk Schulte Nordholt, *Bali, an Open Fortress, 1995–2005: Regional Autonomy, Electoral Democracy, and Entrenched Identities* (Singapore: NUS Press, 2007), 22–24.

7. See Graeme MacRea and Darma Putra, "A New Theatre State in Bali? Aristocracies, the Media and Cultural Revival in the 2005 Local Elections," *Asian Studies Review* 31 (June 2007): 171–89.

8. Interview with General Pastika, Denpasar, 2004.

9. Interview with "Gede," *pecalang* leader, Krobokan, 2005.

10. See Ian Wilson, "The Changing Contours of Organized Violence in Post New Order Indonesia," Working Paper 118 (Perth, Australia: Asia Research Center, 2005).

11. See International Crisis Group, "The Perils of Private Security in Indonesia: Guards and Militias on Bali and Lombok," *Asia Report*, no. 67 (Jakarta and Brussels: International Crisis Group, November 2003).

12. Interview with "Gede," *pecalang* leader, Krobokan, 2005.

13. See ICG, *Private Security*, 2003; also D. Santikarma, "The Model Militia," *Inside Indonesia* 73 (January–March 2003).

14. For a discussion of the links between political instability and local violence, see Schulte Nordholt, *Bali, an Open Fortress*, 43–47.

15. Interview with journalist and academic I Nyoman Darma Putra, 2008.

16. Interview with Viebeke Lengkong, Petitinget, December 2005.

17. For a broad discussion of this issue, see Graeme MacRae, "Art and Peace in the Safest Place in the World: A Culture of Apoliticism in Bali," in *Inequality, Crisis and Social Change in Indonesia,* ed. Thomas Reuter (London: Routledge-Curzon, 2003).

18. See Jeff Lewis and Belinda Lewis, "After the Glow: Challenges and Opportunities for Community Sustainability in the context of the Bali Bombings" (Paper presented at the First International Sources of Insecurity Conference, Melbourne, November 2004), ed. Damien Grenfell (Melbourne: RMIT Publishing, 2004), search .informit.com.au/documentsummary;dn=876201933383235;res=E-LIBRARY (accessed 15 May 2008).

19. Interview with Gede Nurjaya, chief of Bali Tourism Authority, Denpasar, December 2006.

20. Interview with Satria Naradha, BPMG Headquarters, December 2006.

21. Interview with I Nyoman Darma Putra, December 2006.

22. See a more extensive commentary on the ways in which civil society groups such as students, women's groups, and labor collectives are contributing to democratic reform across Indonesia in Mikaela Nyman, *Democratising Indonesia: The Challenges of Civil Society in the Era of Reformasi* (Copenhagen: NIAS Press, 2006).

23. Schulte Nordholt, *Bali, an Open Fortress,* 61–78; MacRea and Putra, "A New Theatre State," 171–89.

24. See discussion in Nyman, *Democratising Indonesia,* chapters 3 and 4.

25. Pamela Allen and Carmencita Palermo, "*Ajeg Bali*: Multiple Meanings, Diverse Agenda," *Indonesia and the Malay World* 33, no. 97 (November 2005); also Graeme MacRae "Understanding Indonesia? Or Imagining Indonesia? The view from Bali," in *Understanding Indonesia,* ed. S. Epstein (Asian Studies Institute, Victoria University, Wellington, 2006) and Schulte Nordholt, *Bali, an Open Fortress.*

26. Interview with Satria Naradha, BPMG Headquarters, December 2006.

27. Schulte Nordholt, *Bali, an Open Fortress,* 6–19; MacRea and Putra, "A New Theatre State," 171–89.

28. I Wayan Juniartha, "Election More Than Just a Democratic Process," *Jakarta Post,* 8 July 2008.

29. I Wayan Juniarta, "Balinese Told to Reconsider Lavish Rituals," *Jakarta Post,* 22 September 2008, www.thejakartapost.com/news/2008/09/22/balinese-told -reconsider-lavish-rituals.html (accessed 22 September 2008).

30. MacRea and Putra, "A New Theatre State," 171–89.

31. Interview with Viebeke Lengkong, Kuta, 2006.

32. See David Saxby, "Youth Indonesian," *Inside Indonesia,* no. 85 (January–March 2006).

33. Tim Lindsay and Simon Butt, "Indonesia's Life or Death Battle against Drugs," *The Age* (27 May 2005); also Laine Berman, "From *Jungkies* to Jihad," *Inside Indonesia,* no. 75 (July–September 2003); Madonna Devaney, Gary Reid, and Simon Baldwin, *Situational Analysis of Illicit Drug Issues and Responses in the Asia-Pacific Region* (Canberra: Australian National Council on Drugs, 2005).

34. Harriot Beazley, "The Construction and Protection of Individual and Collective Identities by Street Children and Youth in Indonesia," *Children Youth and Environments* 15, no. 1 (Spring 2003).

35. International Narcotics Control Board, "Indonesia," *The Report of the International Narcotics Control Board 2007* (Vienna: United Nations, 2007), 491–540. See also Devaney, Reid, and Baldwin, *Situational Analysis of Illicit Drug Issues.*

36. I. M. Setiawan, J. Patten, A. Triadi, S. Yulianti, I. P. G. Adnyana, M. Arif, "Report on Injecting Drug Use in Bali (Denpasar and Kuta): Results of an Interview Survey," *The International Journal of Drug Policy* 10, no.2 (April 1999), 109–16.

37. Berman, "From *Jungkies* to Jihad." See also, United Nations Office on Drugs and Crime, *Strengthening Judicial Integrity and Capacity* (2004 Report), www.unodc .org/unodc/corruption_projects_Indonesia.html (accessed 5 June 2007).

38. Laine Berman, "Deals and Denial: Who Is Really Responsible for Indonesia's Drug Epidemic?" *Inside Indonesia* (January–March 2007); also MacRae, "Understanding Indonesia?"

39. Berman, "From *Jungkies* to Jihad."

40. ICG Report, *Private Security*, 2003; D. Santikarma, "The Model Militia," *Inside Indonesia*, no. 73 (January–March 2003).

41. See Fugly Bali, www.fugly-bali.org/police.html (accessed 20 June 2007).

42. Interview with General I Made Mangku Pastika, Denpasar, December 2005.

43. Bill Guerin, "After the Tsunami: Waves of Corruption," *Asian Times Online*, www.atimes.com/atimes/Southeast_Asia/HI20Ae01.html (accessed 20 September 2006).

44. See "Mixed Results in Govt's Anticorruption Campaign," *International Corruption Watch* (6 June 2006), www.antikorupsi.org/eng/mod.php?mod=publisher&op =viewarticle&artid=473 (accessed 10 June 2007).

45. Pseudonyms have been used to protect the identity of the German and his Balinese wife.

46. Despite repeated appeals, Schapelle Corby remains in prison with an expected release date of 2024. In August 2008, she was awarded a three-month reduction of her sentence as part of Indonesia's Independence Day Celebrations.

47. T. Lindsay, "Fact and Fiction in the Corby case" *Fairfax Online* (*SMH*, 27 May 2005), www.smh.com.au/news/opinion/fact-and-fiction-in-the-schapelle-corby -case/; also T. Lindsay, ed., *Indonesia: Law and Society* (Sydney: Federation Press, 1999); T. Lindsay and S. Butt, "Justice System Not Getting a Fair Hearing in High Profile Drugs Cases," *Fairfax Online* (*SMH*, 3 May 2005), www.smh.com.au/ news/opinion/justice-system-not-getting-a-fair-hearing-in-high-profile-drugs-cases/; R. Sackville, "Don't Hold the Bali Court System in Contempt," *The Australian*, 15 June 2005.

48. Donna Leigh Holden, *Change and Recovery: Bali Rehabilitation Fund Project Completion Report* (Canberra: Australian Government, 2006).

49. United Nations Development Program, *Bali beyond the Tragedy: Impact and Challenges for Tourism-Led Development in Indonesia* (Denpasar: Consultative Group Indonesia UNDP-World Bank, 2003).

50. See Jeff Lewis and Belinda Lewis, "At the Edge of the Big Wave: Community Recovery in a Tsunami-Affected Area of Sri Lanka," in *Life on the Margins*, K. Cook and K. Gilbert (Sydney: Pearson Education Australia, 2006).

51. Interview with Satria Naradha, CEO Bali Post Media Group, BPMG Headquarters, December 2006.

52. Interview with Professor Muninjaya, Udayana University, December 2006.

5

Terror, Territory, and God

The Cataclysm of Violence

Certainly, there's no evidence that military personnel planted the Bali bombs, but there's no doubt that it planted the seeds that produced those bombers and their successors. Radical Islam may provide the motivation for terrorism, but Indonesia's armed forces repeatedly supplied the opportunity and means.

—Gary LaMoshi, *Asia Times*, October 2004

This was her first job. I was in the shop two doors along, but she wanted to work in the restaurant. It was good experience. She went to the university to study tourism, and this was her first job. I knew when I heard the bang that she was dead. When I ran down to there, it was already full of smoke and fire. People were screaming but I knew straight away she was dead.

—Wayan, on the death of his daughter in the 2005 bombing

God is great. Allah is the one God. I hate America. I hate Australia. You are all going to Hell. God is great!

—Amrozi, convicted Bali bomber, 2004

FEAR

On the night of the second Bali bomb attacks, we were sitting with some friends in a small restaurant at the back of Kuta Square. The place was full of tourists again, and for all intents and purposes it appeared as though the island had recovered from the 2002 attacks. The monument in Legian Street

5.1.   The Bali Bombing Memorial, Kuta, Bali (2008).
Courtesy of Belinda Lewis.

had assumed the status of a shrine where pilgrim visitors could look and reflect on the names of the dead, imagining a horror that had already been
assigned to history and memory, as though it were already closed in another
cultural space and epoch. By October 2005, in fact, many of these pilgrims
had also returned to the nightclubs and bars. The streets were bustling.
Spruikers had resumed their posts, and once again there were seating delays
at Made's Warung and other popular restaurants.

On the surface, at least, Balinese themselves appeared a little more optimistic about the economy and tourism, believing perhaps that the Islamic
threat had been largely tamed. The ritual cleansing and invocation of the
rwa bhineda (two-in-one) principle[1] seemed to have restored a balance to
the spirit world, appeasing the outbreak of evil that had wrought such destruction onto the community. Shopkeepers were reporting a return to
profit, businesses had begun to hire labor again, and the local gigolos were
back on the beaches plying their trade, playing their tricks, winning the
hearts and favors of lonely foreign ladies seeking their own share of the romance idyll. The *kupu kupu malam* and drug dealers were also back, whis-
pering to clients and slipping through the shadows and nets of the night
traders.

The Indonesian government and Bali Tourism Authority had invested heavily in this recovery. They had assured the international tourist market that it was safe to return, that harmony had been restored, and that Bali was again the Island of Gods—welcoming, peaceful, and friendly. Only one Brahmana priest with whom we spoke had remained skeptical. "Evil," he said, "was once in the roots of the tree. Now it has spread through the trunks and leaves." For this priest, at least, the excesses of development and modernization remained potent, and the "recovery" had simply returned the island to a state of malevolence and chaos. "Impurity is everywhere," he told us solemnly. "We are no longer Balinese." Evil, he believed, circulated through the hearts of all men, in their greed and hunger, in their breath and in their speech. This evil had not been subdued, but lived in the dark corners, waiting to inflict harm on all humanity.

Then chief of Bali police, Inspector General Made Mangku Pastika, had confirmed this skepticism, telling us in 2004 that he expected another attack in Bali within twelve months. And while it seemed that Jemaah Islamiyah had refocused their interests on Jakarta, with attacks on the Marriot Hotel and the Australian embassy, Bali remained a potential target. This view was certainly confirmed by government travel warnings in the United States, United Kingdom, and Australia. International tourists, however, subsumed these warnings within the more familiar and sensory mantra of Bali harmony/Bali paradise. Tourists, it seemed, had become so engaged in the Bali harmony discourse that the violence and horror of the 2002 attacks was best understood as historical aberration, an event that could be transformed and closed within the frieze of an historical relic and glorified remembrance. The Legian monument performed this role, as it collapsed the complex meanings of the bombings into a cool, fixed, and extemporized inscription which glorified the dead, their deaths, and the underlying ideology of nation and nationhood. The monument, that is, removed the event from history, inasmuch as it cleansed the details in favor of a polemical motif in which the dead were victims and heroes. In this way, the remembrance, which draws the tourists to the site, is equally a monument to historical forgetfulness.

This forgetfulness, however, was simply another part of the official recovery plan, a plan that appeared to be working brilliantly until 1 October 2005. With simultaneous attacks at Jimbaran Bay and Kuta Square, the Islamic militants had again shattered the illusion of Bali harmony. By the time we arrived at the square, thick smoke was already billowing through the streets and buildings. People were huddling in the dull, amber light, their eyes fixed in disbelieving horror at the rising flames. Some were trying to flee through the jammed traffic, but most stood motionless, trapped by inertia, outrage, and a profound sense of helplessness. The customers and staff who had been in the restaurant were now sprawled outside. Some were screaming. Others just sat, shaking quietly and holding their faces. Already there were corpses on the roadway, their bloodied bodies half covered by cloth. One man was screaming: "This is my daughter. This is my daughter." We could see other bodies in the flames, charred, and twisted in that terrible moment of death. The blasts in Kuta Square and Jimbaran Bay killed twenty people and seriously injured nearly a hundred more. Jemaah Islamiyah had once again imposed itself and its powerful ideology on the island and its diverse peoples.[2]

THE SOURCES OF INDONESIAN TERROR

The first bombings occurred on 12 October 2002. A van loaded with explosives was detonated outside the Sari Club in Legian Street, Kuta. Just along the street at about the same time, a suicide bomb attack ignited propane gas cylinders at Paddy's Bar, creating a hideous and deadly fireball that burned alive many of the patrons who had survived the initial blast. The official death toll was 202, though the figure is likely to be higher as many non-Balinese Indonesians remained unaccounted for. Around eighty-eight Australians were killed; the other major nationalities included British, American, Japanese, Brazilian, German, and French. The attacks occurred as the United States, United Kingdom, and Australia were preparing to invade Iraq and extend the parameters of the global war on terror. Clearly, the 2002 and 2005 attacks were designed to instill fear in the coalition governments and their citizens, creating a mood of insecurity which would ultimately shatter the nexus that had formed between Bali and the "West" within the broader economy of pleasure.

Fear, thereby, is the essence of modern terrorism. While there are many different definitions of terrorism, the most plausible of these present a terrorist act in terms of its political and communicational objectives. Terrorism within the contemporary context, therefore, possesses the following attributes:[3]

- Terrorism is fundamentally communicational. To this end, modern terrorism is a form of political violence which uses the networked media to communicate particular ideas, perspectives, emotions, ideologies, and beliefs to audiences who are not the immediate victims of the attack. In this way, the current phase of global terrorism is constituted around complex wars of meaning and "language" as they are amplified through the modern media. However, while former British prime minister Margaret Thatcher famously stated that "publicity is the oxygen of terrorism," this "oxygen" is the life-source of all modern politics; terrorism is a player in a political sphere that is constructed essentially around the broadcast media and other global communication systems.

- The violence may be perpetrated by governments, subnational and transnational groups. While the U.S. Department of Defense and State Department both refute this point, it is very clear that elected and authoritarian governments have frequently committed acts of terror against their own and foreign citizens. As we have noted, the Dutch colonial government and the Suharto regime deployed various forms of violence in order to impose their will and interests over the Indonesian people. Suharto, in particular, imposed a vicious and unflinching military order which silenced criticism through the perpetual threat of violence. Equally, the Indonesian occupation of West Papua and the annexation of East Timor were sustained through a terror campaign that targeted and murdered civilians as part of the regime of enforcement. The regime attacked and terrorized citizens in order to publicize their power and subdue dissidents. Other groups who exercise terror may be transnational, such as Jemaah Islamiyah and al-Qa'ida, or largely intranational such as Darul Islam and Laksar Jihad (see below).
- The direct victims of terrorist violence are non-combatants, who are often randomly selected from a social group that has strong symbolic value for the militants. To this extent, the Jemaah Islamiyah leaders and strategists attacked the tourist zones of Bali in order to demonstrate their disdain for "the West," to disrupt the tourist economy, and inflict fear on the peoples and governments within the U.S.-led Coalition of the Willing. In the broadest sense, the injury and death inflicted by the attacks were designed to persuade these governments to cancel the war on terror and expel themselves from all the holy Muslim lands, including Indonesia. However, while JI sought to inflict fear through the mediated amplification of their attacks, they also hoped the bombings would attract new recruits into the Islamic cause, one of the primary motivations of the al-Qa'ida attacks on New York.
- The terrorism associated with the Bali bombings and the 9/11 attacks on New York are part of a much broader symbolic order that has been generated through the modern global media networks. The cultural and political context of these attacks invokes a powerful historical dialectic which is constituted around a grand civilizational divide between the East and the West. While this divide has several incarnations—Islam-Christian, Orient-West, Islam-Modern—it has been largely generated by warrior groups as the symbolic or cultural validation for disputes over territory and material resources, the most recent of which is oil. It is within this broader symbolic order and its contending manifestations of the "war on terror" and global "jihad" that the current complexion of political combat is being waged. History is being radically reduced through these simplistic dichotomies, creating an impression that terrorism and political violence more

generally are the expression of an "Evil" that is bound essentially to an underlying and inescapable cultural ontology: that is, culture is composed out of essential differences, rather than difference being created through culture.

This impression, however, is entirely the construction of the opposing parties, each accusing the other of some immense cosmological contamination. This is not a "clash of civilizations" as Samuel Huntington so famously pronounced, but the *imaginary* of such a clash; by perpetually invoking difference as unbridgeable and constructed through divine power, each party dehumanizes their opponents and hence validates the inhumane treatment of their enemy.[4] Thus, the U.S. administration and the al-Qa'ida leadership speak extravagantly about the universal evil and inhumanity of the other party, centering their accusations on the deplorable exercise of terrorist violence. Within this symbolic order, terrorism is not merely an act of violence perpetrated against the enemy's people: it is an invocation and deployment of history and culture for the sake of polemical interests.

Clearly, this notion of terrorism is part of the intensely agonistic process of global modernization: as we have frequently heard, one person's terrorist is another's freedom fighter. Even so, the attacks in Bali and elsewhere in Indonesia by militant Islamicists[5] need to be understood in terms of a crisis of culture within which Indonesia's specific modernization is taking place. Bali's own "forbidden crisis" is, thereby, integrated into the broader sphere of transition in Indonesia and a history which binds the two territories—Java and Bali—into a disjunctive and profoundly volatile political compound. The relationship between Bali and Java is in many respects the essence of the Indonesian nation since it represents a complex contiguity of continuities and differences, the resolution of which forms the basis and validity of the Indonesian state ideology (*Pancasila*) as well as the constitutional fabric of Indonesia's democratic statehood. The Islamic militant attacks, therefore, were not merely a threat to life and economy: they were an assault on the very essence of the Indonesian state and its politico-cultural integrity.

In fact, the attacks that were perpetrated in Bali by associates and members of Jemaah Islamiyah (literally Islamic community) are symptomatic of a thoroughly modern context of political violence. While Bali had resisted the lure of Islam and the military-political power of Java for several centuries, this independence was finally compromised in the 1908 *puputan* when Dutch imperial soldiers conquered and invaded the southern areas of the island (see chapter 1). While always marginal, a sentiment of Balinese secessionism has continued through the period of Dutch occupation and national independence into the present, expressing itself most consistently in terms of Hindu anti-Islamicism. Bali's status as a minority Hindu enclave within a vastly dominant Muslim archipelago has clearly contributed to a pervasive sense of territorialism and a powerfully resistant cultural identity, both of which express themselves through a deep suspicion of the political and military power of Java generally and the national government based in Jakarta in particular. The Balinese genocide of 1965/1966 intensified these suspicions, cleaving the society between those who were the allies and beneficiaries of the New Order and those, especially among the lower caste, who were its victims.

While an actual secessionist movement remains largely peripheral, the psychology of its anxieties is widespread within the Hindu Balinese community. In this sense, modernization has created new contradictions for a people who are the economic beneficiaries of global participation, but who nevertheless remain loyal in varying degrees to customary and ritualistic belief systems. The militant attacks have further intensified these complex sensibilities, reinvigorating older prejudices and modes of Muslim scapegoating while nevertheless imploring the national government for assistance and "solutions." In this context, many Balinese have been active participants in the *Reformasi* democratic process, most particularly the electoral process in which vigorous public debate was conducted around the respective worth of particular candidates and policies. After the 2002 bombings, however, the Balinese vote became less predictable, turning somewhat against their 1999 preferred presidential candidate, Megawati Soekarnoputri, who had failed in the view of many voters to adequately address the problems of security and remilitarization.

In either case, the Balinese attraction to secular presidential candidates, such as Megawati and Susilo Bambang Yudhoyono, is not surprising, as the Balinese remain threatened by the surge and power of political Islam. While these anxieties have their roots in religious and cultural history, the militant attacks also represent an assault on Balinese secularism, most particularly the new economy and cultural forms being generated through global participation and modern tourism. Thus, even though many Balinese viewed the first attacks as primarily an assault on "Westerners," there was also an uneasy and persistent sense that the Islamists were attacking the Balinese lifestyle that had been created through their interaction with the West.[6] In this way, Western fears over growing Islamism in Indonesia were conflated through the Balinese's own sense of threat both for their religious integrity *and* their more secular aspirations—economic security, sustainable livelihoods, and new forms of consumer-based pleasures.

The results of the 2004 presidential elections might seem in some respects to have justified these anxieties. There are clear indications that post-Suharto Indonesia is evolving a particular political dialectic which is common across many Muslim nations: that is, between secular and Islamic political representation. In table 5.1 below, we can see clearly that this dialectic is a central feature of Indonesia's political scene.

Table 5.1. Percentage of Votes for the Major Parties in the 1999 and 2004 Elections

Party	Key Person/Orientation	% Votes in 1999 Legislative Elections	% Votes in 2004 Legislative Elections
Golkar	Wiranto/Tandjung	22.4	21.6
PDIP	Megawati	33.7	18.5
PD	Yudhoyono	7.5	
Subtotal	*Votes for Secular Parties*	*56.1%*	*47.1%*
PKB	A. Wahid (Gus Dur) (Pluralist Islam)	12.6	10.6
PAN	A. Rais (Pluralist Islam)	7.1	6.4
PPP	Hamzah Haz (Moderate Islamicist)	10.7	8.2
PBR	Zainudin Mz (Moderate Islamicist)	2.8	
PBB	Yusril Mahendra (Radical Islamicist)	1.9	2.6
PKS	Hidayat Nur Wahid (Radical Islamicist)	1.4	7.2
Subtotal	**Votes for Islamic Parties**	**33.7%**	**37.8%**

Note: Adapted from Greg Barton, *Indonesia's Struggle: Jemaah Islamiyah and the Soul of Islam* (Sydney: University of New South Wales Press, 2004).

Religion is clearly an important part of civil life and the political process in Indonesia. However, although nearly 40 percent of voters chose candidates with Islamic credentials, these figures indicate that it was the secular parties that remained dominant. Perhaps more importantly, the political power of moderate and more radical Islamicists remains relatively constrained within the electoral process. The change to direct presidential elections in 2004 (as opposed to appointment by the legislature in 1999) clearly confirms the electorate's preference for a secular leader. In particular, the electorate expressed its anxieties about security and social instability through the choice of the "clean" ex-general, Susilo Bambang Yudhoyono (34 percent first round votes) over Megawati (29 percent) whom many believed to be weak and susceptible to remilitarization.

It is apparent, therefore, that many Muslim and non-Muslim Indonesians see considerable value in the separation of religion and state. Many Indonesians, including the Hindu Balinese, are hoping that a modern secularist government might best deliver social reform, stability, anticorruption, prosperity, and protection from the more extreme effects of Islamic radicalism. Thus, while the Muslim pluralists, represented by Abdurrahman Wahid, are regarded in relatively benign terms, the more radical parliamentary Islamic parties are viewed with greater suspicion. This is particularly the case when these parties maintain dialog with—and on occasions directly articulate—the views of an even more pure version of Islam which rejects the parliamentary process altogether. For these "purist" groups, there can be no authority or legitimate power which is not linked directly to God. Secularism and parliamentary democracy, therefore, are viewed as fundamentally sacrilegious, an offense to the true teachings of the Prophet Mohammed. Within this general class of purist Islam, however, are the more dangerous factions which advocate violent *Jihad* in order to eradicate social impurity and establish a true Islamic state.

In late 2008 the Indonesian parliament finally passed the *shari'ah*-style antipornography bills, an event which coincided with the execution of three of the Bali bombers (see chapter 3). These events marked an important moment for Indonesian civil processes and the power of the Islamic political and militant forces. On the one hand, the passing of the antipornography bills might be seen as a victory for purist Islam, while on the other side the executions could be regarded as a victory for secular judicial processes and law enforcement. In either case, the events underscore the complexity of cultural and institutional politics in Indonesia. Undoubtedly, candidates in the 2009 presidential elections have been careful not to offend the Islamic lobby and risk alienating Muslim voters: the pornography laws and the executions are directly implicated in the difficult balance between faith and modern secular politics.

MODERN ISLAMICISM

There has been over many years a frequently repeated myth that Muslims in Indonesia are essentially moderate, far more moderate than their counterparts in Malaysia, Pakistan, and the Middle East. This view largely falsifies the complexity of Indonesian Islam and the diversity we have outlined above. Certainly, some Indonesian Muslims are pluralist and there are gradients of observance to libation and ritual. But within this pluralist framework, there exists a powerful genealogy of purist Islam which has strong links to Shi'ite religiosity and Saudi Islamic scholarship. In some cases, such as in Aceh, these purer or more distinctly *shari'ah* modes of Islam are regionally based. In Aceh at the northern end of Sumatra, for example, the local form of Islam is more closely linked to Muslim India than it is to the ritual styles in the eastern islands of the archipelago. Thus, to speak of a universally moderate Islam says more about the West and its own political-cultural ideals than it does about Indonesia. In many respects, these ideals seek to confirm themselves and the high value of modernization through the moderation of others: a belief in Indonesia's secular modernization confirms the importance of the West and its own ideology and historical trajectory.

In fact, Indonesia's transitions and modernization, as in the West, are replete with contradictions and inconsistencies. As we have noted, the Islamic radicalism that has accompanied the rise of modernization is not simply a retreat to tradition, but a manifestation of internal agonisms which work in and through the processes of modernization and change: that is, radical Islamicism is another player in the broad landscape of Indonesia's modern political field. To this end, the invocation of traditional Islamic law (*shari'ah*) and the literalist application of the Qu'ran are not of themselves antagonistic toward the processes of modernization. Rather, they are expressions of an internal belligerence which seeks to ground itself in a higher political order and in "deep time." In other words, radical Islam, like the religious politicism in Western countries such as the United States, uses tradition, history, and the divine as political weapons within the general momentum and condition of *modern* language wars. The particular set of interests which are represented by radical Islam should not be simply seen as "antimodern," except inasmuch as modernization itself is gestant with its own internal contending elements and internal modes of resistance. That is, radical Islam is not merely reactive to modernization and modernism—rather it may be seen as an inevitable part of modernism's own propensity for agonism, dispute, internal contention, and warfare.

In chapter 1 we discussed the relationship between Romanticism and modernization, suggesting that the reactionary naturalism associated with European Romantic philosophy was an inevitable dimension of modernization. Our discussion of class politics and Romanticism clearly indicates that the historical momentum of modernism has been disjunctive, complex and often discontinuous, forging itself through an astonishing cacophony of claims for domination and resistance. As in the West, modernization in developing societies is characterized as much by struggle and belligerence, as it is by a momentum toward universal ideology and political conditions. Modernization bears with it the sources of its own destruction.

To look at this more precisely, Western modernism bears a dialectical lineage which opposes and seeks to resolve a profound tension between Romanticism and rationalism. As we have noted in earlier discussions, Romanticism emerges in Enlightenment Europe (seventeenth through nineteenth centuries) as the legacy of religious and aesthetic transcendentalism and as a reaction against the philosophical and technological rationalism which was beginning to dominate the new historical epoch. In particular, Romanticism reacted against the cultural and environmental degeneration associated with urbanization and industrialization. Philosophers like G. W. F. Hegel and Immanuel Kant proposed an epistemological (knowledge-based) and cosmological reunion of mind, body, and spirit. Romantic artists, poets, and philosophers advocated the restitution of nature and religious ecstasy against the degradation of a modern social decay and alienation.

The experiences of social disconnection and alienation, which accompanied the evolution of industrial cities and the nation state in Europe, were also central to the emergence of other countertheories and forms of social resistance. Marxism, in particular, was an essential component of the new class politics which challenged the ascendancy of economic liberalism and liberal democracy. Existential philosophy sought to confront the Western experience of alienation and offer some form of aesthetic or epistemological elision from its most negative effects in warfare or mental illness. Even the religious revivalism implicit in New Age or born-again Christian Evangelism seems somewhat to extend the Romantic-rationalism dialectic, proposing to liberate the soul from the nihilistic effects of excessive materialism and the decline of community.

In many respects, this very modern dialectic is also evident in the resistance being proffered by radical Islam. In particular, the more pure forms of radical Islam set their solutions to oppression and alienation in an apocalyptic vision which purges evil and elevates the human soul above the degrading effects of poverty, despair, and Western economic imperialism. History is thus invoked as a "pure origin" in which the self becomes grounded in a collective condition—Islam. This communion of self and society is also a key component of modernization which intensifies the individual within the general momentum of collective economy and mass society (national and/or global). Islam, in this sense, is the ideal modern antidote to the modern condition of social overflow and individual separation. Like other twentieth-century solutions—communism, Nazism, nationalism, Zionism—Islamicism rejects the ideology of an infinitely liberated self by fixing subjects back into a history of struggle and conquest. Radical Islamic theology engages in the modern dialectic, therefore, through its own double helix of alienation and elevation: the problem and the solution rising like snakes in a basket through a deadly and entangled embrace which obscures the source of their difference.

And indeed, the tactics and technologies that are employed by radical Islam are entirely modern and often highly sophisticated. Funded by plutocrats like the royal family of Saudi Arabia (who are themselves key players in the modern global economy), many of these radical Islamic organizations have developed complex communications networks and information strategies. In Indonesia, in particular, these organizations have

- established free education schools and universities across Java;
- numerous personnel in senior and technical roles who have studied at international universities, especially in Saudi Arabia, Australia, and the United States;

- developed very sophisticated Internet communication strategies and technical expertise;
- established their own media channels and PR machinery;
- developed and applied sophisticated military and ballistics expertise, employing weapons that are far from medieval.

Thus, while using the rampart of history to launch their claims, both violent and nonviolent Islamic radicals are engaged in a modern warfare in which territory, culture, and the future are at stake. The agonisms associated with *jihadism* and the "war on terror" are not a matter of tradition against modernity; rather, they are a manifestation of language wars that are as intense and confused as the battleground of bodies they elicit.[7]

Wahhabi and Salafy: Pure Islam in Indonesia

While there is no consensus on how best to define the embryo of radical Islamicism in Indonesia, two terms—Wahhabi Islam and Salafy (Salafi, Salafism)—are most commonly applied. The former term derives from the theocratic regime represented by the House of Saud, the dynastic government of Saudi Arabia. This form of pure Islam is based on the teachings of Muhammed Abd al-Wahhab (1703–1791), a Muslim scholar who advocated the restoration of a mode of religious observance deemed to be closest to the original prophecies and teachings of Muhammad. Al-Wahhab sought to cleanse Arabian society of the various interpretations and mystical practices supposedly derived from the Qu'ran. According to al-Wahhab, Arabian society and Qu'ranic scholarship had been degraded over the past twelve centuries, especially through its interactions with Greek philosophy, Christian Byzantine theology, Persian and Indian mysticism, and peasant folklore. Al-Wahhab's purification of the Qu'ran stimulated a scholarship of literalism which has contributed significantly to the ideal of the *shari'ah* state.

The force and resonance of al-Wahhab's *shari'ah* cult is, however, political, rather than theological. The adoption of the cult by the House of Saud ensured its amplification as a mode of political expression. The enormous oil reserves and wealth generated through Saudi Arabia ensured, further, that its distinctive form of governance would impress itself on the global economy and hence international geopolitics. The Saudi family's own theopolitical ambition inscribed itself on world politics, most particularly as a platform for resistance to the colonial and neocolonial policies of world powers like Britain and the United States. More locally, this mode of antimodern modernization is also evident in the politics of the Egypt-based Islamic militant group, the Muslim Brotherhood. Particularly through the leadership of Sayyid Qutb, the Brotherhood emerged during the twentieth century as a fearsome organization which was determined in the first instance to impose a pure Islamic style of government on Egypt, and ultimately the whole of the Arabic world. Qutb's radicalism and militant methods became the inspiration for many militant Islamicists across all Muslim countries. The violence advocated by Qutb and others in the Muslim Brotherhood inspired the Islamic *mujahadin* fighters in the Afghan-Soviet War, a critical event in the evolution of contemporary terrorism (see below).

The other term that is popularly applied to this form of pure Islamicism is Salafy. While Salafy as a form of pure Islam has become increasingly prevalent over the past three decades, it is nevertheless part of a more general form of puritanical Mohammedism that extends back centuries in Indonesia. The term, while not entirely interchangeable with Wahhabism, is nonetheless associated with a particular form of religious politicism that links many of its adherents to Saudi funding and the Saudi scholarly Ulema. It should be noted, however, that the term Salafy has an official status in Indonesia's Ministry for Religion, referring specifically to schools which have an exclusively religious curriculum. Indonesians themselves often use the official and more general meanings interchangeably, believing that the religious schools are merely manifestations of the broader Salafy mission.

In this context, Salafism in Indonesia is a form of pure Mohammedism which denounces modern innovations in social, political, and religious life. At its purest, Salafist theology is characterized by the following:

1. It rejects electoral or democratic politics as there can be no authority that is not derived directly from Allah through the Prophet Muhammad and the Qu'ran. Secularism is thus abhorred because the word of God cannot be parenthesized. While some commentators regard this principle as a form of pure "apoliticism," it is rather an expression of cultural politics as we have defined it in this book.
2. This cultural politics expresses itself through the process of rejection. Through their exclusive allegiance to Allah, the community of the faithful is the primary social unit. A Salafy Muslim cannot swear an oath of allegiance to any leader other than God. Salafists, in principle at least, belong to a transnational or globalist community.
3. Salafy rejects modern innovations and invokes the pure Islam practised during the first two centuries following the death of Muhammad. This older form of Islam invokes *shari'ah* law, the strict control of women, and literalist punishments for wrongdoing. It advocates the dedicated study of the Qu'ran and rejects the four schools of law which have become the foundation of Muslim orthodoxy. At this level, a number of Salafy scholars distinguish their own mode of pure

Islam from the Wahhabi which constructs its conservative paradigm around one of the four schools (the *Hambali*). According to some Salafy, the Wahhabi interpretation applies a weak interpretation of the Qu'ran and the *hadith* (traditions) without a clear and direct engagement with the origins of the holy text.

4. Salafism's invocation of a "traditional culture" leads to a rejection of other cultural elements in technology, style, and self-presentation. Like other traditionalist religious cults such as the Christian Amish, Salafy prescribes strict dress and behavior codes: men wear beards and women are usually required to wear the full covering of the *chadar*. Technologies like photography, video, television, and music are banned as in Taliban Afghanistan. (As we have outlined above, this puritanical approach to technology is rarely followed by the militant *jihadists*.)

5. The pure Salafy reject violence against fellow Muslims, except for defensive purposes and as punishment for crime. In this sense, the Salafy apply the notion of *jihad* (literally "struggle") for the protection of Muslims who are under attack. This defensive mode would necessarily exclude violent rebellion against Muslim governments. It would also preclude preemptive or offensive attacks such as those carried out by al-Qa'ida on American citizens in New York.[8]

It is around this final point that the purity of Salafy is most frequently challenged. Indeed, while some Salafy adherents have compromised this purity by engaging in Indonesia's civil and electoral processes, others have diverged into various forms of political violence. Perhaps the purest and most radical Salafy remain strictly faithful to the principles which seek an evolutionary reinstatement of the *hadith* traditions through a gradual process of education and conversion. For those other Salafy or Wahhabi who have been inspired by the actions and "successes" of organizations like the Muslim Brotherhood, the deployment of violence seems a more certain strategy for the establishment of their pure Islamic state.

DARUL ISLAM, THE JAKARTA CHARTER, AND STATE POWER

As we have noted, the Muslim scholarship and funds provided by the Saudi royal family have been instrumental in the rise of Salafism and Wahhabism in Indonesia, particularly since the 1980s. However, radical and militant Islamicism had been evident in Indonesia during much of the twentieth century. Persatuan Islam or Persis, established in 1923 in Badung, for example, was one of several rebel groups in West Java which challenged the authority of the Dutch colonial rule. The Persis scholarship group established Indonesia's first *pesantren* (Islamic boarding school) in 1936, promoting a curriculum which excluded secularism and the four orthodox models of Islamic law. The Persis *pesantren* provided a model for Islamic boarding schools which have become the organizational framework for Indonesian Salafism and the militantism practiced by groups like Jemaah Islamiyah. At least one of the JI Bali bombers, Imam Samudra, has direct family links with the Persis movement.

Islamicists were also active during the nationalist revolution following the defeat of Japan in 1945. In seeking to maintain the integrity of the Indonesian state, the nationalist leader, Sukarno, proposed a *Panca Sila* (Sanskrit: "five principles"), the first of which prescribed a vaguely articulated "belief in God." Sukarno's strategy was to ensure that all Indonesians, including Christians, Buddhists, and especially Balinese Hindus, would become engaged in the establishment and maintenance of a pluralist and fundamentally secular Indonesian nation. The purist Islamic leaders, however, felt largely discontent with the first *sila*, proposing an addendum which proscribed, "A belief in God with the obligation for adherents of Islam to carry out the *Shari'ah*." Known as the Jakarta Charter, the addendum was met with fierce opposition from many in the nationalist movement and, following the declaration of independence on 17 August 1945, it was formally replaced with the phrase: "A belief in God Who is One." This compromise admitted the integrity of a single god which implied, though did not specify, the status of the Muslim deity.

Even so, there remained many traditionalist Muslim leaders in Islamic organizations like Persis, Nahdlatal Ulama, and Muhammadiyah who remained skeptical, not only about the constitutional framework of Indonesia (*Pancasila*), but the ultimate role of Islam in the political machinations of the state. While supporting the revolutionary expulsion of the Dutch colonists during the revolution, the traditionalists formed their own distinctive communities and points of resistance once the common enemy had been expelled. In particular, schisms developed between the more modernist and urban members of the Islamic community and those provincial *ulama* (orthodox religious scholars within Islam) who felt somewhat demeaned by the secularist and modernist disposition of the Sukarno government that was established in 1949. When elections were finally held in 1955, however, the two major Islamic parties Masyumi (more modernist) and Nahdlatal Ulama (more traditionalist) failed to win a majority, and hence questions over the political role and status of Islam and the Jakarta Charter remained largely unresolved.

A more militant schism was formed by a prominent Islamic rebel who had been actively resisting the colonial occupation of the Dutch and the Japanese. Sekarmadji Maridjan Kartosuwirjo helped to establish Hazbullah, a militia group with strong links to the peak Islamic organization, Maysumi. While initially supporting Maysumi's participation in civil processes, Kartosuwirjo became frustrated by the secularist and democratic framework, returning ultimately to the military framework that had guided his years of colonial resistance. In 1949, Kartosuwirjo established the Negara Islam Indonesia (Islamic State of Indonesia) in West Java: the districts within the protectorate of his troops were declared Darul Islam (abode of Islam), the name popularly adopted to describe his secessionist rebellion. In south Sulawesi another former Hazbullah leader and nationalist warrior, Kahar Muzakkar, dissatisfied with the treatment of his troops by the official Indonesian military (TNI— *Tentara Nasionalis Indonesia*) announced his support for Darul Islam, declaring the province a part of Negara Republik Indonesia.

The secession was, however, sporadic and not broadly supported. While Kartosuwirjo engaged the TNI in various skirmishes for over a decade, he was finally captured in 1962, and Darul Islam basically collapsed around him. In many respects, Darul Islam resembles the later secessionist movements in Aceh where the nationalists believed they were fighting for the formation of an Islamic state, if not a distinct Islamic province. The lasting impact of Darul Islam has been shaped in two ways. First, Darul Islam provides a vocabulary of Islamic resistance, especially for those who believe in armed struggle. To this end, Kartosuwirjo shared in the propagated glory of anticolonialism and the nationalist revolution, but as an Islamicist his heroism was elevated by the greater glory of Allah and the divine jihad. Secondly, Darul Islam is itself martyred by the actions of a repressive (and demonic) secular government.

Thus, while Kartosuwirjo's capture under Sukarno generally quelled the Islamic rebellion, it was regenerated through the mythic and durable power of his popular beatification. The ruthless and oppressive authority that Suharto wielded over the population merely intensified this belief in Islamic martyrdom and divine retribution. As we discussed in chapter 1, the political genocide perpetrated by Suharto virtually annihilated leftist opposition in Indonesia, but the Islamists were able to retreat into the shadows and silences of the mosque and the *pesantren*. For no immediately obvious reason, Suharto's anxieties over this latent Islamic threat expressed itself in 1977 when he decided to flush out the remnants of Darul Islam resistance. Working through his special operations leader General Ali Murtopo, Suharto enticed the old Islamic fighters out of hiding on the pretext of enlisting their support against a resurgent communist threat. Once they had identified themselves in this way, the former Darul Islamists and their sympathizers were accused of belonging to an organization called Kommando Jihad and were arrested for sedition. As Martin van Bruinessen has noted, Suharto's deceit stimulated an even more formidable consciousness among the radical Islamicists, refurbishing an identity of resistance which was constituted around antisecularism and antimodernism.[9] This consciousness, which now had its own local martyrs, became the cognitive framework for a new network of radical opposition. The Iranian Islamic revolution and the financial support of the Saudi Arabian oil-rich government enabled the Indonesian militants to build their own revolutionary ideals beyond provincial boundaries. The new Islamic movements that emerged through the latter half of the Suharto regime were thus able to contemplate a *shari'ah* state that incorporated all Muslims across the region and the world—something that was probably never considered by Kartosuwirjo and his soldiers of Darul Islam.

THE FOUNDATIONS OF JEMAAH ISLAMIYAH

The repressive assault perpetrated by Suharto and his secret police during the 1970s laid the foundations for a new, more modern and globally connected mode of Islamic militancy in Indonesia. The organization loosely called Jemaah Islamiyah was founded during this period. While somewhat nascent and unfocused, this "community of Islam" was formed in the late 1970s by two Darul Islam sympathizers, Abu Bakar Ba'asyir (Bashir) and Abdullah Sungkar. Sungkar, originally a resident of Brebes in Central Java, was among the 185 Darul Islamists arrested in Murtopo's sting. While we will discuss JI's evolution into a terrorist organization in greater detail below, it is worth noting here that both Sungkar and Ba'asyir were part of the general ferment of purist and radical Islam which emerged during the late 1970s and 1980s in Indonesia and more generally through the Middle East and South Asia. This ferment was directly catalyzed on the university campuses of Java which perhaps provided some intellectual refuge from the dangerous and repressive political environment imposed by the Suharto state autocracy.

As Suharto effectively closed down civic debate within Indonesia and brutally repressed political activism in universities, the mosque became a center for discussions on religion and the associated cultural politics. And indeed, during this period of ferment there was still little obvious difference between the various Islamic purists as both militant and nonmilitant Salafy scholars focused their study and political energies on scripture, education, and recruitment. Of particular importance was the Islamic Propagation Council of Indonesia (*Dewan Dakwah Islam Indonesia*) which became increasingly active in promoting Salafism in universities such as Bina Masjid Kampus. The DDII provided funding for Indonesians wishing to fight the Soviets in Afghanistan, and for the distribution of translations of militant scholars such as Sayyid Qutb and Hasan al-Banna of the Muslim Brotherhood.

Equally potent in the rise and spread of Salafism in Indonesia was the establishment in 1980 of a campus of the Saudi-based Imam Muhammed bin

Saud University in Jakarta. Receiving generous funding from the mother university in Saudi Arabia, the Indonesian campus (LIPIA) attracted many students to its inexpensive and intensely religious program. While establishing strong community links and outreach programs with prestigious universities such as the University of Indonesia, LIPIA was able to thrive, even in the midst of Suharto's continuing efforts to repress Islamic politicism. Working with and through the Islamic Propagation Council of Indonesia (DDII), LIPIA became increasingly absorbed by the theology and political ideals of the Muslim Brotherhood. The Brotherhood's founder, Hasin al-Banna, had pioneered the notion of an Islamic political movement called *harakah*, by which small social units or "families" (*usroh*) would live by *shari'ah* law. These units would thus become the communal basis for a broader and more sweeping Islamicism that would ultimately unite whole peoples and nations. It was precisely one of these *usroh* that formed the basis of the Jemaah Islamiyah organization established by Sungkar and Ba'asyir.

It is, however, the *harakah* and the influence of the Muslim Brotherhood which ultimately alienated many of the LIPIA graduates and teachers. As in Gajah Mada University in Jogjakarta, central Java, this split in the Salafy ranks resonated throughout the purist Islamic community. Even among those committed Islamicists who joined the mujahidin fighters in Afghanistan, there were significant divisions over the legitimacy of violence perpetrated against Muslim governments and countrymen in Indonesia. The Muslim Brotherhood was committed to the overthrow of orthodox and secular government in Egypt and ultimately across the Middle East. This preparedness to kill fellow Muslims in order to transform the society into a genuinely *shari'ah* state has been rejected by many Salafy on both theological and humanitarian grounds. The incidental killing of Muslim Indonesians in the Jemaah Islamiyah attacks in Bali and Jakarta evince precisely this same division of theological and strategic orientation. For many Salafy, as well as orthodox Muslims, the killing of ordinary Muslims in these attacks is patently wrong and an offense to the true teaching of the Qu'ran and *shari'ah*.

The split is also apparent across the community of Islamic boarding schools or *pesantren* which have increasingly populated the Javanese countryside since the 1980s. Again, as a primary conduit for the dissemination and promotion of a purist Islam, the *pesantren* have notoriously become engaged in the training of militants—but these *pesantren* are a distinct minority. Most famous among them is the Pondok Ngruki, established by Abu Bakar Ba'asyir just outside Solo in Central Java. The Pondok Ngruki provided a locus for the solidification of the Jemaah Islamiyah organization, which until the mid- and latter 1980s had been largely an aspiration of Sungkar and Ba'asyir and a fantasy of the Suharto security paranoia.

JEMAAH ISLAMIYAH AND THE BASIS OF THE BALI BOMBINGS

The rise in militant Islamicism in Indonesia can be summarized in the following terms:

1. The purist forms of Islam, while a continuous presence in Indonesia, became fortified in the later 1970s and 1980s through the influence of Saudi-based Wahhabism and Salafism
2. While Saudi support was initially scholarly and theological, it also manifests itself as a form of cultural politics. The spread and influence of these purist forms was largely financed by the oil wealth of the Saudi royal plutocracy.
3. The theology and tactics of the Egyptian-based Muslim Brotherhood exerted particular influence over those Indonesian purists who considered armed struggle (Jihad) to be a legitimate tactic for establishing a *shari'ah* Islamic state. These views were reinforced by the success of Islamicists in the Iranian Revolution and later the Taliban victory in Afghanistan.
4. The repressive political environment in Indonesia during the Suharto period created a new class of Islamic martyrs, while simultaneously forcing civic debate and political critique into the refuge of the mosque.
5. The strategy of establishing Islamic *usrah* communities and networks through universities and boarding schools (*pesantren*) enabled the *imam* leaders to influence and recruit increasing numbers of young people to the purist cause.
6. The Soviet-Afghan War was particularly important as it trained considerable numbers of Indonesians, along with many other South East Asian Muslims, in the tactics and technical mechanics of civil warfare. In particular, it provided training in ballistics and bomb-making skills. These skills were effectively adapted for the terrorist attacks perpetrated by Laskar Jihad in Maluku and by Jemaah Islamiyah in its various assaults across Indonesia, including Bali.

Afghanistan appears to have been the cauldron for much of the ideological and military development of many in the current jihadist leadership, including Osama bin Laden and Abu Bakar Ba'asyir. Sungkar and Ba'asyir were not only inspired by the success of the mujahidin army in Afghanistan, but also the theological and tactical integrity of the Taliban forces. Inspired by the Gama faction of the Muslim Brotherhood and its theological-ideological reiteration and realization through al-Qa'ida, Sungkar and Ba'asyir returned to Indonesia following the fall of Suharto and embarked on a deadly campaign to purify the Indonesian state. While Sungkar died in 1998, Ba'asyir presided over an intensely radicalized mode of Islamic puritanism, one which attracted converts from across the region, the Middle East, and Australia. Clearly sponsored by the interests of al-Qa'ida, this group included Rhaman al-Ghozi, arrested in 2002 for bombing attacks in Manila; Hambali, who was the main al-Qa'ida link in Indonesia and a key figure in the bombing attacks in Jakarta and Manila, and under suspicion for a planned attack in America; al-Jibril, who is the main financial courier for al-Qa'ida in South East Asia; and Agus Dikwana, who is under detention in the Philippines for alleged association with Manila and Jakarta bombings.[10]

While initially focusing on Christian groups and other non-Muslims in the region, Jemaah Islamiyah made its most spectacular contribution to the global Jihad with the bombings in Bali. As we have indicated, however, JI's campaigns of violence began in earnest around 1999 when, after returning from the Afghan-Soviet war, a number of its key leadership group devised a new strategy of political militancy. Led by Indonesian nationals and organized loosely around more or less autonomous cells, JI has been linked to a series of fatal attacks in Malaysia, the Philippines, and Indonesia. Most notably, in the Christmas Eve attacks of 2000, JI bombed churches and attacked priests across eleven Indonesian cities in six separate provinces. These attacks indicated a reasonably high level of organization and coordination across a wide area of the country.

The International Crisis Group report of 2002 confirmed much of the intelligence information on JI, noting in particular that the organization is structured around three distinct tiers.[11] The first of these tiers includes Ba'asyir, Muklas, and other key strategists such as Noordin Mohammed Top and Azahari Husin who were key figures in the second bombings of 2005. These strategists are mostly Indonesian nationals who now reside primarily in Malaysia. Beneath this loosely organized leadership, a second tier of trusted foot soldiers is responsible for managing operations, delivering money, and co-opting local operatives. The third group of operatives and suicide bombers is usually comprised of young men from the local *pesantren*; clearly, they are the ones most at risk of arrest, injury, and death in the operations. These operatives are usually devout, young men who have a psychological predisposition to obedience and fidelity to the Imam and the faith. While not exclusively the case with Islamic suicide bombers, this level of the JI hierarchy is usually drawn from poor, rural areas. Their knowledge of the world, prospects, and education are forged by the JI Imam and the *pesantren*.[12]

ABU BAKAR BA'ASYIR AND "CREEPING ISLAM"

Few Indonesians approve of the violence being perpetrated by sectarian and radical Islamists. However, there is a remarkable public interest in, and sympathy for, many of the ideas and social programs offered by Islamist Imams such as Abu Bakar Ba'asyir. Indeed, while Ba'asyir is seen as a demonic figure in Australia and other Western nations, he has achieved a reverential, almost heroic, status among many Indonesians. Ba'asyir's now formidable propaganda machinery has successfully presented the aging cleric as avuncular and caring, a religious figure who rails against the excesses of Western materialism and exploitative economic practices. For many Indonesians, still suffering from the effects of the 1997 financial crisis and the thievery and oppression of Suharto's military dictatorship, Ba'asyir's message offers some genuine alternative to the ongoing conditions of penury and civil disorder.

While in the 1980s Ba'asyir was a largely inconsequential leader of a marginal religious sect, he has now become mainstreamed through the clarity, simplicity, and consistency of a vision. In the wake of disasters like the Aceh tsunami (2004) and the Jogjakarta earthquake (2006), the Islamists provided genuine and ongoing community care and support. Long after the international aid workers had retreated, Jemaah Islamyiah and other groups governed by people like Ba'asyir remained, offering family support, health care, and welfare to the victims. This work was not paraded by the expensive vehicles and weekend parties that are often associated with international aid workers, but was conducted through the community, side-by-side with the victims and their families. In many respects the Islamist model contrasts significantly with other NGOs and political organizations which remove themselves from ordinary people in order to exercise their power and privilege as a form of social preeminence.

In this sense, Bakar Ba'asyir and Jemaah Islamiyah represent a genuine spiritual and political alternative to a corrupt and indifferent government apparatus, and a Western cultural ideology which promises much but delivers very little to the majority of Indonesians. The increasing notoriety and popularity of Ba'asyir—which clearly contributed to the pardon in 2006— is a form of "Islam by stealth." It is rising through the community and ingratiating itself through good work and the vision of a better future. In the current context, Ba'asyir has assumed a benign and somewhat avuncular demeanor for many Indonesians, who simply reject his association with *jihadist* atrocities as another dimension of Western propaganda and hegemony. Ba'asyir remains a significant spiritual and symbolic figure in the JI's own propaganda war. In an important sermon delivered in late 2007, Ba'asyir exhorted young Muslims to assault Western tourists, describing them as "worms, snakes, and maggots" who defile the Muslim lands by showing their skin on the beaches of Bali. In the same sermon Ba'asyir extolled the moral virtues of martyrs and suicide bombers, and warned that there would be vengeance if the Bali bombers were executed.[13]

While there are broad speculations about the primary motivation of Jemaah Islamiyah, it is clear from evidence presented at various trials that the members' motives include political, social, and religious interests. A deep faith in Muslim values and the strict interpretation of holy law is often combined with a strong sense of social justice and desire to overthrow oppressive political powers. The operatives have adopted the ideology of anti-Americanism which is frequently articulated as anti-Christendom and pro-Islamicism. The massacres of Muslims by Christians in Maluku, North Maluku, and Poso had been used as a primary motivation for many of the attacks on Christians in Indonesia.[14] The recruitment and training of general operatives has also incorporated discussions and videos about the Maluku and Poso killings, pointing directly to the violence that Christians have perpetrated against local Muslims. These events also inspired the activities of the larger but less well-trained jihadist organization, Laksar Jihad. The Maluku civil conflicts were clearly escalated through the participation of various Islamic militant groups, including JI. These conflicts, in fact, served a similar purpose for the younger militants in JI, as Afghanistan had for the older leaders: it provided valuable in-the-field training in ballistics, strategy, and guerrilla warfare, as well as motivation and propaganda for recruits from the *pesantren*.

The al-Qa'ida attacks on New York in 2001 provided a stimulus for rethinking both the focus of the JI violence and the means by which it might achieve its objective of establishing a *shari'ah* state in Indonesia. It is certainly clear that at the time of the attacks al-Qa'ida was itself in a state of attrition, even disarray. Financially strained and alienated from many parts of the Islamic world, al-Qa'ida placed enormous hope in the "big job"; failure would almost certainly have threatened the survival of the network and its notional leader, Osama bin Laden.[15] As we have noted, modern terrorism is fundamentally a communicational event, and the atrocity of the 9/11 attacks ensured that the militants' message was heard across the global media networks. The Jemaah Islamiyah leadership, while somewhat divided about timing, became convinced that the al-Qa'ida strategy of striking directly at international targets should be adopted in their own region. The testimony of a number of the Bali bombers has confirmed that the new strategy of striking international "soft" targets would achieve better outcomes than simply focusing on Indonesian Christians. According to Amrozi and other Bali bombers, the attack on international targets was adopted in order to more effectively achieve the three key Jemaah Islamiyah key objectives—to avenge Western attacks on Muslims, to generate fear in the Western enemy, and to destabilize the secular Indonesian government. It was generally believed that an attack based on the 9/11 model would be highly effective for the recruitment of new operatives and martyrs willing to surrender their lives for the glory of Allah. To this end, the tyranny of America and Australia became the key focus of video training in the *pesantren* after 9/11.[16]

RESTORING BALI'S *RWA BHINEDA*

While there are more than 200 Jemaah Islamiyah operatives either in custody or dead, Jemaah Islamiyah remains brutally focused and dangerous. Recent interrogations have revealed that JI has a greater depth and a larger membership than had previously been recognized. The links with al-Qa'ida have been substantiated, although it is also clear that the cellular structure of JI enables considerable local autonomy and capacity for independent decision making. While it appears to be undergoing internal reorganization, JI links in Australia, the Philippines, Singapore, and Southern Thailand mean that it is still the most threatening and widespread terrorist organization in South East Asia.[17] The deployment of pedestrian bombers in the 2005 attacks in Bali also illustrate that the group can adapt to changing circumstances and has a broadening repertoire of strategies and targets. And while funding is a continual challenge, Jemaah Islamiyah is generally well supported, making further attacks a distinct possibility, especially in Jakarta and Bali.

The strategic and symbolic value of these targets is manifest within the social and economic framework of Indonesia itself. As the second highest income earner after oil, tourism has been a critical industry for Indonesia generally and for Bali, in particular. As we have noted, the tourism boom since the 1980s had significantly improved Bali's economic situation. Before the bombings in 2002, poverty rates in Bali were less than 4 percent, considerably less than Indonesia's national average of 16 percent. With over a million foreign tourist arrivals per year, development in Bali has occurred rapidly and in an uncontrolled manner, resulting in vastly inequitable distribution of wealth. The JI strategists believed that an attack in Bali would destabilize the Indonesian government along with its political and administrative institutions. As table 5.2 indicates, the immediate downturn in visitor numbers and serious economic impact of both attacks might seem to have vindicated the strategy.

Clearly, the attacks in 2002 and 2005 produced both an immediate decline in aggregate tourism numbers as well as a noticeable interruption to the rates of development and growth. More broadly, the figures disguise the cultural and social impact of the attacks, including significant changes in

Table 5.2.   Foreign Tourist Arrivals to Bali, 2002–2007

2002	*2003*	*2004*	*2005*	*2006*	*2007*
1,286,000	993,000	1,458,000	1,386,000	1,260,000	1,664,000

Source: Bali Provincial Government 2008, *Statistik Pariwisata*: "Direct Foreign Tourist Arrivals to Bali by Month," www.baliprov.go.id/informasi/stat_par/index.php?op=stat_2 (accessed 20 May 2008).

the nationality, demographics, and character of the tourist population. Since the first attacks, in particular, the Indonesian government and Bali Tourism Authority have sought to increase the numbers of domestic tourists as a way of compensating for the retreat of Western tourists who may have been frightened off the island. Along with the continuing acceleration of Japanese tourists and a very noticeable increase in Chinese, Taiwanese, and Korean visitors, the Javanese represent a marked change in the ethnic character of Balinese tourism (see table 5.3). The southern end of Kuta beach, in particular, has been transformed from a scantily dressed Anglo-idyll to a more conservative (though no less playful) and covered-up domain in which the Muslim headdress is common. Even more telling, perhaps, is the reinvigoration of the resort areas through the increased presence of Asian tourists. While many of these tourists avoid the cheaper and somewhat scruffy beach zones of Kuta and Legian, as we noted in chapter 2, these resort tourists tend to huddle and spend their money in the comfortable terrain of the hotel shopping malls and restaurants, rarely venturing beyond the gates to deliver income to the Balinese themselves.

In fact, the impact of the bombings in Bali itself reached well beyond the measurable slump in tourism numbers.[18] Specifically, Bali has experienced an economic, social, and spiritual crisis which both broadens and exposes the underlying crisis of modernization that we have been examining throughout this book. Most obviously, the downturns affected employment and family incomes across Bali, as well as nearby Lombok and the farming communities of East Java which supply raw materials, craft products, vegetables, and other foodstuffs to supply the demand from Bali. In their 2003 report, the United Nations Development Fund reported that in the year following the bombings, over 30,000 Balinese lost tourism-related jobs and there were dramatic increases in levels of bankruptcy, underemployment,

Table 5.3. Foreign Tourist Arrivals by Nationality, 2006–2007

Market	Rank	2006	Share (%)	2007	Rank
Japan	I	255,767	20.29	351,604	I
Australia	III	132,236	10.49	204,421	II
Taiwan	II	141,979	11.27	138,842	III
South Korea	IV	89,911	7.13	134,454	IV
Malaysia	V	72,724	5.77	104,949	V
PR China	X	40,687	3.23	84,254	VI
United Kingdom	VI	62,772	4.98	70,841	VII
Germany	VII	62,568	4.96	68,135	VIII
France	VIII	50,858	4.04	61,805	IX
United States	IX	47,071	3.73	56,208	X

Source: Bali Provincial Government, *Statistik Pariwisata*, "Direct Foreign Tourist Arrivals to Bali by Nationality" (2008), www.baliprov.go.id/informasi/stat_par/ (accessed 20 May 2008).

poverty and hardship, school dropouts, and various forms of social dislocation. As we discussed in the previous chapter, many younger Balinese, along with transmigrants from elsewhere in Indonesia, were stripped of their livelihoods in Bali. While many of these people simply returned to their villages, others survived through their involvement in petty crime, the sex industry, or begging. Many rural village families had already sold their farms to raise funds for the education of their children or provide capital for small businesses. They had been dependent on remittances provided by these young people. With neither productive land nor cash flow, these families were profoundly affected by the bombings.

In the months following the 2002 bombings, a range of recovery plans were formulated by various levels of government, aid agencies, and the business community. Financial support for the recovery was pledged by the Indonesian central government, international aid donors (such as UNDP, USAID, AUSAID), and transnational financial corporations such as the World Bank. The UNDP/World Bank report, Bali: Beyond the Tragedy (2003) recommended a tourism-led recovery supported by heightened security, strengthened social safety nets, and a range of small development initiatives to diversify Bali's economic base and strengthen its ability to cope with fluctuations in the tourist economy. The report stated that tourism, while remaining a cornerstone of the economy, should be supplemented by a more vigorous social and commercial environment. The report was clearly situated within the broad ideological framework of a globalized and transnational development perspective. The underlying values of the report were fixed within the ideology of a modernization that privileges global market capitalism and development. In accordance with the Indonesian government's own economic objectives, the UNDP report views culture in much the same way as the Dutch colonialists and the Suharto plutocrats: that is, culture and cultural preservation are largely constituted around marketability and the commercial value of commodities.

Not surprisingly, therefore, the recovery process that has been sponsored by the Indonesian government, international relief agencies, and development financiers has been largely focused around a "business-as-usual" model. The Indonesian government, in particular, invested considerable sums of money into an international tourism promotion campaign. Seeking to stimulate domestic and international tourism markets, the government and the Bali Tourism Authority constructed the campaign around the highly predictable motif of "Bali Harmony–Bali Peace–Bali Paradise." Within this motif, the Bali idyll, which had been so successfully marketed during the 1980s and 1990s, was again mobilized, albeit with a softer and more tranquil tone designed to reassure visitors that Bali was once more a safe and comfortable destination and that the terrorist attacks were merely an historical aberration. To this end, the graphic media imagery of burning bodies, death, and profound grief was rearticulated in the Bali Bombings monument—a stable and durable relic that had been absorbed and marketed as a site for pilgrim-tourists to stand before and photograph in a state of respectful and reverential awe.[19] In the six months prior to the second bombings in October 2005, it appeared that the promotion campaign had worked its magic—at least in terms of the restoration of tourism numbers. According to the Bali Tourism Authority, the 2005 peak tourist season (just prior to the bombings) was the most successful on record.[20] Similar tactics were employed after the 2005 attacks, and as the figures in table 5.2 indicate, 2007 represented the highest ever number of international tourist arrivals in Bali.

However, behind the smiling faces of the Balinese, the trauma of the bombings remains unresolved. Immediately following the first bombings, many Hindu Balinese had invoked the spirit world and customary rituals in order to both understand and cleanse the horror of this outbreak of evil. While some of these ceremonies were clearly generated by the Tourism Authority as part of their global public relations and marketing campaigns, others were more substantially motivated by a desire to engage with the historical moment of this crisis. In particular, there was a sense among many of the more devout Hindu Balinese that the terrorist attack represented a much broader release of evil and that somehow the *bhuta kala* and other demon beings had disturbed the cosmological balance and natural order of things. While it needs to be said that the *bhuta kala* are not considered entirely evil, and their antithetical gods not entirely good, there was nevertheless a sense in which a contagion of evil had been spreading across the island and that the terrorist attacks were simply the most recent and dramatic manifestation of this condition.[21]

For the Hindu Balinese, this contagion is largely expressed as "imbalance," where the infinite dialectic of good and evil (*rwa bhineda*) is disrupted, creating terrible consequences for both the living and the dead. Good and evil are neither entirely distinguishable nor independent; rather, the two cosmological forces are interdependent conditions which must be managed through complex rituals and forms of human-social management. While the cultural and environmental degradation associated with rapid tourism development has been endured by the Balinese for several decades, it has always been accompanied by a profound anxiety about ultimate cosmological consequences. The bombings, therefore, were a clear sign that the *rwa bhineda* (two-in-one principle) had succumbed to a long period of human mismanagement and offense to the divine. In an effort to restore the social and cosmic balance articulated through the *rwa bhineda* the Balinese adapted a range of rituals to include interfaith ceremonies involving Westerners and non-Hindu Balinese. In the changed state of their cultural and spiritual environment, many Balinese created hybrid (modern) forms of ritual cleansing that were designed to give voice and sincerity to the Bali harmony ideal. These included ceremonies, rock concerts, international surfing competitions, and smaller, local initiatives.

In many respects, the Balinese were bewildered by "the tragedy," as they euphemistically called the 2002 bombing. But the recourse to a divine aesthetics was not simply a retreat from the hard reality of global geopolitics; nor was it entirely a retreat from Bali's own complex and often violent relationship with Muslim-dominated Java and the national government. Rather, the drawing together of traditional ritual and new, globally constituted cultural elements was part of the island's own broadly evolving cultural politics. The convocation of traditional and modern cultural forms was a clear response to, and expression of, Bali's integration with the global economy and correlative engagement with the transnational terror and current modes of political violence. The rituals, in this sense, were profoundly political, representing an ideal of civil society, harmony, and social reform which is, again, a central feature of the Romantic dimensions of modern political ideologies. It was a statement of a pluralistic ideal, a utopianism, which seeks to transcend the destructive and negative conditions of the island's own history. It was, in essence, a forceful expression of a politically constituted cultural identity.

To this end, the ritual cleansings following the 2002 bombings—which were also repeated after the 2005 attacks—were a "natural" response to the disaster.[22] Many Balinese believed that the tourists—especially Australians and Americans—were the real focus of the attacks. But they also understood that the Balinese themselves were collateral to those targets. The atrophy of tourism and the economic declines which accompanied both attacks were part of the corollary of their association with tourism and its "guilty pleasures." Indeed, many Balinese saw the attacks and the economic disruption as a punishment for the mistreatment of the island, their culture, and its beauty. It is precisely this psychological and spiritual dimension of the crisis which was still exposed, even as the tourists returned in 2005. I Made Mangku Pastika, in his role as chief of police in Bali, predicted the second bombings, not merely because JI were still rampant and merely waiting for their international targets to return, but also because Bali itself had not recovered its sense of value and cultural dignity. According to Pastika, who was elected governor of Bali in July 2008, it was the weaknesses within the culture that rendered Bali vulnerable to the calumny of this other evil.

ETHNIC TENSION AND THE FALSIFICATION OF BALI HARMONY

Various formal and informal commentaries on the recovery process in Bali have praised local communities for their restraint and good management of the crisis, arguing that these virtues are largely examples of the Balinese people's very particular social and moral character. In their report on the 2002 attacks, the United Nations Development Fund praised Hindu Balinese, in particular, for avoiding a "widely expected" outbreak of sectarian and religious violence.[23] According to the UNDP, this was largely attributed to the religious and community leaders in Bali who were proactive in directing the emotions of their people toward a more positive and enlightened response. As a result, there were very few reported attacks against Muslims despite an obviously troubled history and the deep hatred expressed by the militants for the Balinese themselves. For many outside observers this restraint was a measure of the Balinese people's own intrinsic capacity to create harmony through the essence and purity of their culture and belief system. The Balinese recognized that the attacks were perpetrated by extremists who did not represent *all* Muslim people. According to a number of scholars and commentators, harmony has been quickly restored through interfaith dialog and the supreme charity that is intrinsic to Balinese spiritualism.

This assessment of the post-bombings periods, however, seriously misreads the complex mood of the Balinese and the ongoing conditions of crisis. Antagonism toward Muslim Javanese (and vice versa) is a smoldering and often unacknowledged cultural constant across the archipelago. While this antagonism to Javanese hegemony is dramatically evident in Aceh, East Timor, and West Papua, there have been strong secessionist movements and moods in various parts of the archipelago, including Bali. Although it can't be claimed that Balinese secessionism is either mainstream or a majority aspiration, it nevertheless exists as a feasible option in Balinese political thinking. The violent absorption of Bali's distinctive religious and cultural heritage into the Dutch colonial aegis (completed 1908) continues to provide secessionists with a grounding for the construction of a contemporary political identity. Indeed, antagonism toward the Javanese has its own historical codings and density. From the early days of modern tourism, the Balinese established a myth that they were essentially honest and decent, while the Javanese were treacherous, dishonest, and malingering; according to the Balinese, it was always and exclusively the *orang Jawa* who committed crime and spoiled the moral integrity and cultural beauty of the island. From the 1970s, violent and summary punishments—including executions— have been imposed on non-Balinese caught stealing or merely found in the vicinity of a crime. With the blame being placed on Javanese, tourists were conditioned into thinking that any problems on the island were almost exclusively the fault of the *orang Jawa*. Even today, senior Balinese officials will speak from the corner of their mouths as they blame the Javanese for any number of social or community problems—drugs, prostitution, major crime, official corruption, the price of fuel are all the fault of the Javanese. Balinese concerns about outsiders were intensified during the economic slump after the 2002 and 2005 bombings and incidences of brutality and murder inflicted by civilian vigilante groups on outsiders, including children, have been documented in recent reports.[24]

There is an undercurrent of tension and distrust between the Balinese and non-Balinese, especially the Javanese. From their respective positions—the Javanese are treacherous; the Balinese are lazy, stupid, and inflated with their own privilege. As outlined in chapter 4, these subterranean and ongoing tensions are necessarily linked to a modernization which has been largely imposed and driven by Javanese interests and military force. The massacres of 1965/1966, which paralleled the arrival of modern, mass tourism, announced in the most brutal terms to the Balinese that their independence and independent will were fundamentally subordinate to the interests of the Indonesian state. Like the people of Aceh, the Balinese were suddenly awakened to the raw facts of their integration with Indonesia; the nationalist revolution, which bore itself through the great and progressive ideals of liberty and equality, revealed its other self as the ogre of tyranny and state power. This, of course, was the shock Europe had already experienced in its own incandescent modernization: Increased interaction between variable social, ethnic, and religious groups created an imperative toward larger and more complex social formations, most notably the nation-state and empire; this imperative, however, created the conditions for greater security and insecurity as it created a volatile mix of populations, resource competition, and territorialism.

Modernization, in this sense, has a multiple trajectory in which the state, communities, and individuals are drawn together in a dangerous and often unstable political nexus. The profound insecurities being generated by *Jemaah Islamiyah* and other Islamic militant groups are, in many respects, a manifestation of this complex interaction of the state and its constituent elements. As we noted in our discussion of the 1965/1966 political genocide in Indonesia (chapter 1), the greatest shock for the Balinese was the alliance that had been forged between their own elite social groups and Suharto's authoritarian militarists. The treachery of the Java-based state had entirely inverted the social bonds that had maintained the sense of Balinese culture and society. The resonance of this treachery, in fact, continues to compromise the potential for trust, even into the present. Relations between the Balinese and Muslim outsiders remains fraught, trapped in historical amplitudes which threaten at any moment to disrupt the imposed and inescapable continuities of nation and state. The breakout of ethnic-sectarian violence around the 1999 presidential elections and the attacks in 1999 on Muslim street traders at Kuta beach are indications of this simmering hostility.

To this end, many Balinese continue to be suspicious of Javanese politicism and state power. As we noted in the previous chapter, they regard the judiciary and police as the corrupt arm of a dubious, Java-based political system. Even in the recent presidential elections, the majority of Hindu Balinese continued to vote for Megawati (despite her dubious competence) because of her familial links with Bali. Of course there are friendships between Hindu and Muslim Balinese, but these tend to be constituted as modes of tolerance rather than substantive communal bonds. According to Wayan, a female market stall worker in Kuta, her Javanese boss is "ok" but— "I just keep it inside. Because I don't want to talk too much. If talking too much there will be problem for me. Just quiet. Better no talking, ya? In Bali it's OK. They're OK here."[25]

The Muslim communities in West Bali and in the east on the island of Nusa Penida do promote an ideal of tolerance and dialog with their Hindu neighbors. But the attitudes on both sides remain largely concessional, reflecting a generally convivial but distinctively distanced communal relationship that is clearly being strained by international political events. Indeed, many local Muslims have experienced considerable duress and anxiety over the bombing attacks, recognizing that, despite the range of interfaith initiatives to prevent reprisals and community tension, relations with the Hindu Balinese have considerably cooled.[26]

Hindu-Muslim Community Tensions

In 2006, our own research in Medewi, a mixed Hindu-Muslim village in West Bali, exposed deep anxieties about the state of interreligious relations in the community. While there is little direct conflict and considerable mutual support between religious groups in the *desa*, each group maintains its respective rituals and territory through very careful communal management strategies. Muslims and Hindus attend each others' weddings, funerals, and significant events, providing mutual support and security for their respective religious ceremonies. Structures are in place to facilitate dialog between the elders of both communities in order to minimize conflict. When tensions arise, particularly between youth, they are quickly settled. The head of the village (*kepala desa*), who is Muslim, will call the leaders of the Hindu *banjar* to a "small meeting" to discuss the problematic issues and plan immediate action to resolve tensions. Nonetheless, both sides report that the potential for conflict is always present and that this has been exacerbated by the economic tensions since the bombings. According to one *kepala desa*:

> You can feel the difference. It's hard, but we notice it. They don't do things directly, but it's more a general thing. . . . But fighting is normal. Sometimes we just talk, we explain and they understand. We'll all say OK, we're sorry. . . . We live together. We have separate parts of the village but we work together for the

village. Whether we are Hindu or Muslim, we are all Balinese. We look after each other.[27]

One Muslim community worker, associated with a well-respected Balinese NGO providing trauma counseling after the 2002 bombings, told us that as soon as he heard of the 2005 attacks he went immediately to his office and barricaded the door for fear of reprisal—even from his Balinese friends and colleagues. In many respects, this was not a surprising response as there were a range of incidents reported after the 2002 attacks around Kuta and Denpasar. While most of this was sporadic and perpetrated by youth gangs, somewhat more systematic violence was also carried out by the community officials or *pecalang*. As outlined in chapter 4, the *pecalang* has evolved a new community role in the *Reformasi* period, merging the protection of religious rites and duties with the protection of secular interests and property. According to the International Crisis Group, the Kuta *pecalang* was largely responsible for the violence perpetrated against Muslim street traders in 1999, and various *pecalang* in the Badung district became active in security, surveillance, and vigilante-style community policing after the 2002 bombing.[28] Through these various activities, the *pecalang* have become feared by many non-Balinese transmigrants working in Bali. Young Muslims, in particular, report that they have been beaten by the *pecalang* if they cannot produce their migrant identity card (KIPP) and residency permit. A number of our interview respondents described simmering tensions and outbreaks of gang fights with Balinese youth who have become increasingly territorial and violent in the midst of the economic downturn:

> Ya, the Javanese are afraid of the Balinese guys. At night, you know, at first they're OK and then they have some drinking and it's like, "You're fucked. You bombed us." And then there's some fighting.[29]

These acts of violence, however, have caused considerable consternation within the Balinese community itself. Many Balinese remember the violence of 1999, which caused an immediate reduction in tourist arrivals and calls for the *pecalang* to restrain their behavior for the good of the economy. In this light, the much-applauded restraint of the Balinese following the bombings is as much a matter of sound commercial strategy, as it is a reflection of elevated sensibility. Bali's restrained response to the Islamic militant attacks reflects a pragmatism that has been learned over several decades of oppression and externally controlled economic development.

In many respects, as we noted in chapter 4, the Balinese are still coming to grips with the end of the Suharto period and the transitions to civil society that are taking place in a very uneven manner. The continuation of inept and illicit practices in the law enforcement and judicial agencies fortify

Balinese suspicions that Java and the Javanese political hegemony are fundamentally incapable of decent modes of governance. After the second round of bombings in 2005, thousands of Balinese protestors gathered around Krobokan Prison and demanded the immediate execution of the convicted 2002 bombers—Muklas, Sumadra, and Amrozi. "Gede," who played a leading role in calming the mob violence at the protest, is a secessionist and member of the local *pecalang*. While claiming that the protests were not associated with his broader political and community position, Gede insisted nevertheless that Bali's problems could be attributed directly to outsiders and the Java-based national government. Echoing the concerns of many Balinese, Gede explained that the Hindu rituals and culture of Bali were distinct and were the primary attraction for international tourists. Bali, he argued, would be better off if the island was independent:

> We can control the border points for outsiders who come. Then it would be easy to detect terrorists. It would be better if there were no Muslims—the only people in Bali were Hindu Balinese and foreign tourists.[30]

GOVERNMENT AND SECURITY IN BALI

While there is a strong mood of self-censorship in Bali, it has become increasingly clear that the current conditions of insecurity are linked to the complex processes of modernization. The resonance of historical tensions between Bali and Java has woven itself into a tapestry of cultural and political anxieties. Clearly, Bali's integration into the Western-dominated global economy, manifest in the large numbers of Australian and American tourists, has caused particular offense to the Islamic militants who attacked the island. But these assaults may also be viewed as another iteration of ongoing tensions between the two territories. As we have argued above, they are part of the amplitude of progress and modernization—the contiguity of reforming peoples, politics, and cultures. This crisis of insecurity represents a volatile compound of historical and contemporary elements.

Paradoxically, the demise of the Suharto regime and the liberation of expressive political spaces have contributed to this increased instability. Thus, while Islamic radicalism appears to have festered within the oppressive conditions of Suharto's prohibitive regime, the *Reformasi* has provided opportunities for its more explicit expression. As we have noted, the liberation of these expressive modes has been generated through parliamentary processes, civil society, community engagement, and political violence. In this sense, it is wrong to assume that a terrorist organization like Jemaah Islamiyah is one-dimensional, or has no presence in civil and community life. In fact, "Jemaah" literally means "community," and like many other Islamic militant organizations such as the Muslim Brotherhood (Egypt), Hezbollah (Lebanon), and Hamas (Palestine), JI is very active in education, welfare, and community affairs. The very concept of Jemaah Islamiyah is confusing for many Indonesians who regard it as a loosely formed ideal in which good community work is conducted in the name of the faith. This integration with the community is a critical part of the JI political ideal, demonstrating the complex and often diffuse nature of legitimate and illegitimate political expression in a modernizing social environment. It is for this reason that Jemaah Islamiyah has not been officially banned by the Indonesian government—even its identification by an Indonesian court in 2008 as a terrorist organization remains somewhat ambiguous, not the least because Indonesia does not have a common law system.[31]

As we also noted in the previous chapter, groups like Jemaah Islamiyah and the Defenders of Islam Front have moved into the security spaces vacated by the military; in the new civil society these organizations emerge from the complex matrix of Indonesian community life; they commit their atrocities and then retreat back into the fabric of everyday communal life. For citizens and governments that have been targeted by *jihadists*, this impression of a relatively benign community-based resistance force seriously perverts the reality of their crimes, as well as the critical deficiencies in Indonesia's security policy, policing structures, and general standards of governance. The U.S. and Australian governments were extremely critical of the Wahid and Megawati presidencies for failing to control the spread of terrorist organizations in their country.[32] The U.S. government, in particular, is leveraging its financial, aid, and diplomatic powers to ensure that President Yudhoyono fulfils his international obligations and cracks down on Jemaah Islamiyah and other terrorist organizations.

However, neither the Australian nor U.S. governments is prepared to concede that its own foreign policies over several decades have clearly contributed to the conditions which have stimulated Islamic extremism in Indonesia. In the first instance, their support for Suharto and a willingness to overlook human rights abuses, genocide, and profound corruption have clearly contributed to a social environment which fosters political extremism and violence. At the time of the 1965/1966 mass killings, the Australian government went as far as to congratulate Suharto on his tough stand against communists. In the second instance, the U.S. and Australian governments supported the mujahidin in the Afghan-Soviet War, a war which provided the training, relationships network, and ideological grounding for many high-profile terrorists in al-Qa'ida and Jemaah Islamiyah. Combined with the U.S.-led invasion of Iraq, the Afghan-Soviet War has proved the most powerful catalyst for the radicalization of Muslims in Indonesia.

In the post-Suharto period, many of these grievances were finally released. And of course, in the *Reformasi* context an abundance of conspiracy theories have emerged which seek to connect the military (TNI) and others in the Jakarta elite with various forms of political agitation, terrorism, and insecurity. As we noted in the previous chapter, for example, the former Vice President Hamzah Haz provided considerable public support to convicted Bali bombing conspirator, Abu Bakar Ba'asyir. There are also clear links between the military and the now disbanded Laksar Jihad, most particularly in the sectarian violence in Muluku and Central Sulewesi. Some of these theories suggest that the TNI has actually provoked sectarian violence in order to stimulate a social instability which only they can quell. In this view, the military wants to be able to justify a return to military rule in Indonesia, either through parliamentary or revolutionary means. The International Crisis Group have raised questions about direct military participation in the Jemaah Islamiyah Christmas Eve bomb attacks in 2000 (especially in Medan), and other attacks on the Malaysian Embassy and Indonesian Stock Exchange in Jakarta.

Whether these accusations are true or not, it is very clear that many Balinese believe that the military and other social elites are somehow implicated in the bombing attacks of 2002 and 2005. And while there is little hard evidence to support this claim, the belief itself indicates a very powerful degree of distrust among the Balinese toward the military and the Java-based government itself. In this context, the military continues to hold a very strong and privileged position in post-Suharto Indonesia. As much as anything else, this was evident in the 2001 impeachment of President Wahid which, despite official explanations outlining multiple concerns about his capacity to govern, was considered by many commentators to be the result of his demilitarization initiatives. Indeed, even within its own ranks, the military is a polyglot of competing political and financial interests, the force of which is constantly demonstrated to the elected government and the Indonesian people at large. These competing fiscal and ideological interests have clearly contributed both to the insubordination of the military leadership and the astonishing autonomy that is often attributed to the TNI. Even in the post-Suharto period, the massacres and human rights abuses in East Timor, West Papua, and Aceh might be more clearly attributable to an autonomous regional military leadership than to the government which is supposedly its master. The notion of a national security agency dedicated to the eradication of civil violence seems somewhat pallid in light of these horrors.

To this extent, there is a clear link between the failings of Indonesia's civil processes and the insecurities being generated by Islamic militancy. In conditions where rule of law is a fantasy of the political minority, insecurity flourishes. Even within the penal system, Abu Bakar Ba'asyir was able to continue his campaigns of hate and social violence. Prior to his release and pardon in 2007, Ba'asyir had continual access to the media and his supporters, presenting himself as a victim of Western oppression and the Indonesian government's supine obedience to U.S. political hegemony. Similarly, through a peculiar confluence of religious sympathy, celebrity culture, and penal mismanagement, the three condemned bombers—Muklas, Samudra, and Amrozi—were able to conduct regular press conferences up until the final days before their execution. Even more disturbing, however, was a 2006 International Crisis Group report which claimed that convicted Bali bomber, Imam Samudra, was in constant contact with other Jemaah Islamiyah operatives, including Noordin Mohammed Top, the mastermind of the second attacks in 2005. This report was later confirmed by senior prison wardens who found Samudra with a laptop computer which he was using to make satellite connections with the JI leadership. Having been inside Krobokan Prison, we know that it is entirely implausible that the prison guards were not aware of this communication; it is far more likely that they were receiving significant payments for the privilege.

JEMAAH ISLAMIYAH, NARCO-TERRORISM, AND
FUTURE THREATS TO BALI

In May 2007 the International Crisis Group released an update on the state of Jemaah Islamiyah and terrorism in Indonesia.[33] Reporting on police raids earlier in that year on JI safe houses in Central and East Java, the ICG argued that Jemaah Islamiyah may be undergoing a significant reorganization of its internal structure and military strategy. Evidence gathered from arrests, seized documents, and arms caches suggests that JI is switching focus, as it tries to recover from the elimination of key leaders and strategic operatives such as Mohammed Top and Azahari Husin—key figures in the 2005 bombings. In fact, the cumulative effect of the bombing campaigns has exposed Jemaah Islamiyah to considerable organizational, ethical, and financial stress. In particular, many militant and nonmilitant Islamicists were angered by the collateral killing of Muslims in the Bali Marriot Hotel and Australian Embassy bombings. Even in the villages and urban neighborhoods of Central and East Java, where Jemaah Islamiyah has enjoyed considerable sympathy for its cause, if not its tactics, the incidental killing of Muslims has created considerable consternation. This weakening of support has placed further strain on an organization that depends heavily on community favor for funding, personnel, and as a shield from police investigations.

As the ICG report demonstrates, the sheer costs of a major bombing attack demands a secure funding line within a broadly based organizational network. While remaining potent in Indonesia, Jemaah Islamiyah's funding has been truncated in various ways, particularly through threats to its external supports like al-Qa'ida and the House of Saud. It is therefore cheaper and more convenient for the organization to commit relatively simple and lower-level attacks on individuals rather than on more complex and larger targets. The attack on the Australian Embassy, for example, cost around USD$8,000, while the assassination of the head of the Central Sulawesi Protestant Church only cost around USD$25. As the ICG report notes, the change in focus toward a more military and precisely targeted mode of violence is more financial and pragmatic, rather than ideological or ethical. Jemaah Islamiyah remains committed to military and religious training, but its violence is being constrained by circumstances.

Because of the complexity of Indonesian society and culture, and the chameleon capacities of *jihadist* organizations like Jemaah Islamiyah, the ICG report recommends the development of flexible counterterrorism strategies. The use of former JI members to advocate against terrorism and speak openly with the media and young Islamic radicals is clearly an attempt by the Indonesian security agencies to neutralize the appeal of terrorism in this way. Specifically, Ali Imron, who drove the explosives van to the Sari Club in the 2002 Bali bombings, has been recruited by the Indonesian counterterrorism forces to challenge the extremist Islamic beliefs which inspire and underpin *jihadist* attacks. In many respects, too, the agencies have employed Imron and his "return to true faith" in order to counter the culture of apocalypse and "martyrdom" that was advocated by the condemned Bali bombers—Amrozi, Samudra, and Muklas. While the three executed bombers claimed their martyrdom as the privilege of serving Allah, Ali Imron continues to present a more sanguine view of the *jihadists*, describing their attacks in Bali as deluded, irreligious, and inhumane.[34]

Apocalypse and Ecstasy in Bali: The Executions and Beyond

Many Balinese and other Indonesians welcomed the execution of the three bombers—Muklas, Samudra, and Amrozi. Their celebrations, however, were tempered by updated travel warnings in Australia and the United States, which encouraged tourists to defer travel to Indonesia because of the increased risk of terrorist attack. Indeed, many moderate and purist Islamicists regarded the executed bombers as religious warriors and martyrs, who had justifiably fought against the infidels and their moral contamination. The more militant among these groups, of course, howled for vengeance against Westerners and the Indonesian government, calling on their supporters to avenge Allah and His martyrs. And while it is unlikely that Jemaah Islamiyah has the resources to carry out an attack like the 2002 bombings, its various splinter groups are certainly capable of causing considerable harm through assassinations and other forms of politically directed violence. Jemaah Islamiyah itself maintains strong social and community networks which it is using to attract new recruits and rebuild its criminal capacities.

For Westerners, the executions have proven a double bind. In countries like Australia, where the death penalty is prohibited, the desire for retribution had to confront a broader sense of social responsibility, civility, and the rule of law, which are the foundation of a modern, democratic state. While many Australians and Americans were baying for blood, others were more circumspect, recognizing that absolute vengeance would activate the terrorist cause even further, as it compromised the moral authority of their own nations. This was particularly problematic for the Australian government at the time, which was engaged in a delicate diplomatic dialogue over the death sentences of several of its own citizens in Indonesia.

Thus, with a number of Australians facing execution for drug-based crimes in Bali, many Westerners believe that the Indonesian legislature and judiciary are both corrupt and perverse. This is particularly the case for the drug courier group known as the Bali 9 who were arrested in Bali in April 2005. This group of relatively young Australians had been recruited by an international drug trafficking syndicate to courier a quantity of heroin from Bali to Australia. Gravely concerned that their son was at risk of becoming involved in illegal activity, the parents of one of the young recruits contacted the Australian Federal Police. Commissioner Mick Keelty, the highest official of the AFP, informed his Indonesian counterparts who waited until the couriers were in possession of the drugs and then arrested them at a Kuta hotel and at Bali's Ngurah Rai airport.

Clearly, Keelty's decision exposed the young couriers to processing by the Indonesian law enforcement agencies and the judiciary. By having them arrested in Indonesia, rather than waiting until their arrival in Australia, Keelty and his officers knowingly exposed the young Australians to the death penalty. Circuitously, this decision was largely forged around the issues of terrorism and regional security: Keelty appears to have believed that the arrest would enhance trust and collaboration between the Indonesian and Australian police, creating a better working partnership in the war on terror. While several of the Bali 9 have had their capital sentences commuted through appeal, many Australians and other Westerners believe that Indonesia remains soft on Muslim terrorists while it excessively punishes and demonizes Westerners through its hard-line approach to drugs.

This overlap between illicit drugs and terrorism, however, extends well beyond judicial practice. Indeed, the financial imperatives of political violence appear to be leading many global terrorist groups toward a greater involvement in organized crime, particularly drug trafficking. While this sort of activity may seem anathema to the religious principles of Islam, the financial pressures outlined above have prompted organizations like al-Qa'ida and the Taliban to adopt a more pragmatic approach to drug trading.[35] According to

Indonesia's Narcotics Board, the drug trade is not only contaminating the health of an entire generation of young Indonesians, it also provides an important economic infrastructure for criminal and terrorist organizations across the region. Peter Chalk, who has conducted an analysis of "narco-terrorism" in Indonesia, locates this confluence of crime and political violence in the open spaces of the post–Cold War context:

> One specific threat that has assumed greater prominence on South East Asia's broadened security agenda . . . has been transnational organized crime. The increased salience of this particular issue stems, in many ways, from the region's overriding predilection with financial power and influence. Combined with the existence of severe and widespread disparities in economic wealth, situations have increasingly arisen where people have been motivated more by the need to possess dollars and less by considerations of the means used to acquire them. The net result has been the gradual evolution of a parallel underground economy, which is currently being powered by syndicates dealing in everything from humans to drugs, gems, timber and weapons.[36]

In fact, as they have sought to consolidate a stable funding source, many terrorist organizations have simply appended their interests to preexisting criminal practices and networks. Al-Qa'ida and the Taliban have, most notably, engaged in the illicit heroin trade in Afghanistan, exploiting the clandestine trading and communication networks that reach across to Burma and on through South East Asia. Within Indonesia and South East Asia itself, the dealings of *jihadist* organizations in arms and explosives have brought them into contact with the illicit financial and money-laundering network known as the *hawala*. Operating as a traditional and clandestine trading network, the *hawala* deploys a complex system of trust and coded messages to facilitate the bulk transmission and trade of very large sums of illegal finances in a very short period of time. According to Peter Chalk, terrorist organizations are now using the *hawala* to support both their financial and political activities.

This convergence of political and economic violence in Indonesia is seen frequently as a convenient alliance of antigovernment and criminal dispositions, which challenge the authority of the state and its "legitimate" modes of order and social reconstruction. As we have noted in the previous chapter, this alliance is all the more worrying as there is clear evidence that members of the Indonesian political and economic elite are implicated in high-level crime, illicit drug trading, and acts of political violence, including *jihadism*. And while Indonesia's Anti-Corruption Commission is approaching these issues bravely, its evidence and investigations are constantly frustrated by the power of its suspects. As noted above, there are persistent and voluble rumors that the Indonesian Army (TNI) has actually provoked ethnic and religious violence in places like Ambon, creating the conditions of insecurity that only the military can resolve.[37] While the military's involvement in narco-terrorism is proving difficult for the Anti-Corruption Committee to corroborate, our own research has demonstrated very clearly that Indonesians themselves are demonstrably convinced that members of the military and police, through various ranks, are heavily involved in extortion, illegal arms trading, and drug trafficking. Thus, while civil and community groups continue to seek solutions to the double-headed hydra of political insecurity and organized crime, their efforts are continually undermined by the sheer power of their adversaries, including the Indonesian military.

Further Attacks in Bali?

Indonesia is a honeycomb of variable networks and systems. Thus, the overt and publicly enunciated processes of civil and democratic reform are bound in very complex ways to equally formidable but far less visible networks of sedition, violence, and criminal commerce. While Western media and policymakers too often seek to simplify these multiple codings in order to render "Indonesia" comprehensible, it is also clear that the cultural density of the archipelago resists precise formulation and monadic analysis. What is evident, however, is that organizations like Jemaah Islamiyah and its various offshoots will continue to attack Indonesia's fragile civil and economic infrastructure. The organization's current focus on military training and individual assassinations does not preclude more spectacular and percussive attacks in the future. Indeed, there are many in the organization who crave the dramatic media impact of the Bali attacks and the notoriety it delivered to Jemaah Islamiyah. Our own sense is that there will be another *jihadist*-inspired attack in Bali, though the timing and nature of that attack is uncertain. Bali is simply too tempting for the *jihadists* as it represents all that is abhorrent about the West and the global economy of pleasure. Thus, the "Kuta culture," which is replete with drugs, crime, and sexual licentiousness, can no longer protest its innocence.

For the Islamists, Bali is considered a blight in a Muslim land, a festering sore which must be lanced in order to release the poisons that have accumulated in the streets surrounding the Kuta monument. That holy monument: a shrine to the dead tourist visitors and vector of religious ecstasy for the Islamist bombers. For most Hindu Balinese, however, the concrete and gold memorial is another work of cultural grammar, another inscription on the broad trajectory of time. And in this time, good and evil maintain their holy rage. The *bhuta kala* demons scramble through another installment of smoke and blood, converging bodies in hate and desire, the maddening pulse that lays human flesh to waste. Now, of course, the Siren song of the nightclub returns, the young eyes trawling the night-light and shadows.

Beneath the eye and ire of the monument, the victims and the perpetrators scratch their lives together in an indistinguishable rhapsody of hope and despair. The purification rituals and civil processes that should have cleansed these killings have merely protracted and accentuated their absurdity. Like a Greek chorus, the monument gazes back on the street, announcing the convocation of violence and prayer—a history that is fated and degraded as much by global ideology and impulse as by the fantasy of benign or demonic spiritual beings. In this historical condition, the Balinese have encountered themselves walking along the opposing pathways of the same cultural tributary, the same wending and wistful laneway.

Civil society is an emissary of these changes, rather than an end. Like all modernizing social groups, the Balinese are experiencing an intense and profoundly confronting cultural rupture; in order to limit the dangerous excesses that issue from such historical ruptures, however, civil processes and effective governance must be blended through the rich and historically resonant power of the Balinese aesthetic. Customary cultural elements and practices may mutate or even vanish through these transformations, but it is the Balinese themselves who must be granted the dignity of self-actualization. For better or for worse, the Balinese must have a greater say in the privilege and responsibility of determining their own destiny.

NOTES

1. Within Hindu-Balinese cosmology, the *bhuta kala* demons represent the dynamic interplay between good and evil which allows for the possibility of "harmony." To this extent, the demons are not considered intrinsically evil, nor are their spiritual nemeses considered entirely wholesome. Rather, the dialectic of evil and good which characterizes Balinese Vedic culture is formed through an eternal interdependence: evil is not subjugated, redeemed, nor eradicated from the human body or spiritual world more generally since it is the eternal predicate of good. The principle of *rwa bhineda* or "two in one" conceives of good and evil in terms of a mutual identification which seeks merely to minimize the harm that evil may inflict on the living (and the dead). See Jeff Lewis and Belinda Lewis, "Transforming the Bhuta Kala: The Bali Bombings and Indonesian Civil Society," in *Interrogating the War on Terror*, ed. Deborah Staines (Newcastle-on-Tyne, UK: Cambridge Scholars Press, 2007).

2. The attacks in Kuta Square and Jimbaran Bay (a few kilometers south of Kuta) were perpetrated by suicide bombers, who walked into the open restaurants and detonated explosive backpacks. The explosions propelled nails, ball bearings, and other shrapnel intended to maximize the injuries to restaurant patrons and workers. As in the 2002 attacks, the 2005 killings precipitated a radical downturn in tourism arrivals which lasted 18–24 months.

3. This discussion is adapted from Jeff Lewis, *Language Wars: The Role of Media and Culture in Global Terror and Political Violence* (London: Pluto Press, 2005).

4. Samuel Huntington, *The Clash of Civilizations and the Remaking of the World Order* (New York: Touchstone, 1996). For a counterargument, see Tariq Ali, *The Clash of Fundamentalisms* (London: Verso, 2004).

5. The term "Islamicism" refers to the beliefs, ideology, and attitudes of those followers of the Muslim faith who seek to ensure that their religion has a central role in government and law. Islamicism, therefore, represents the political expression of the Muslim faith. In keeping with a general orthodoxy that has appeared in scholarly writing over the past few years, we will use the term "Islamism" to refer more specifically to those radical Islamicists who have adopted militant and violent strategies in order to impose their beliefs and establish an Islamic political state. Thus, while all Islamicists might prefer a system of Islamic law (*Shari'ah*) and mode of governance, Islamists (Islamic militants) use violent methods to achieve this end.

6. See our primary research in Bali. See Belinda Lewis and Jeff Lewis, "After the Glow: Challenges and Opportunities for Community Sustainability in the context of the Bali Bombings," (Paper presented at the First International Sources of Insecurity Conference, Melbourne, Vic. November, 2004), ed. Damien Grenfell (Melbourne: RMIT Publishing, 2004), search.informit.com.au/documentsummary;dn= 876201933383235;res=E-LIBRARY (accessed 15 May 2008).

7. Jeff Lewis, *Language Wars*.

8. For an elaboration of this point see International Crisis Group, "Indonesia Briefing: Why Salafism and Terrorism Mostly Don't Mix," *Asia Report*, no. 83 (Jakarta and Brussels: International Crisis Group, September 2004).

9. Martin van Bruinessen, "Genealogies of Islamic Radicalism in Post-Suharto Indonesia," *South East Asia Research* 10, no. 2 (2002). See also Greg Barton, *Indonesia's Struggle*; Zachary Abuza, *Militant Islam in South East Asia: Crucible of Terror* (New York: Jamestown Foundation, 2003); International Crisis Group, "Indonesia: Jemaah Islamiyah's Current Status," *Asia Briefing*, no. 63 (Jakarta and Brussels: International Crisis Group, March 2007).

10. See Jeff Lewis, *Language Wars*.

11. International Crisis Group, "Indonesian Backgrounder: How the Jemaah Islamiyah Terrorist Network Operates," *Asia Report*, no. 43 (Jakarta and Brussels: International Crisis Group, December 2002).

12. Recent studies on suicide bombers have demonstrated that poverty and low levels of education only partly define the profile of a suicide bomber. Some suicide attackers, such as those who flew the airplanes in the September 11 attacks in America, are very well educated. Others are not. The psychological profile, however, is somewhat more consistent: for whatever social reason, suicide attackers tend to be susceptible to authority and religious-military conditioning. See Scott Antran, "Genesis of Suicide Terrorism," *Science News* (7 March 2003).

13. Natasha Robinson, "Bashir Urges Attacks on Infidel Australians," *The Australian*, 24 March 2008, www.theaustralian.news.com.au/story/0,25197,23421343 -601,00.html (10 May 2008).

14. These attacks have been ongoing but were intensified in 1998 and 2000, 2004/2005. See International Crisis Group, "Jihadism in Indonesia: Poso on the Edge," *Asia Report*, no. 127 (Jakarta and Brussels: International Crisis Group, January 2007).

15. See Alan Cullison, "Inside Al-Qaeda's Hard Drive: Budget Squabbles, Baby Pictures, Office Rivalries—and the Path to 9/11," *The Atlantic Monthly* (September 2004), www.theatlantic.com/doc/200409/cullison (accessed 10 May 2008).

16. International Crisis Group, "How the Jemaah Islamiyah Terrorist Network Operates."

17. International Crisis Group, "Indonesia: Jemaah Islamiyah's Current Status."

18. United Nations Development Fund, *Bali beyond the Tragedy: Impact and Challenges for Tourism-Led Recovery in Indonesia* (Denpasar: Consultative Group Indonesia UNDP-World Bank, 2003).

19. See Jeff Lewis, "The Bali Bombings and the Terror of National Identity," *European Journal of Cultural Studies* 9, no. 2 (2006); Adrian Vickers, "Being Modern in Bali after Suharto," in *Inequality, Crisis and Social Change in Indonesia*, ed. Thomas Reuter (London: Routledge-Curzon, 2003); Jeff Lewis and Belinda Lewis, "The Crisis of Contiguity: Communities and Contention in the Wake of the Bali Bombings," (Paper presented at the First International Sources of Insecurity Conference Melbourne, Australia, November 2004), ed. Damien Grenfell (Melbourne: RMIT Publishing, 2004), search.informit.com.au/documentSummary;dn=876183300411977; res=E-LIBRARY (15 May 2008).

20. Interview with Gede Nurjaya, head of Bali Tourism Authority, Denpasar, 2006. See also Bali Provincial Government, "Statistik Pariwisata."

21. See Lewis and Lewis, "Transforming the *Bhuta Kala*."

22. For a full account of the Balinese response to the bombings see Lewis and Lewis "After the Glow." This paper is based on interviews conducted in 2003 and 2004.

23. UNDP, "Bali beyond the Tragedy," 2003. For a fuller argument on the recovery process associated with both bombings, see I Nyoman Darma Putra and Michael Hitchcock, *Tourism, Development and Terrorism in Bali* (London: Ashgate Books, 2007).

24. For example, see Degung Santikarma, "The Model Militia," *Inside Indonesia*, no. 73 (January–March 2003); also, International Crisis Group, "The Perils of Private Security in Indonesia: Guards and Militias on Bali and Lombok," *Asia Report*, no. 67 (Jakarta and Brussels: International Crisis Group, November 2003). There have been a range of violent assaults and even killings associated with ethnic and religious tensions. The most notable was the murder of two Balinese Muslims during the 2004 presidential election campaign. Our own research has exposed a raft of violent crimes being perpetrated against young non-Balinese who live on the margins of society.

25. Interview with Wayan, Kuta, Bali 2006.

26. See Lewis and Lewis, "After the Glow."

27. Interview with "Nyoman Muhammad Khalim" (*kepala desa*), West Bali, 2006.

28. International Crisis Group, "The Perils of Private Security in Indonesia."

29. Interview with Donno, tourism worker, Kuta, 2006.

30. Interview with "Gede" (*pecalang* leader), Krobokan, 2005.

31. The head of the International Crisis Group in South East Asia, Sidney Jones, welcomed the court's decision. It is yet to be seen, however, whether the court's decision will translate to other judgments in cases involving members of *Jemaah Islamiyah*.

32. U.S. Secretary of State Colin Powell was extremely critical of the Indonesian government's management of terrorist organizations and security, threatening to withdraw American financial support if Indonesia did not improve its security efforts. The Australian government was equally forceful in its criticism. See Stephen Sherlock, "The Bali Bombing: What It Means for Indonesia," *Current Issues Brief*, no. 4 (Canberra, Australia: Department of the Parliamentary Library, 2003).

33. International Crisis Group, "Indonesia: Jemaah Islamiyah's Current Status."

34. In 2007, Ali Imron was temporarily released from prison. During this time, he spoke to several Indonesian and foreign journalists. See ABC Radio, *Background Briefing*, "Talking Indonesian Terror," (23 September 2007), www.abc.net.au/rn/backgroundbriefing/stories/2007/2037572.htm (20 May 2008).

35. Peter Chalk, "The Politics of the South-East Asian Heroin Trade," in *Globalisation and the New Terror: The Asia Pacific Dimension*, ed. D. M. Jones (Cheltenham, UK: Edward Elgar, 2004).

36. Chalk, "Politics of the South-East Asian Heroin Trade," 256.

37. See International Crisis Group, "Indonesia Briefing."

Conclusion

Visions of the Eternal Spirit

GLOBAL BALI AND THE ECONOMY OF PLEASURE

In December 2007, Bali hosted the United Nations Conference on Climate Change. Convened in the luxury resorts at Nusa Dua, the conference featured many significant global leaders, including delegates from the world's heaviest polluters—the United States, European Union, and Australia. All the world leaders espoused their commitment to effective climate change management, testing their policy strategies against the ideas of UN experts, scientists, and specially invited environmental activists who added a sense of pageant and freedom of expression to the affair. In many respects, the Bali conference was an ideal opportunity for Indonesian president Susilo Bambang Yudhoyono to showcase the new civic state and parade the maturity of his nation's status in the new global order. The Nusa Dua Bali, therefore, provided both a convivial context for the international parley, as well as a symbolic template for the merging of East-West, modern-developing cultures and interests. Bali's own intensely appealing spiritual and cultural aesthetic elevated the material and often-fractious rhetoric of the conference through a more refined or universal ideal. Within the security walls and rolling lawns of Nusa Dua, the Climate Change Conference was ennobled within the vortex of the Bali harmony mythology. The violence, grubbiness, and degradation of the island was safely excluded from the view of the delegates—and the conscience of the world's great polluters.

When we visited the conference, we were of no great interest to the security agencies that had amassed to protect the global dignitaries. An explosives expert investigated our taxi driver's glove box and lunch bag, but otherwise we were able to enter the conference largely unencumbered. We had spent much of the previous day at Krobokan Prison speaking to convicted drug traffickers, social workers and wardens. Over the two-year period that we had been visiting the jail, we had witnessed a remarkable transformation. In 2006, when we first visited Krobokan Prison, none of the wardens could speak English, and there was a steel-tight unofficial system of prison trade and entry control managed by senior wardens. The presence of high-profile Australian inmates has radically expanded the prison's economy, and there is now a broader and more inclusive system of payoffs and internal trade, which has created a constant and peculiar *pas de deux* between the official and unofficial systems. For a period, Australian and other "Western" tourists were visiting Krobokan's celebrity inmates, providing necessities for survival in the jail including food, toiletries, and various types of contraband such as alcohol, drugs, and communication tools. Even the female prison wardens had developed a nuance in the island's economy of pleasure, with the routine security pat-down for single female visitors featuring a lingering focus on breasts and hips.

So, our visit to the Climate Change Conference was a compelling contrast to our previous day at Krobokan Prison. The brutality and profoundly violent psychosis of the prison setting were etched in our thinking as we wandered around the perfectly arranged gardens and conference schedules of Nusa Dua. Without any accreditation other than our white skin, we were able to attend various gatherings and speeches. We spoke with a number of delegates and a protest group from the United States who had been granted permission to perform street theater about the felling of forests. They told us that most of the protests had packed up by mid-morning in order to avoid the midday heat. We adopted this sensible approach to social change, and used our white skin and spoken Indonesian to enjoy a lavish buffet lunch and air-conditioning in one of the conference venues. We only wished that we had brought our swimmers and surfboards.

Feeling a little morally bruised, we returned that evening to Kuta Beach and a free rock concert that had been promoted as the Global Warming Extravaganza. There was a big crowd on the beach, mostly young Balinese and other Indonesians, and there was the usual frolicking and cacophony of sunset football, dalliance, and bathing. The beach-sellers were packing up, and the shadows were stretching wide across the sand. As the light muted gold and crimson, and the stage was illuminated, a strange truth revealed itself. Young sales promotion girls were handing out cigarettes and ashtrays marked with the logo *AMild*. The MC suddenly appeared on stage in a plume of green smoke. He too tossed out a handful of *AMild* cigarettes as the first shrill chord of an electric guitar pierced our ears.

It turned out that the Global Warming Extravaganza was actually being sponsored by Sampoerna (Indonesia), a division of the multinational tobacco giant, Philip Morris. *AMild*, their new brand of menthol cigarettes, was being actively promoted to a youth market and the many accompanying young children at the event. Despite their commitment not to advertise to minors, Philip Morris advertises everywhere in Indonesia—billboards, in bus stops, on television, and at promotional events such as this. Indonesia's lax tobacco control laws continue to help the company remain true to its claim of lawful advertising. The marketing team for Sampoerna and Philip Morris had clearly identified climate change as an effective branding signal which could alert the interest of young people, linking youth markets to contemporary styles and cultural practices. With declining consumption in the West, international tobacco companies have targeted their market growth in the developing world and especially young consumers whose addiction would ensure continued sales over a lifetime (however brief). Kuta Beach, which has been the ensign of the Balinese pleasure economy, was an ideal place for the promotion of a product that compresses its deadly consequences within an image of personal and social freedom—the ecstasy of choice. The music that evening was great. Another manifestation of the creative and adaptable capacities of the Balinese. But the air was thick with the smoke of new addicts, another generation of consumers who would express their sense of self and modernity in a cultural practice that is inscribed with the black energy of global capital.

This same energy is evident in the great wash-ups that occur annually on Kuta beach at this time of year. The concert lights illuminated the tidal line of rubbish that was being cast out by the Java Sea. The changing currents were now expurgating the volumes of plastics, fish corpses, oil sludge, cargo boxes, and effluent that had been held in its belly for the six months of the Dry Season. The onshore trade winds gently teased the concert crowd with the stench of decay and death. In the morning, the beach vendors would hastily defend their patch, raking the garbage into small piles, burning the plastics, and burying everything else in the sand. By the time the tourists arrived on the beach, it would appear pristine again, at least until the next high tide when the drill would repeat itself, as it does through every December of every year. There was one year, 2006, when the beach garbage was so dense and so rancid that even the beach vendors could not manage it. In that year the beach was closed and earthmovers were deployed in order to deal with the piles of rusted steel, poles, oil, concrete, and other structural material that had been washed onto the sand. In the strange mixing of currents, the Java Sea had finally released a mountain of materials that had been washing about its belly for years, belching out the disgusting refuse that links development to pleasure.

THE CRISIS OF CONTIGUITY

Of course, the verdant and rolling lawns of Nusa Dua represent the sublimation of these stories. For the Indonesian government and the cosmopolitan context of the UN Climate Change Conference the grubby details of tourism development and global transformation are incidental to the more distinguished and optimistic vision of the New Bali. In many respects, the Climate Change Conference and its principal outcome, the Bali Roadmap, might seem to subsume the crisis that rapid modernization has wreaked upon the island communities and their cultures. According to the American Society for International Law, for example,

> The Bali Roadmap marks a milestone in the process of international consensus building, setting forth a multilateral legal framework to address climate change. . . . The building blocks of the Bali Roadmap include: mitigating climate change by cutting emissions; facilitating clean technology transfer; adapting to such consequences of climate change such as floods and droughts; and financing adaptation and mitigation measures. Bali delegates additionally agreed to support activities such as funding developing countries to prevent deforestation.[1]

In this context, Bali has yet another incarnation. The Bali harmony narrative has expanded as a cosmopolitan and consensual vision: global order in which there can be collaborative resolution of common problems. Bali's own crisis of contiguity, shaped by its cultural and geospatial proximity within the Western pleasure imaginary and global economy, has been transformed by the Nusa Dua imaginary into an ensign of political and ecological reawakening.

From our perspective, however, the paradoxes and tragedies that lie behind this delusion could not be more compelling. Thirty years before the Climate Change Conference the Bukit Peninsula and Nusa Dua landscape was dry and harsh. The villages were very poor and the soils supported only sparse agriculture and husbandry. As we discussed in chapter 2, the resorts were created out of brutality and deception. The mangrove swamps that separated the two islands (*nusa dua*) were landfilled, causing immeasurable damage to the estuarine environment and the repurification processes for Bali's south-flowing rivers. The effluent and garbage that is generated through the resorts have placed enormous stress on an ecological system that is already in crisis. Despite these problems, it is very likely that the majority of world leaders and other international delegates who attended the Climate Change Conference were able to travel the multilane causeway that connects Bali to the rest of the world, entirely oblivious of the damage in which they themselves were complicit.

Of course, many Balinese are entirely cognizant of the irony of the Climate Change Conference being convened in the capital of their island's plunder and devastation; in accord with the *rwa bhineda* or two-in-one principle (see chapter 5), the might and momentum of progress is merely returning to its roost. In these contiguities of space and time, Bali's modernization reveals itself as a double-coding of desire and despair. The Balinese, thereby, exist in the midst of a crisis that they dare not speak, but which resonates through the catacombs and minutiae of their daily lives. In this way, the crisis traverses the shopping strips, hotels, and roadways that connect the Bombings monument in Legian Street to the Bukit and Sanur, across the rice fields in the south, west to the rain forests and along the pathways to Ubud and the majesty of Mount Agung and the Besakih "mother temple," turning across the impoverished villages in the northeast around again through Klungkung to Denpasar, Krobokan Prison, and the nightclubs of Kuta. In these spaces and journeys, the old and new Bali cannot be disaggregated but live within the memory of the dead and the energies of the living. It is a crisis therefore that has no boundary, but exists within the material and spiritual being of the Balinese themselves.

In this sense, we can't claim that Nusa Dua Bali is any more or less authentic than the imaginings that are generated through various notions of "tradition" or "Old Bali." It is not, as we claimed at the beginning of this book, that "new Bali," "paradise Bali," or "Bali harmony" are propagated untruths that entirely misrepresent the reality of the island people and their culture. Rather, our argument has been that Bali is a dynamic cultural montage that is shaped around a complex of meanings, practices, elements, and processes of transformation. In this light, the Nusa Dua Bali is as much a part of this montage as the malnourished children in Tianyar, the ancient palm leaf manuscripts, or the foreign drug couriers serving time in Krobokan Prison. Our aim in this book has been to present this complex cultural montage through the lens of crisis, which in our view has been largely underacknowledged or misunderstood by many commentators and visitors to the island. As we said in the introduction to this book, the processes of modernization have been variously experienced in Bali by a broad range of social groups and individuals. We have also argued that the new Bali has not superseded or erased the old Bali. Indeed, we have challenged the whole opposition of old and new, traditional and modern, arguing that the complex of cultural features in Bali is more like the mixing of currents in the Java Sea. The extraordinary beauty and power of older modes of cultural practice, ritual, and expression are not erased by modernization; they are variously adapted, transformed, rearticulated, mutated, and ultimately transformed within the lexicon of alien and reconstituted cultural meanings and expressivities. In this way, contemporary Bali is clearly immersed in the multiple flows and counterflows of globalization, flows that draw together spatial, cultural, and historical elements into a swarming crisis of contiguity, transformation, and renewal.

Of course these changes are themselves embedded in global economy and the rigors of transnational cultural politics. While modernization is a contingency of perpetual change (and hence the perpetual threat of "crisis"), Bali's transition has been particularly acute as it has been experienced through such extraordinary velocity and violence. Nevertheless, it is important to remind ourselves that crisis is not an absolute or entirely negative condition. A crisis necessarily involves the contention of constituent elements; however, the resonance of crisis, even through violence and rupture, may generate positive as well as negative outcomes. Bali's crisis, as we have outlined it in this book, has been created through the radical irruption of the island's cultural, social, and geospatial environments. Even so, the irruption of Balinese culture has provided the impetus for renewal. For the Balinese, in particular, the crisis brings forward the momentum of new opportunities, new expressive modes, and a creative engagement with cultural change. Despite the intensity of this transition, we would argue that the richness and creative dispositions that are intrinsic to Balinese culture are already providing the sort of psychocultural resources necessary for renewal and community recovery.[2]

THE CYCLE OF RENEWAL

For many commentators and leaders in Bali, this sort of recovery and regeneration of self-esteem can be achieved through the propagation of "traditionalism" and "localism." While parading itself as distinctively Balinese, the *Ajeg Bali* cultural revival movement is clearly implicated in processes of globalization. Thus, Bali resembles many other social groups across the world seeking to shield themselves from excessive transnational homogenization. As cultures and peoples across the globe have become increasingly integrated into the global economy, they have felt exposed to the overwhelming and neoimperialist power of U.S.-Western cultural styles, products, and practices. In order to protect, and even generate a distinctive local culture, these social groups have stimulated for themselves and others in their ethnic, religious, or spatial cohort the adoption of a more strident, even chauvinistic, local identity.

As we noted in chapter 4, *Ajeg Bali* might in this sense be understood as an antiglobal movement, a way of shielding the Balinese from the excesses and standardization of U.S.-dominated global culture. In a peculiar way, however, *Ajeg Bali* is also a part of this globalization momentum as it may be seen as part of a global trend toward religious revival. Moreover, the traditionalism that *Ajeg Bali* propagates is very distinctively part of the tourist fantasy: the "old" or "authentic" Bali that hotel guests pay to observe. This sort of cultural preservationism is a clear feature of modernization's double-coding which propels a culture forward through the grounding of a particular and notionally stable past. As we have noted throughout this book, the predisposition of modernity toward perpetual change is facilitated by an imagination that it has a solid social base and an origin that determines the direction of these changes. In many respects, this counterbalance of change and stability is represented in the survival in modern, secular societies of religion and religious practices. As much as anything else, *Ajeg Bali* represents the same sort of religious evangelism that emerges in Western secular states, particularly when they are dealing with crises like 9/11. In this sense, *Ajeg Bali* promotes itself as a form of spiritual revivalism which can save the Balinese from the outbreak of evil and restore their sense of cultural cohesion and faithfulness.

The great difficulty for *Ajeg Bali*, as with other cultural revivalist movements, is that it fundamentally misrepresents contemporary Bali—and the past. Thus, while *Ajeg Bali* enjoys some popularity, especially among the elite, it has barely penetrated younger and more cosmopolitan Balinese groups who see it as antiquarian and of very little practical benefit. Moreover, the religious, prosaic, and somewhat didactic overtones of *Ajeg Bali*, offer a peculiarly provincial and tepid defiance to the momentum of globalization and the crisis it elicits. Indeed, the new cosmopolitanism is probably a far more productive expression of the continuities and force of Balinese aesthetic and creative capacities. Thus, the rising generation of Balinese artists, designers, and writers has integrated older motifs and styles into a more contemporary and reflective aesthetic, one which more clearly accords with the complexity of the island's cultural montage. In this sense, these more cosmopolitan groups of artists and creative thinkers are, like many of the world's artistic communities, working through local and global influences in order to produce original and innovative expressive forms.

In this context, for example, the Bali Arts Festival has had a significant influence on development of the performing arts in Bali. Each year, the festival *Pesta Kensenian Bali* (PKB) presents traditional dance along with "new" (*kreasi baru*) innovative forms and hybrids that capture contemporary cultural politics. New dances continue to emerge, such as the Gambuh Macbeth which retains the integrity, formality, and costumes of the traditional Gambuh, but the story and its themes draw from Western traditions. After the 2002 bombings, Balinese performers and artists created new tools for healing using modern forms of Hindu Balinese traditions to help people come to terms with the tragedy. Dances developed in the 1970s were adapted, modernized, and used to strengthen community morale and maintain social cohesion.[3] Traveling troupes performed the *Wayang Dasa Nama Kerta* in which customary *wayang kulit* shadow puppets explored the theme of "overcoming the demons within us" with audiences of Balinese children. In schools across Bali, puppeteers on skateboards were projected onto huge screens via laptop computers, and accompanying DVDs were distributed. The transformative power of new technologies was harnessed in a significant deviation from the rituals defined by the traditional *adat*, while maintaining respect for traditional community values and cosmology.[4]

This sort of creative resilience is an essential part of community recovery, sustainability, and growth. There is no single mechanism for resolving or progressing beyond crisis. Our own feeling is that Bali will continue to evolve in a way that is exhilarating and ultimately hopeful. Sometimes we'll sit on the beach, watching the Kuta sunset and chatting with our old friend Ketut. Ketut's family originally owned a coconut plantation on the coastal strip between Kuta and Legian. As we chat, we inevitably drift back across the many years we have sat in this same place and conjured the changes, the people, the pleasures, and the loss. The family's coconut plantation and fishing operations were transformed by the arrival of the surfers and backbackers. As a teenager, Ketut exchanged the fishing nets for a vendor's tray, sweets, and Coca-Cola. His first wife owned and operated a small *warung* on the beach and eventually, Ketut became a tourist driver for the small guesthouse that had replaced the coconut plantation. He now owns several cars, a number of small shops, and he has recently taken a second wife in accordance with his personal prosperity and the rules of the local *adat*. On the night of the Global Warming Extravaganza, following our day at the Climate Change Conference, we had been sitting on the beach with Ketut discussing the Westerners who were waiting on death row in Krobokan Prison. As we parted that evening, he told us, almost incidentally, that his mother had recently died and he invited us to the cremation. When we expressed our sorrow for his loss, Ketut looked strangely bemused, even embarrassed: "This is the way," he reminded us. "She will come back. It is sad, but it is for the best."

And of course, this is the story of Bali.

NOTES

1. Elizabeth Burleson, *The American Society of International Law Insight* 12, no. 4 (March 2009): 1.

2. We have written about this specifically in terms of the Bali bombings. See Jeff Lewis and Belinda Lewis, "Taming the *Rwa Bhineda*: Recovery after the Bali Bombings," in *Rethinking Insecurity, War and Violence: Beyond Savage Globalization*, ed. Paul James, Tom Nairn, and Damian Grenfell (London: Routledge, 2008).

3. In 1978, I Wayan Dibia, the author of *Balinese Dance, Drama and Music*, created a final exam piece depicting demons dancing in the middle of the night and spreading disease. Shown widely on local television, it created substantial controversy. Two decades later, his approach has been mobilized for community healing.

4. Kemausiaan Ibu Pertiwi (YKIP) in partnership with UNICEF, took performances to thirty schools. Along with an accompanying DVD, the performances reached 500,000 people. Messages were embedded about stress, anxiety, conflict, and how to restore balance via cooperation and harmony. The primary focus was on posttraumatic stress disorder, helping people to recognize the condition and effectively seek assistance. Performances were also accompanied by counseling for children and their families.

Index

political protests. *See* protests

pornography: definition of, 127; youth and, 110. *See also* antipornography bill

prostitution. *See* sex work

protests: against antipornography bill 129–31; against development, 58–63; demanding execution of Bali bombers, 214

public health: capacity building for, 173–79; issues and problems in Bali, 71–74, 111–19, 132–33, 163–69, 173–79

puputan, 17–19

Putra, I Nyoman Darma, 36–37, 93, 123, 153

Reformasi period, 144–57, 171, 176, 189, 213–15

religion, 14–42, 142, 151, 157, 160, 190–96

rice growing and *subak,* 55–59

rituals, 68–71. *See also* ceremonies

rwa bhineda. See cosmological balance

Sanur, 3, 16–17, 31–36, 52–53, 62

secession: movement in Bali, 154, 188, 210–14; threats after the porn bill passed, 129–31

Serangan Island, 43, 71–74

sex: changing attitudes and practices, 85–98, 109–12, 121–36; colonial period and, 83–89; cultural politics of, 80–83; under New Order, 92–95; sexual health, 97–99, 111–19, 132–33; tourism and, 103–9, 111–12, 121–27; traditional beliefs and practices, 93–103; virginity and sex before marriage, 96–99, 109–11. *See also* sexuality

sexuality: homosexual, 113–15, 117–20; idealization of Balinese sexuality, 85–92; transgender, 94–96, 113–20; transvesticism and *waria,* 113–15, 120–21; youth, 92–112

sex work and workers, 91–105, 119, 121–27

Shari'ah law: increasing influence of, 112, 127–33, 142–47, 175, 191–204. *See also* antipornography bill

silencing: 1965 killings, 36–39, 41n2; Balinese culture of, 36–59, 75, 155, 209–14

social inequalities, 27–32, 124, 151–58, 163–67, 176, 206

Soekarnoputri, Megawati (former president), 144–52, 189–90, 212–15

Spies, Walter, 24–26, 51, 113–19

subak. See rice growing and *subak*

Suharto (former president), 2–15, 30–76. *See also* New Order

Sukarno (former president), 13–19, 27–33, 93–95, 141–45, 197

Tanah Lot, 58–62

terrorism: definition of, 186–90; the media and, 186–94. *See also* narco-terrorism

terrorist attacks in Indonesia, 200–204. *See also* Bali bombing

terrorist organizations. *See* al-Qa'ida; Defenders of Islam Front; Islam: Darul Islam; Jemaah Islamiyah

Tirta Gangga, 107–9

tobacco industry, 228–30

tourism: 1960s and 1970s, 48–52; 1980–1998, 52–54; development phases, 62–67; development under Suharto, 30–36, 46–47, 52–54; domestic, 78n17, 132, 206; downturn, 63–65, 176, 205–9; international, 205–9; recovery, 151, 176, 185, 205–9, 232–34

transgender. *See* sex

transmigration, 68–76, 148, 207, 213

transvesticism. See *waria*

"two-in-one" principle. See *rwa bhineda*

Ubud, 24, 32, 51–54

About the Authors

Jeff Lewis is a professorial research fellow in the Global Cities Institute, School of Applied Communications, RMIT University, Melbourne. In 2006, he was visiting professor at London School of Economics. Jeff is an established scholar who has lived and worked in Bali and Indonesia since the 1970s. He has written numerous short stories and magazine feature stories based on his experiences in Bali and Indonesia. Jeff has an international reputation as a leading cultural studies scholar. He has authored many research papers and books, including the critically acclaimed *Cultural Studies* and *Language Wars: The Role of Media and Culture in Global Terror and Political Violence*.

Belinda Lewis is a researcher in health promotion and international health in the Faculty of Medicine at Monash University, Melbourne. Belinda has a doctorate in health promotion and has wide experience working with a wide range of major public health agencies, aid organizations, and community groups. She has lived and worked in Indonesia and Bali over a fifteen-year period, and has conducted extensive qualitative research on crisis, community recovery, and health in Bali and other parts of the Asian region. In collaboration with Jeff Lewis, she has published numerous essays, book chapters, and articles on the deeper impact of the Bali bombings and recent social and cultural transitions in Bali.